Haywains &
Cherry Ale

Binder Twine &
Rabbit Stew

JOAN KENT

ARROW

Published by Arrow Books in 1999

1 3 5 7 9 10 8 6 4 2

Haywains & Cherry Ale © Joan Kent 1980
First published in the United Kingdom in 1980
by Bailey Brothers and Swinfen Ltd, Century edition 1996

Binder Twine & Rabbit Stew © Joan Kent 1976
First published in the United Kingdom in 1976
by Bailey Brothers and Swinfen Ltd, Century edition 1994

This omnibus first published in 1999 in the United Kingdom by
Arrow Books Limited
20 Vauxhall Bridge Road, London SW1V 2SA

Random House, Australia (Pty) Limited
20 Alfred Street, Milsons Point, Sydney,
New South Wales 2061, Australia

Random House New Zealand Limited
18 Poland Road, Glenfield, Auckland 10, New Zealand

Random House, South Africa (Pty) Limited
Endulini, 5A Jubilee Road, Parktown 2193, South Africa

Random House UK Limited Reg. No. 954009

Papers used by Random House UK Limited are natural, recy-
clable products made from wood grown in sustainable forests.
The manufacturing processes conform to the environmental
regulations of the country of origin.

ISBN 0 09 929600 4

Printed and bound in Norway by
AIT Trondheim AS

Haywains &
Cherry Ale

Contents

To Alan, the blacksmith's eldest son.
With love.

Introduction

When I found a skein of green beads beneath the torn lining of a woven work basket Mum had bought for next to nothing at an auction sale, she dismissed them as a paltry bonus, for fancy jewellery had no place in her hard working life. I, her afterthought, the youngest of her nine children, was a compulsive traveller on flights of fancy, a persistent weaver of dreams wherein the necklace sparkling like raindrops on beech leaves bursting from their buds in springtime, provided the means of solving my parents' farming and financial problems, making us all extremely rich.

I sometimes disentangled the string of beads from unwound cotton bobbins, buttons, lengths of elastic, darning wool and stay laces that conglomerated in a treacherous tangle. Making sure that they were safely hidden from sight, I wore the beads to school, certain that I was the only pupil sitting in that draughty village schoolroom with a string of fabulously precious gems hung around my neck.

Inevitably the fraying thread parted company with the clasp as I hurried home across the meadows at the end of the day's lessons. Many of the scattered beads were lost in the long grass. Those I retrieved were put into a gaudy vase that held a multitude of hat pins, awaiting the time when Mum could find thread fine and strong enough for the skein to be restrung.

By the time that happened, the top heavy vase had been tipped over so often that many more beads had disappeared. My left-handed attempt to restore the necklace produced a loose string lacking sequence, and too short to fasten around anyone's neck. They remained in the 'oddments' drawer of the front room table for years on end with no one questioning their value or establishing their worth.

When the new brooms of a changing, post war era brushed aside all that my parents had strived for in their life span, the string of green beads was just another broken link that was swept away.

I experienced too many hard winters to harbour any illusion of that vanished country world being a rural Arcadia, yet there was always laughter bubbling just beneath the surface; a great sense of purpose, pride, and wellbeing abounding in the timeless beauty of that slower, smaller sphere. One learned to differentiate between riches and true worth.

So the skein will never be complete again, for so much was lost, with no one questioning the losing.

Just as once I tried to rethread a broken skein of beads, so in this my third book, have I attempted to restring with clumsy fingers, small cameos of times remembered, knowing that only the fickle thread of fraying memory prevents them from being lost in the long grass.

JOAN KENT
BEAM ENDS

The Shearing of Sister Eve

I had five older sisters who would chatter like sparrows round an unthatched oat stack, but they always closed their adult ranks and changed the subject whenever I asked the plain and simple question:

"How will I know when I have grown up?"

I thought I had found some useful information when I scanned through some pages of *Poppy's Weekly Paper* that had come home wrapped round our Friday herrings. It said that no youthful person could hope to become a real young lady until she put her hair up neatly, remembering always to wear a hat when she went out. To illustrate the point, there were photographs of several smartly elegant females wearing magnificently decorated millinery that was anchored by enormous hat pins on either side of their heads.

Growing like a small cloud on my mind's horizon, a preposterous suspicion began to take shape in my brain. A vase on the front room overmantel shelf seemed to confirm my fears. It was crammed with hat pins of every length and colour, from small gilt ones to lethal-looking weapons ornamented with gob-stopper-sized 'jewels'.

These began to hold a terrifying fascination, making me so apprehensive that I kept taking surreptitious glances in the damp-speckled overmantel mirror, convinced that I had discovered the process by which one changed from a child into an adult girl. I searched anxiously for the first signs and symptoms of having 'hat pin holes' develop just above my ears on each side of my head. I knew that Mum had pierced ears, and wondered if one underwent some secret similar operation, or if they appeared suddenly, like holes in worn out socks.

It became an obsessive interest to watch Mum and my sisters anchoring their hats to their long hair with a gaudy assortment of hat pins that were prodded into one side of their craniums, and emerged on the opposite side. Hat pin holes could well explain why Mum always wore her hair swept up onto the top of her head in a top-knot bun. This style probably kept out draughts and helped prevent her catching colds in the head. It would also explain why I alone still had my hair washed in the Saturday bathtub, while my sisters indulged in the luxury of their Friday night shampoos.

It was understandable now that I could endure enamel jugs of rinsing water being poured over my unperforated head, but with hat pin holes to contend with such drastic treatment might well waterlog my sisters' brains. No wonder Friday evenings were such a ritual of boiled rainwater and vinegar rinsings. Lorelei, circa nineteen thirty, they sat round the fire drying their long tresses, showing their short sleeved cotton vests, their camisoles and lace edged petticoats. Curling tongs cooled on the fender, steel toothed 'rat trap' wavers were tightly clamped to encourage corrugated ridges in their hair. Home made setting lotion, owing much to corn starch, was scented with 'Ashes Of Roses' to hide the homely plain-Jane smell of soft soap shampoo.

Dad bought soft soap by the barrel because it had several veterinary uses. As a shampoo it gave our hair a shining sheen like the coat of a well-groomed horse. Dad was inordinately proud of his daughters' long tresses, leaving no one in doubt as to his disappointment and displeasure if any of them was daft enough to take notice of the latest craze and attempt to have it cut.

Shop-bought make up was considered to be sheer extravagance, daring if not decadent, but *Zebra* black lead stove polish served to accentuate line of brow, or length of eye lash, while petals from the red geraniums on the kitchen window were sometimes pressed into colouring my sisters' cheeks and lips. It puzzled Mum why her prized pot plants always showed such budding promise, but produced such tatty blooms. Not made to go to bed as long as I kept quiet and turned the phonograph handle as required, I watched the world of grown-ups from behind the barrier of being 'small'; a world I had become convinced that I would need hat pin holes to join. This did not appeal to me at all.

Our old phonograph was so worn with use that it sometimes developed hiccoughs, but we never tired of the cylindrical records that it played. We sang along with Enrico Caruso, Lily Morris, Dame Nellie Melba, Count John McCormack. Florrie Ford, Nellie Wallace and the rest. At that time my sister Eve worked in the city and could purchase records at a discount. These were added to the dozens already stacked up among Mum's wine and cherry ale brews in the huge old cupboard known as 'the glory hole'.

My strait-laced Aunt Florence was staying with us when Eve brought home the record of a new dance that a dashing young electrician had shown her. The phonograph churned out the music of The Charleston until it faltered from the strain. In trying to keep the rhythm going until her sisters had mastered the new technique of dancing. Eve leaned over the phonograph, catching her long hair in the machinery of the roller. With yards of hair wound into its entrails, the phonograph slurred to a stop. Held fast, her head within inches of the machine, Eve had to be hacked free with Mum's dressmaking scissors. She looked like a badly sheared sheep that had escaped half way through the operation, so the only solution was to cut the rest of her hair off short.

Eve was delighted, for who could dance the Black Bottom or The Charleston, shedding hair pins as they went. Dad's displeasure was muted by the fact that Mum had done the shearing, but he maintained that short hair made Eve look like the back view of a bob-tailed old sheepdog. I was scared to look too closely, worrying that Eve's hat pin holes would now be exposed and let in the rain.

Watching the phonograph being jammed into eternal silence, Aunt Flo expressed the belief that this was divine retribution for the sinful music it had been made to play. The sight of my sisters 'cavorting like pagans' had made her expect some more wrathful form of judgement to descend on our old farmhouse like a thunderbolt from the sky. Looking at Eve's shorn head, my aunt rooted around in Mum's workbasket and got busy knitting a huge shapeless 'tammy' hat that could cover the wanton shamelessness of Eve's naked neck.

"Will it be good and thick enough to cover her ears and keep the wet out?" I asked as I watched Aunt's needles flying. Bolt upright in her iron maiden corsets that forbade any slouching, she glared at me, saying:

"If you've no more sense than to pester a person counting stitches, you can take yourself off and worry your Dad.'

Fraught with anxiety about the situation, this I did. He assured me that my fears about hat pin holes were completely groundless, but admitted that he had often wondered how women managed to use such vicious looking weapons to anchor their hats. He knew that none of the females in our family had leaky craniums, so I had no need to worry on that score. Even if the worst of my fears became reality, he reminded me about the gaping hole in the cart shed roof that he had mended with felt and pitch. Short haired, or still retaining their 'crowning glory', all his daughters were quite safe. As for knowing when I had reached the stage of being grown up. Dad reckoned it to be more of an attitude of mind than birthdays.

"Jo," he said. "There are some folk who were born old. Your Aunt Flo never seemed young and carefree. She was probably weaned on crab apples. You can be young at heart if you are ninety, so just you stay as you are for as long as you can."

A great weight lifted from my heart as I went back into the lamplit kitchen where Aunt's disapproval hung in the atmosphere like a grey, wet blanket and everyone seemed subdued. I had seen Mum looking happier in the middle of a wet washing day. She suggested we might please Aunt Flo and occupy ourselves by making music of our own. But none of my sisters had progressed far beyond playing 'A Maiden's Prayer' on the front room piano.

Instead they sat round the kitchen table making felt cloche hats, or attempting to disguise the fact that they were shortening their skirts to a more fashionable length. Sitting on the broken-springed old sofa under the window, Stan tried his hand at learning the ukelele in ten easy lessons, making little progress because his finances did not run to buying the actual instrument, but only the manual of instructions, and even that was second hand. Billy, the quietest, most serious-minded of my brothers, was so engrossed in the book he was reading that he was oblivious to everything else. Harold was trying to drum up enthusiasm for his idea that making a crystal wireless set was not beyond his capabilities, but our censorious aunt disapproved most strongly, remarking that anyone dabbling with dark forces would be sorry.

For once, I was glad to be youngest, first to leave the dismal, alien atmosphere of our kitchen and go to bed. Offering consolation as she came upstairs to take away my candle. Mum said that Aunt Flo would only stay a few days more. The reason for her visit was an auction sale in a nearby country mansion, where she hoped to find some 'bargain lots'. A real gramophone that played flat records instead of round ones was listed in the catalogue of the sale, and providing that we all promised not to antagonise our crusty visitor. Mum said she would try to buy it. We spent the next few days acting like ministering cherubs.

"There, Liza!" Aunt Flo crowed. "You can see now that you would have a fairly presentable family if you were not as soft as butter! See what wise words and firm handling can do!"

When Stan drove the horse and cart to fetch Mum and Aunt Flo from the auction sale. I rode with him and helped him stack their trophies in the cart. Stan brought out a Hudson's Soap box packed with flat records, then carefully placed a small mahogany cabinet beside it. Next came a huge tin horn that looked like a green convolvulus blossom. I was warned to guard it carefully, and the safest way I could think of was to ride back wearing it like a pixie hat wedged on my head.

By lamplight that evening. Harold put the mahogany cabinet on the red velvet table cloth, then carefully secured a steel needle in the sound reproducing box. He wound the handle and started the turntable, while we all sat awe-struck at the volume of noise that could come from a green tin horn.

Since the instrument had been owned by 'gentry', the second hand records ranged from light classical to downright heavy. These were not what any of Mum's family would have chosen, but we sat and listened, for they seemed to give her a new dimension to living, offering an entrancing, instant escape from her humdrum hard-working world.

Various fiancés, girl friends, and 'intendeds' swelled our ranks that evening. Eve had used all her Friday wages to have her hair properly shingled and buy some flat records of her own choice. Short haired and thoroughly modern, she entertained us by singing. "You called me baby doll a year ago, boopy-doop, boopy-doop." she carolled, quick-stepping round the kitchen with her low-waisted, short frock showing bare leg above flesh-coloured stockings held up with garters sporting bold embroidery and blue silk bows. Skeins of beads swung defiantly around her throat, marking the beat of the music as she danced.

Aunt Flo watched this display in stupified silence, then rose majestically to prod the sound box of the gramophone with her knitting needle as if it was some foul pest. The needle scratched across the record, repeated a couple of phrases, then stopped.

"Shameless wanton!" Aunt declaimed. "Just suppose that you were 'took' this instant – and you should be – you would be cast into the everlasting pit like the whore of Babylon! Think on that!"

Dad said firmly that there would be no more of that kind of talk in this house, so Aunt adopted the attitude of an over-worked avenging angel returning from a particularly arduous earthly assignment to find the gates of Heaven slammed shut.

Mum tried to smooth ruffled feelings by suggesting that we listen to a boy soprano singing 'Jerusalem', but she picked up the wrong record in her confusion. Aunt Flo looked as if she had been mentally pole-axed as Marie Lloyd belted out the chorus of 'A Little Of What You Fancy Does You Good'. She stood stock-still for a second, then deliberately sat down on a pile of records Mum had placed on a nearby chair. There was an ominous crack beneath her and, rising slowly, she turned to inspect the damage, saying:

"Dear me! I seem to have sat in your 'Monastery Garden' Liza, and me a strict noncomformist too!"

Mum quietly picked up the broken pieces, then closed the gramophone lid. We all knew that it would stay shut until our prickly aunt went home. This decision came quite suddenly the following morning. Harold eagerly agreed to load all her luggage and sale bargains in the tip cart, then drive her to her pristine city home. Waving a somewhat relieved farewell as she watched Aunt departing down the farm lane. Mum told us why.

"I just mentioned that I felt really slovenly because everyone else who takes pride in their home has finished spring cleaning, and I haven't begun. Nor has Flo for that matter," said my mother guilelessly, "but now she's hurried home to put that right!"

Dad took her in his arms, lifting her off her feet to hug her, the pair of them giggling all the while. I knew then that growing up had nothing to do with hat pins. My parents could still laugh like children. I would be the same, and stay young all my life.

Welcome, Stranger

We accepted that, during the lengthening days when hares go mad, Mum's rites of spring transformed her to a cottage-loaf-shaped Nemesis, stirring up the contents of the house from attic to doorstep. Eiderdowns, rugs, feather beds, pillows, and blankets were likely to be pitched out of upper windows, to be beaten or brushed to death in the yard below. For the last few years however, Mum's routine of spring cleaning had been thoroughly disorganised by the fact that there was a sudden spate of family weddings.

Each one was an excuse to scrub and shine anything with a solid surface, shake and thump that which was moveable but unlaunderable, and use tubs full of soap suds to drown anything that would wash.

Soon after my twelfth birthday, we were subjected to a particularly violent recurrence, but this time the driving force was my sister June. By then June and Nora were the only two sisters left unmarried. Mum's three youngest daughters were known as 'the pretty one', 'the stylish brainy one' and 'that skinny little one with the ears!'

June suddenly became so houseproud that Mum could only offer the illogical explanation that the girl must be in love. Being blessed with so many brothers and sisters, romance was a phenomenon I had often witnessed, but it had never before inspired any of them to re-arrange the kitchen or attempt to persuade the rest of us that meals would taste much better if we ate them in the cold front room, June had either been bitten by a very virulent love bug, or there was something extraordinary about her young man.

It transpired that, while all the rest had chosen life partners from within the county boundaries, June was being courted by a civil servant, an unknown species, alien to our way of life. Dad was apprehensive, wondering if his daughter intended bringing home one of the brainless, nosy individuals who sat on their backsides in Ministry offices dreaming up stupid forms demanding information on everything on the farm right down to the last hogget, shearling, and one-toothed gimmer. He made it clear from the outset that his welcome would be luke-warm. June's intimation that her young man was attached to the Indian Civil Service did nothing to help matters. She took down the bobbled fringe drape from around the shelf above the fire place, saying that it was old-fashioned. A string line hidden beneath it had always been used for warming and airing our clothes, but we were all expected to make sacrifices in the cause of June's new love.

Everything cluttering the mantel shelf was ruthlessly cleared. The paper spills for Dad's pipe, bills, receipts, and a strange shaped fossil Stan once found in the brook. Even the vase of hat pins was banished to the dark depths of a cupboard.

June did her best to give the place such a stately image that it did not feel like home at all. I even earned the unbelievably large wage of one shilling and sixpence for colour-washing the interior of our 'outback' privy, a glorious salmon pink. Applied with enthusiasm, this trickled through the cracks of the lap-boarded walls, overlaying the tarred exterior with irregular pink stripes which I considered helped to brighten up that particular aspect of the garden immensely, but no-one else shared my view. Nor was my finishing touch of 'quick drying' mahogany stain varnish appreciated. The label illustration showed an overalled painter clutching a shaft of forked lightning in front of him, the motto of the produce being 'It dries in a flash.'

Bitter experience showed that it didn't. The seat of the 'outback' proved an embarrassingly sticky hazard with no hope of impressing our expected visitor, when a bottle of white spirit, clean rag, and a small mirror were vital impedimenta kept in constant readiness on the 'outback' shelf.

June worked in the city all week, so Sunday was the day chosen for her young man's initial visit. This allowed as many as possible of our relations to inspect the rare specimen June had caught.

I had a hastily sewn new white dress for the occasion and my usually plaited hair was twisted and turned into scalp-torturing curling rag knots, to emerge as a shock headed frizz.

June went to meet her sweetheart in a state of nervous apprehension as various aunts, uncles and cousins arrived. Flushed and flustered in the kitchen, Mum stood basting a large hunk of sheep. It took up so much room in the oven that there was scarcely room to roast the potatoes, so our dessert had to be something that would cook on top of the stove. Mum settled for her version of fig pudding.

'Figgy Duff' consisted of flour, lumpy suet, brown sugar, dried figs and as much milk as it took to bind the ingredients together in a cloth. This boiled and chuntered away, needing but cursory attention, giving Mum the opportunity to meet June and her escort on his arrival, then dart back to the kitchen and compare opinions with Dad.

The young man was frightfully 'upper crust', striding around in brown and white shoes and loud checked socks matching the pattern of his tweed plus-fours. Speaking with a strange accent, he called Dad 'Sir', but this cut no ice with my father. If Mum wanted his opinion, yonder chap was nought but a fly-by-night bird catcher, with no more chance of getting his permission to take June off to India than anyone else had of ever walking on the moon.

"I can't understand the girl!" he remarked glumly. "She should have the sense not to get lumbered with stock lacking good teeth, no matter if it has got a good bloom to its coat."

Alternately stirring gravy and custard, I felt a pang of disillusion. The dashing young man's gleaming white smile had reminded me of Douglas Fairbanks, but there seemed little romance in the thought of June watching him remove his dentures each night. Mum's only comment was that she was glad she had chosen 'Figgy Duff' as afters. She smiled gleefully as it expanded to lift the lid of the old two-handled iron pot.

Nora had set the front room table, adding a centrepiece posy of flowers as an artistic touch. Aunt Flo, who would not have missed so interesting an encounter for all the tea in China, deplored the sinful waste of roses and madonna lilies that might have made a lovely wreath.

The first course of that Sunday lunch was eaten in disconcerting silence, with most of us anxious to use our knives and forks correctly although the specially polished cutlery left a metallic taste in our mouths.

As I carried empty plates to the kitchen, I found Mum facing the problem of a Figgy Duff that had expanded to such an extent that she could not remove it from the pot. I thought that removing the water around it might make it more amenable, but our kitchen lacked such modernities as sink or waste pipes so, each holding a handle, we carried the heavy oval iron pot out to the 'sump', a shallow indentation in the back garden, where the slightest shower of rain made a tiny trickling streamlet saunter through.

Prodding, shaking, and tilting, Mum tried to manoeuvre the pudding from its iron prison. One desperate tug on the pudding cloth made it fall 'ker-plop' into the almost stagnant green water. Mum grabbed at it, then used her apron to wipe off the worst of the slimy water weed.

She surveyed it in silence for a moment, then solemnly remarked:

"It doesn't appear to have lost anything. No one will notice a drop of sump water if we cover it in custard. What won't fatten will fill!"

I pleaded loss of appetite, watching the others eating their Figgy Duff with relish. There was, however, one exception. June's admirer removed a stray blade of grass to the side of his plate, then took a tentative mouthful but seemed loath to chew. Instantly my parents began bombarding him with questions: Was the pudding to his liking? Had he hunted tigers? What was the price of wheat in Baluchistan?

As befitting a mainstay of the British Raj, he tried manfully to answer, but his conversation dried up under the torture of fig seeds between his dentures and his gums.

Mum detailed me to spend the afternoon keeping close to June and her young man wherever they might wander. Mo, my cousin, volunteered to accompany me. We were much the same age and he shared my interest in collecting cigarette cards and climbing trees.

The pretence that we were Red Indians stalking two white settlers across the prairie soon became boring because the young man would keep stopping to kiss June's ears. When the pair of them had sat on the same stile holding hands for over an hour, Mo and I decided to go sailing in sheep troughs on the pond in Church Field. Mine sank, ruining my new dress with the same green weedy water that had clung to Mum's Figgy Duff.

Mum seemed less bothered by my ducking than by my dereliction of family duty. She explained the implications of June marrying the smooth-talking gentleman who had damned all his chances with Dad by acting as if he was granting June a great honour by considering the possibility of making her his wife.

"Do you want her to sail off to India, that red blob on the other side of the globe and become a memsahib?" Mum asked with some urgency. I did not. Before my brother Billy left home, I had found one of his paperback novels in his bedroom cupboard and had a crafty read of the contents before Mum used it as 'ammunition' in the outback. The title of that epic was *The Memsahib Slave*, and it dealt with the traumatic adventures of a poor young lady constantly being pursued and captured by a Rajah. The front cover illustrated a huge, coloured gentleman towering above a crouching fair-haired female, draped in what appeared to me to be white lace curtains. In no way did I want my beautiful sister June to go to a place where girls dressed as scantily as that.

I discussed the situation with my cousin, but Mo was as bereft of ideas as myself. Watching June's young man slipping down the garden path to the outback, Mo thought he should be warned about the mahogany varnish but I called him back. A few seconds later we strolled down the garden path to feed the rabbit in its hutch by the privy, nonchalantly chatting as we walked. I said loudly that Mum was sure that a nice sea cruise to India would do wonders for June's attacks of the screaming hysterics, and might even reduce them to less than one a week.

Mo asked if being in love had stopped her heavy drinking.

Just for good measure we threw in some garbled yarn about Dad's hopes that a wealthy new son-in-law might save the family farm from the bailiffs. With an inspired stroke of perfidious genius, we added ten years to June's real age.

As June's swain emerged from the outback, still wiping his hands on the turps rag, we acted out our guilty embarrassment, expressing the loud and fervent hope that he had not overheard our conversation because Dad would be furious if another of June's catches slipped the hook. The disillusioned Romeo feigned sickness, departing at tea time, and Mum's Figgy Duff was blamed.

Nora took June into the front room to cry in privacy and comfort. I could hear them trying to play duets on the piano and singing weepy songs of unrequited love. June's grief lasted for at least a fortnight, then she met up with a smart young man in the city's Silver Band. Dad proposed that she brought this one home for inspection quickly because another bout of refurbishing, privy varnishing, and never knowing where his boots, pipe lighters, or working jacket were likely to be hidden, was more than a tolerant chap like him could stand.

The Five Legged Rabbit

Thirza Kittle seldom encountered any sort of traffic as she plodded through the quiet lanes on her weekly shopping expeditions, so the excitement of hearing the warning bell of the town ambulance ringing ever closer made her risk life, limb, and her best lisle stockings to scramble up in the thorny hedgerow to watch the box-sided vehicle approach.

As it slowly progressed along the roughly surfaced track, she was able to peer through the sepia tinted side window long enough to identify the patient on the stretcher in the back. This confirmed a local 'confidential' rumour that the village nurse had been taken so sadly that she might well require major surgery for some unmentionable female complaint.

In a parish so placidly peaceful that two dogs fighting constituted a major excitement, the village shop was the social centre, a meeting place where Thirza could chat with her cronies, spicing mundane grocery shopping with a sprinkling of local gossip and companionship each Friday afternoon. The fact that a quarter-mile-long farm track separated Thirza from her nearest neighbour never prevented her from finding the most intriguing and interesting snippets of information to mull over with her friends.

Her anxiety to break the news that the community would be without the services of its ministering angel added speed and impetus to her usual ponderous pace. Overweight and on the far side of sixty, hurrying played havoc with her puffy legs and throbbing feet but, having occupied her mind by thinking of every possible symptom and complication that the nurse-turned-patient might endure, Thirza limped into the shop. Pushing past her friends she eased her perspiring bulk up on to the top of a bin of dog meal and sat panting, trying to regain her breath.

The state of Thirza's lower extremities had often provided fuel for flagging conversations, but on this particular occasion it was a subject she was not keen to pursue.

"It ain't my poor old feet that makes my heart bleed!" she remarked sombrely. "It sets me off of a shake to think of that poor dear woman being bumped and bounced all the way to the hospital, knowing that when she gets there some doctor will be waiting to take all her insides away! How are the rest of us to manage should we get struck down sudden, with no trained help at hand?"

Seeing that the perplexed shoppers looked suitably awestruck, Thirza leaned forward, brushing aside a dusty dangling flypaper that had long since lured its last victim to a gum-stuck death.

Straightening a wide-brimmed straw hat that drooped over her ears like a cosy covering the spout and handle of a tea pot, she paused to heighten the dramatic effect.

"And what about our weekly descriptions?" she continued. "Will we still be covered? Can anyone answer that?"

"Descriptions?" The shopkeeper looked as nonplussed as her customers.

"Ah!" said Thirza. "And well might you ask! You pays your penny a week into the Country Nursing Fund box the same as the rest of us, but do you think we're likely to get a halfpenny piece in change while we're without a nurse?"

Within minutes every anatomical detail of the nurse's ailment had been discussed, then the subject veered to the effect her absence would have on those village women who were in 'the family way' and near their time. The assembled shoppers could think of only one such case facing this predicament, and then the patient was unlikely to have problems. With eleven children already, it was the Friday shoppers' considered opinion that 'Slap-Cabbage Sal' would find her twelfth confinement as simple as a sun-dried broom seed popping from the pod.

Thirza kept her own counsel on that particular subject. Sal might be a 'slap-cabbage' slattern, wed to a leery, loutish, work-shy husband, but she was cousin to Thirza's late husband and therefore a relative of sorts. Skilfully changing the subject, she suggested that the most urgent problem was likely to be old Grandad Walls, should the weather turn nasty and bring on one of his bronchial spells again.

Sadie Walls, the old man's daughter-in-law and a Friday reg-ular, agreed that when it came to applying a kaolin poultice to his chest, the district nurse was the only female that the cantankerous old curmudgeon would trust to lift his nightshirt higher than his knees. Sadie hoped that nurses from adjoining areas might keep an eye on the village or a temporary replace-ment nurse might be sent to help out.

By virtue of the fact that Thirza's nephew was courting a kitchen helper at the town cottage hospital, she was believed to have access to information denied others. The rest looked at her expectantly.

"Ah!" she said enigmatically. "We shall have to wait and see!"

At the next Friday shopping session, Thirza offered a graphic description of a surgeon's stitchcraft that had made the nurse-turned-patient's stomach resemble an embroidered patchwork cushion. This did not make the dramatic impact she considered it to deserve. It seemed that everyone else had seen, heard, or met the new nurse who had arrived in the village without her knowing, but this fact Thirza tried to keep to herself.

The others looked incredulous as she admitted, "I can't say I've noticed her about."

"Once seen never forgotten!" the shopkeeper retorted. "You must have heard her roaring around the place on that noisy motorbike."

The thought of a nurse straddling one of those fearsome, smelly objects seemed to Thirza to be downright unladylike, undignified and vaguely indecent.

"Well, her certainly don't ride it side-saddle, Thirza." Tilly Hackett giggled, elbowing the other Friday regulars within nudging distance. "She was over at Grandad Walls' place as I came across the green. If we keep an eye and ear open for her leaving, then you can judge for yourself." Thinking aloud as the motor cyclist stopped outside the village store, Thirza was sure that in all her days she had never seen an apparition like the tall, broad-shouldered figure in knee boots, cavalry riding breeches, leather gauntlets, blue melton cloth donkey jacket and a gaberdine nursing uniform hat.

"If you want my honest opinion," Thirza said earnestly, "There's a bit of jiggerypokery going on somewhere. That's no nursing sister! They're trying to palm us off with some weirdy kind of chap."

Standing six feet tall in her studded boots, the nurse strode into the shop, and not knowing that shopping was an afternoon-long session for the Friday regulars, said she would take her turn in the queue. Unanimous in agreement that the nature of her work gave her top priority, the cronies watched with interest to see what she would buy.

"Five dozen dust combs, bug rakes, nit crackers, or whatever you like to call them," boomed the nurse, more baritone than contralto.

A couple of small-toothed combs, discoloured on a card, had hung unsold in the shop for so long that the price mark had faded completely. The prospect of selling five whole cards at one go made the shopkeeper check that she had heard aright.

"That's it!" The nurse re-affirmed. "Sixty will ensure that each pupil at the village school can be checked at home. I'm damned if I like having to hack off a child's hair because its head is crawling with lice!"

Taking this as a slur on the local women, the lady shoppers protested that there were only one or two suspect families in the parish. The rest were scrupulously clean. "They are the poor blighters that get infected by the others! I plan to eliminate the infestation at the school if I have to kill lice singly by stamping on them with my fairy feet!" The nurse spoke cheerfully, her laughter rumbling like the echoing tide in some deep cliff-face cavern. "Incidentally, can anyone direct me to a Mrs. Thirza Kittle's house?" Thirza made herself known and, as the nurse asked her to step outside for a moment, speculation among the other Friday shoppers ran riot.

The nurse's main preoccupation was with nursing the sick, killing nits, or delivering babies. Thirza was so healthy and wholesome that she was unlikely to be troubled by the first two contingencies, she was also far too long in the tooth to be involved in the third.

When Thirza returned to her shopping, she was extremely subdued, dismissing her chat as being just a bit of friendly consultation, but venturing the opinion that under the nurse's mannish, hearty exterior, was a thoughtful soul with a heart to match her size.

The truth was that on her ante-natal visit to 'Slap-Cabbage Sal', the nurse had taken one look at the horde of lethargic, ill-nourished children swarming amid the squalor and knew that she must find some good-hearted soul to offer her mistreated, thoroughly defeated patient a helping hand.

Enquiries had shown Thirza to be remotely connected with this problem case, so the nurse could only prevail on the tenuous 'cousin by marriage' link and rely on the humanity of this good hearted, if garrulous soul.

Thirza realised that her cronies were not satisfied with her brief explanation, but family shame for the pigsty conditons surrounding Sal's imminent confinement called for prevarication. She told them she had consented to do some voluntary assistant nursing, providing her poor old feet would stand the strain. She then maintained the discreet silence demanded by medical ethics and let her friends ruminate over that.

On the day Sal's twelfth child made up its mind to start arriving, the nurse rode over for Thirza in a hurry. Perilously perched on the pillion of the twin-engined 'Brough Superior' motor cycle, Thirza was convinced that she would die of fright if her lights and liver were not jolted and jarred to atoms, but had to admit that covering the mile and a quarter journey in two minutes was a lot easier on her throbbing feet. Any discomforts of the journey were soon forgotten as she hobbled over the threshold of Sal's poverty-stricken home.

Thirza bustled around, stoking up the corner copper to boil water, coping with the children that swarmed under her feet like ants. Sal's labour was surprisingly long and protracted in the early stage, so the nurse donned a sackcloth scrubbing apron and set to helping Thirza clean house. They even managed to launder a load of bed linen, and by evening a hovel with all the charm of a rubbish dump became a reasonably presentable place.

As Thirza and the nurse sat waiting for Sal's contractions to increase in intensity. Thirza remarked that although she had no personal experience of childbirth, it seemed to cause Sal less discomfort than she was personally suffering with her feet.

"Let me take a look at them, Thirza!" Friendly as it was, the nurse's voice brooked no argument. Thirza rolled down her stockings to reveal a pair of feet that her overweight state had prevented her from reaching down to tend for years. Before she could object they were soaking in a pan of hot soda water, while one of the round-eyed, runny-nosed small spectators watching this exceptional operation was dispatched to the village blacksmith for the loan of the kind of iron rasp the farrier used to file down the horses' hooves.

The nurse needed all her strength to prune back the calcified ingrown nails that had been so long untended that they had extended over the top of each tortured toe. Thirza did far more groaning than the woman in labour, and when the baby suddenly arrived just as the nurse finished filing Thirza's tenth toenail, there were three patients, all bawling with relief.

Feeling nimble as a young filly, Thirza trotted around looking after Sal and her brood, but found time to collect her weekly Friday groceries the next afternoon. To the other shoppers eagerly awaiting a grunt-by-grunt account of Sal's confinement, she announced that a miracle worker had come among them.

"There she was," she enthused, "calm as you please, curing my poor crippled old paddlers and delivering soft headed Sal's little one all in a matter of moment, with no fuss or commotion. That's what I call a proper nurse."

The shopkeeper suggested that it might be more useful if the nurse could cure Sal's loutish husband of his drunken depraved habits, for he had been caught acting like an old tom cat with a servant up at The Hall according to some. If the nurse could work a miracle or two in his direction there would be fewer drunken brawls, black eyes, or babies for 'Slap-Cabbage Sal', and a good-hearted soul like Thirza would not be traipsing back and forth to clean up a midden or mind a parcel of kids. If Thirza was expected to make an answer, the assembled women were disappointed. She had never been one to stand idly by when folk around her were in trouble and, while she personally favoured castration for Sal's husband, she kept her opinion to herself.

Another Friday shopper, Tilly Hackett, filled the awkward silence that followed with the comment:

"My Tom's old mother wouldn't agree that the nurse is an angel, Thirza! She's up at Foxley End chuntering something chronic, calling her a ham-hoofed cart horse and suchlike. For my part, I ain't much of a praying woman, but I tell you straight that for this last few days I've given thanks on my knees that this new nurse came!"

Glad to have the focus of attention taken from her own disreputable relatives, Thirza urged Tilly to explain. As everyone knew, Mrs. Hackett senior always took her bad back to bed at the first cold twinge of winter every year. The previous nurse had popped in to give her 'creaking screwmatics' an occasional oiling with embrocation and Mrs. Hackett had stayed bed-bound, suffering in comfort until spring. She considered it a small trifle to ask of her daughter-in-law that she tended fires, cooked, cleaned and cared for her when Tilly and Tom lived not more than a two mile step away.

Tom's mother had sent for the new nurse because an autumnal spell had driven her to bed. The nurse had shown less interest in the patient's carefully listed symptoms than in the sagging springs of the bed. She bounced the mattress up and down until the brass bedknobs rattled and, when Mrs. Hackett made groaning sounds appropriate to suppressed agony, diagnosed a classic hypothetical condition that needed drastic action right away. As she watched the nurse clump out of her bedroom, Mrs. Hackett snuggled under her coverlet and wondered what kind of treatment she might expect.

She had not heard the like of the bumping and thumping noises coming from downstairs since the village carpenter and undertaker had brought coffin boards up the narrow staircase on the night her husband died. It had been something of a shock to learn that she had an affliction that the nurse could put a name to, but it was disconcerting to think that the clod-hopper in a starched apron believed her to be as far gone as that. She was relieved to see the nurse re-enter the bedroom with the top board of her scullery trestle table, but when brawny arms that brooked no argument lifted her bodily from her bed to sit on the seat of her commode, she was not so sure.

Mrs. Hackett watched her precious goose feather bed being hauled into the damp back bedroom. The trestle boards were shoved beneath the hard, unyielding horse hair under-mattress, and within minutes she was tightly tucked into a pillow-less comfortless bed. Questioning the nature of her ailment and her treatment, she was told there was a simple alternative to staying where she was. The best remedy for her creaking joints was to give the house a clean and polish from top to bottom. Activity was the best cure the nurse could recommend.

Tilly Hackett related how she had arrived to find her mother-in-law up, dressed, and looking as joyful as a second-hand shroud. She confided that it was the 'High Patheticals' that ailed her, and while it was the modern treatment to make a poor tormented sufferer sleep on boards like a parish pauper, no navvy in a nursing apron would deny her the right to sleep on the feather mattress that had been a wedding present from her husband's grandmother, even if it meant gritting her teeth and bearing the burden of her illness by herself.

All Tilly knew was that for the first time since her marriage to Tom, she could look forward to a winter without rushing over to Foxley End in fair weather or foul, walking miles back and forth seven days a week. She reiterated her unstinting gratitude to the new nurse, but wondered how she had managed to cure Thirza's crippled feet, deliver 'Slap-Cabbage Sal's baby, and cope with eleven kids and all sorts of animals running in and out of the place.

Thirza realized she was being invited to make further comment on the intimate details of Sal's confinement, but the squalid misery of the woman was too painful to discuss.

In any case she could not linger for as long as usual because the nurse was taking her back to Sal's when the shopping session was done. And the first problem was evident as soon as Thirza and the nurse arrived there.

A bewildered, unweaned toddler was in his mother's bedroom, screaming to the full extent of his lungpower because every time he clambered on to her bed to nuzzle against her full breasts, he was pushed aside in favour of the new baby that had overnight usurped his place. A waif of a girl, Sal's oldest daughter, tried to pacify him by tying sugar in a snippet of rag like a miniature pudding, then popping the makeshift comforter into his open mouth.

When this failed to quieten him, she let him hold a wriggling rabbit she gently withdrew from above the waistband of her torn and buttonless dress. Frustrated in his infantile fury, wanting only comfort from his mother, the enraged toddler hurled it onto the woman's bed.

Sal shrieked like a soul tormented, terror contorting the features of her thin pale face. Covering her newborn babe with the bedclothes, she cuffed the rejected infant, then flung the rabbit toward her eldest daughter. It hit the wall behind her, landing on the floor to squirm spasmodically for a few moments before it was still. "You bloody stupid ninny, Lizzie. Ain't I got enough troubles without you deliberately wishing another load of misery on my shoulders? Take that devilish unnatural creature out of here or I'll get out of this bed and belt you, straight I will!"

Between sobs, the patient entreated the nurse to make sure the baby was not deformed or birth-scarred and, having ensured that the child was remarkably lusty, the puzzled nurse shooed all the rest of the family into the kitchen and bid her patient rest.

The eldest child sat on the hearthrug, rocking back and forth, crooning softly to the rabbit that lay lifeless in her arms, while Thirza made a start on ironing borrowed bed sheets.

"Get out from under my feet when I'm back and forth heating the flatiron Lizzie!" she said sharply. "For goodness sake take that outside and bury it, it's too scrawny to skin for your dinner. Why on earth did you have to upset your mother, with her in childbed. It's wishing misery on her. She's the last creature on God's earth to want an increase in family within the year! With eleven little brothers and sisters to play with, why did you cart around a thing like that?"

Lizzie's cowed, almost furtive expression made Thirza reassure her that no one was going to hit her, then the girl said quaveringly,

"I had to take it! Poor little dap got borned with five legs!"
Thirza's shriek was almost as hysterical as Sal's had been.

"Lord have mercy on us, Lizzie! No wonder your poor Ma was
in such a turmoil. Don't you know that's just wishing a freak or
an imbecile mite to be born here within a twelvemonth. Fancy
showing her an unnatural thing like that!"

Injecting sanity into the superstition-riddled situation, the
nurse said that rabbits, malformed or otherwise, had nothing to
do with human procreation.

Thirza shushed her, whispering.

"Lizzie may be sixteen, but she's as simple-minded as a six-
year old and has shown no sign of being a woman grown.'

The nurse had first judged Lizzie to be about eleven, but her
real age explained why her hair was still long while all the
school age children of the family had cropped hair to eradicate
the lice.

Lizzie's head would need inspecting. Really studying this thin,
under-developed waif, another thought crossed the nurse's mind.
She had witnessed the stick-thin, pot-bellied poverty among
mining families during the lockouts, strikes, and unemployment
of the nineteen twenties a few years earlier, but this seemed
indefinably different. There was a curious roundness beneath the
tattered dress and a haunted, almost animal fear was written on
the child's undernourished face.

"Thirza, do you mind keeping the others occupied for a few
minutes?" the nurse asked quietly. "I am going to ask Lizzie to
slip off her dress."

The anxious inflexion of her voice made Thirza glance up
questioningly and the message passing between the two women's
eyes was instant and telepathic as Lizzie whimpered.

"No, not you! please."

"Come now child!" the nurse said briskly. Shivering with
terror, abjectively submissive, Lizzie let the shapeless frock fall
off her shoulders. Both women saw the bruising, the hand marks
and the rounded stomach.

"Christ in heaven. Gentle Jesus, help us!" Thirza's voice was
pure anguish as she tried to reject the obvious truth, but with
Lizzie standing in just her knickers, there could be no doubt.

The nurse asked if Lizzie had a regular sweetheart, or was she
one to fool around with the village lads. Thirza was certain that

this was not so. In mind and body, Lizzie was a reticent, simple, almost infantile child, so timid she was incapable of getting herself a job.

Not then fully comprehending the true situation in this benighted and bullied household, the nurse said,

"Perhaps Lizzie's parents can tell me more?"

Lizzie's father had gone off following the threshing machine, his first employment for some time and it seemed to Thirza that Sal's anger was more devious than furious as she railed at her uncomprehending daughter.

"You've been out with them village boys, ain't you Lizzie? Now you admit it unless you want your father to take his strap to you! Do you want to get put away in some institution, locked up for years on end?"

Lizzie, bewildered and frightened, nodded, then shook her head.

"Say it then, say it was one of them boys that did it!"

Turning to the nurse, Sal stuttered.

"Lizzie's sixteen now, remember. I was married at her age and expecting too, not that that matters, except that she's over the age of consent."

Thirza suggested that the trouble might have been caused closer to home.

"You think what you like," Sal started sobbing, "but I've got twelve kids to feed, and when you try to prove what you're hinting, just remember that you might take the bread and butter out of their mouths. Bloody rabbit! I told you what would happen Lizzie, when you brought that thing in the house."

Thirza and the nurse agreed that Lizzie must be taken out of the danger right away, but the Poor Law Institution was the only solution available at the time. Sal made no objections, but the thought of poor inoffensive little Lizzie being incarcerated in the grim old prison-like building in the nearest city, was more than Thirza could bear.

"Lizzie," she said briskly, "your poor Ma has too many burdens and kids to contend with properly. I have none. How would you like to come and live with me for always. I do get a mite lonely at times."

Lizzie made no answer but went to collect her few personal

belongings, a broken string of glass beads and a torn piece of old blanket which she cuddled when she went to bed.

So Lizzie found a home in Thirza's lonely cottage, and there some four months later a premature, puny, brain-damaged child was born. No one could have lavished more love, care and attention than did Thirza, and in the few months that the baby survived, the young mother, still not fully comprehending her situation, cuddled her infant in the summer sunshine as if she was caressing a living doll.

The nurse had been a constant visitor from the day that she first discovered Lizzie's condition, collecting Thirza's weekly grocery order from the village, helping and keeping kindly watch over the ageing countrywoman with her simple-minded niece, and a baby with a life expectancy of nil.

It was easy to forget that hers was a temporary appointment to allow her nursing colleague to recuperate, and eventually the day came when she rode over to tell Thirza that she must soon leave.

She found Thirza washing nappies. Together they went to look for Lizzie who had carried her baby into the meadow beyond the back garden gate.

They found her on her knees amidst the tall sorrels and daisies, crooning tunelessly to the baby lying limp and lifeless in her arms. Thirza held her close as the nurse took the dead child from her, Lizzie looking perplexed by the tears on the nurse's cheeks.

"You said that five-legged rabbit was bad, didn't you Aunt Thirza? He made me take it! It's his fault ain't it?" She looked at Thirza for confirmation.

"Who Lizzie?" The nurse asked gently, hoping to clear up her suspicion of incest. All she got by way of answer was Lizzie whimpering. "I don't want to be hurt bad again, nor locked up!" The subject was dropped. It took all Thirza's courage to take Lizzie for her usual Friday shopping. The regulars were all there, excited and anxious to tell her that Lizzie's drunken father had been knocked down. He had staggered in front of the nurse's motorbike and had landed in Plough Lane ditch.

"No bones broken!" The shopkeeper assured her, "but while he was floundering in the mud half-drowned with panic, the nurse accidentally blacked his eye as she hauled him out. He's got some diabolic bruising, but that's only to be expected when you think of being prodded by that sharp upright metal front number plate.

'Fat lot of thanks she got for her trouble and bothering to look after him this morning. Pearce the postman reckoned he could hear him hollering half a mile distant when the nurse poured liniment over his bruised unmentionables to stop infection setting in. It seems that 'Slap-Cabbage Sal!' won't need to worry now about him breeding babies like some old buck rabbit, or being unlucky enough to have number thirteen for some time to come."

"Talking of rabbits!" Sadie Walls interjected. "Now the nurse is leaving I wondered if we ought to give her a little farewell present seeing how helpful she has been. I've got an old-fashioned brooch that was Grandma Walls. It's a lucky rabbit's foot mounted on silver. Do you think she'd like that, Thirza?"

Before Thirza could answer, Lizzie spoke out.

"Don't give her that or she might get a poor little baby same as I did."

"Lizzie, you do talk nonsense," Thirza interjected. "Come on girl, help me pack these groceries, we must get back now!"

Hand in hand with her ageing Aunt, the artless, immature girl walked back along the country lanes towards the only safe sanctuary of love that she had ever known.

Chains of Daisies

Cast ne'er a clout until May be out was a saying that most country people agreed with, although there were differing opinions about the exact time of year intended. The more venturesome believed it to be permissible to shed a few layers of winter clothing as soon as the blossom on the hawthorn bushes began to bloom. More cautious souls waited for the treacherous month of May to be safely finished before attempting to cast off their winter combinations or flannel petticoats.

Some of my classmates at the village school were literally stitched into flannel undershirts from Michaelmas until June, regardless of any minor heatwave that April or May might bring. My Mum was not averse to protecting my chest with a piece of flannel soaked in oil of wintergreen and goose grease, kept in place with long tapes, and tucked out of sight beneath an itchy woollen vest. My liberation from being muffled in cold weather clothing always came toward the end of May, on one special celebratory day of joyous freedom, a landmark in the year.

I loathed the brown, concertina-wrinkled stockings of winter, since they had to be held up by tight garters that did nothing for my circulation and frequently fell down around my ankles. Otherwise they were held aloft by home-made suspenders sewn to my liberty bodice. Any slight exertion was liable to send the buttons pinging so, whichever method of suspension my mother favoured to keep my long skinny legs encased for the winter, my stockings were always at half mast, leaving a gap between knee and knicker prone to every cold wind that blew.

The fleecy-lined knickers that I wore stretched with each trip to the washtub, extending upwards to my armpits and sagging into a voluminous elastic-gathered bunch around each leg. Vest, combinations and petticoats were topped by a thick skirt and jumper but, come Empire Day, all this was changed. With my winter-clothing chrysalis discarded, the summer 'me' emerged like a scrawny specimen of a Cabbage White butterfly, white cotton vested, knickered and petticoated.

Gone were the drooping winter stockings in favour of cotton socks, and the boots in which, like most country children, I plodded through the mud of winter, were put aside. On Empire Days I was allowed to wear white canvas shoes or sandals that, by comparison, were thistledown upon my feet.

Freedom from muffling winter-weight clothing was but one factor that made the ritual of our Empire Day celebrations seem so special, the one day in the year when I ran eagerly to school.

The year my father donated a flagstaff for School Field I was sure I would burst with pride. I watched while he felled the tallest pine tree on the woodland skyline. I rode beside it as Dad's horses hauled it home on a rumbling timber tug. Weathered, planed and painted, it was taken round to School Field, waiting to be dedicated and erected when that year's Empire Day ceremony began.

I left home early that morning, taking the short cut through a wood green with springtime, where a myriad huge black ants industriously scurried around their teeming mounds in regimented order, where wild anemone and heady-scented bluebells carpeted the woodland floor on each side of the path. As I hurried along past hawthorn hedges heavy with pinky-white blossoms smelling like vanilla junket, unsheared sheep and fat, panting lambs stared steadfastly as if they envied the fact that I had shed my winter fleece.

Under horse chestnut trees, with candle blossom all ablaze in celebration of summer, I ran on through Parsonage Path, flanked by hedges of white and purple lilac, philadelphus and laburnum in full flower, until I reached School Lane. In overcrowded cottage gardens, stocks and riotous-coloured wall flowers were kept in some semblance of order by the Guardsman-straight lines of yellow and red tulips lining either side of the front paths.

Other children had reached School Field before me, wandering in the still-wet grass with their white sandals turning damp-grey in the dew as they picked the longest-stalked daisies they could find. The object of the exercise was to make the longest, strongest daisy chain before the school bell went. Trooping triumphantly into the schoolroom with three or four lengths twined round our necks, the most despicable sabotage one could inflict on a fellow pupil was to nip off the daisy heads, so that the chain fell apart and dropped to the floor.

With our schoolmaster in charge of the proceedings, one would never dare to stoop down and attempt to retrieve it, although the possession of a daisy chain was an all-important factor in this special day.

While pupils stood shuffling, hands on heads, and more than a promise of the cane for anyone caught talking, the 'big boys' helped to carry the school piano out of doors. Marching forth in columns, ever mindful of the fate threatened by the school-master to those who did not mind their manners, we mustered in lines before a circular slab of concrete with a hole at its centre. An assembly of honoured guests sat on chairs brought over from the village hall. Part of the fascination of the occasion was to watch them visibly shrinking as the tips of their chair legs sank lower and lower into the turf. The school governors and managers, Dad among them, the parson, several fussy-hatted ladies and, of course, His Lordship himself: all shrank before us.

The little ceremony ran to a set pattern, starting with the schoolmaster's speech of appreciation of the honour being bestowed on the humble village children by His Lordship's presence. Then His Lordship had his say. Because he too, stuck to a recognisable routine, as soon as his first question left his throat, we were ready with hands thrusting upward, hoping to be the fortunate pupil called upon to answer. Could we tell him why we were all wearing daisy chains this morning?

Of course we could, yet if his silver-topped cane pointed in one's direction, country shyness made the pupil stumble on his words, stuttering and mumbling, while all the rest shouted the answer clear. We knew that there were as many branches of the British Empire as there were petals on a daisy, because he used the same theme every year.

We knew too that each flowering shrub around the perimeter of School Field was planted to commemorate those men who left our village to defend our Glorious Empire in the 1914–18 war. To break their branches was to damage and disparage the names of those who fought for us. It was almost treasonable, and an insult to our illustrious King.

At this point six big boys from the top class struggled to lift and carry the new flagstaff forward to the concrete base. Assisted by Charlie Cartwright, Lordy's steward and my father, they heaved it upright, carrying it forward like a wavering caber, to the accompaniment of mild clapping and infantile cheering. It tilted, wobbled and swayed. The parson stood ready to give his blessing, but ducked as the flagstaff dipped and fell to the ground.

"Damnation!" said my father. "The blasted wood has swelled with last night's dew."

Old Charlie Cartwright suggested that all it needed was a bit of planing, and while one of the big boys was dispatched to fetch a rasp and plane from the school woodwork cupboard, ceremonial faltered. Uncertainly, our honoured guests sat wondering how to maintain the dignity of the occasion to background noises of carpentry and old Charlie Cartwright's comments.

"If this is a plane, I'll stew my grandmother's toe-nails! You could ride bare boned to London on it and not get saddle sore!"

"Better take another smidgin off 'un, Harry. Let's try her now. Up a bit. Back aways. Hold it. Watch out missus. That's more like it."

As the flagstaff came to a vertical position and stayed there, Charlie turned to His Lordship, smiling, and said, "There you are, Sir. Didn't take more than the shake of a nanny goat's tail to do 'un, and ole Harry's flag pole be settled in snug as a flea in a tinker's nightshirt."

Our Empire Day celebration carried on. The parson intoned a diffident blessing and the flag was hoisted to loud applause. We sang rousing patriotic songs, and the more literate among us recited hunks of Kipling. Another prayer from the parson, then the schoolmaster reiterated the rules for our Empire Day race.

Spaced out according to age and sex, the course was ten times round School Field for the older pupils and twice for the smaller tots. Since there was an Empire Shield and a shilling awaiting the winner, the race became a free for all with no holds barred. We all knew that once the race was over and the shield presented, His Lordship would call for three cheers for King George, three more for our Glorious Empire, then ask if we would like a half-day holiday from school.

It happened every year, but we would still express complete surprise and shout "Yes please, Sir!" We willingly gave three more cheers for our bounteous kindly Lordship, and when we had finished the boys bowed and the girls all curtseyed to our honoured guests. Still wearing our daisy chain garlands we were free to race off home.

My pride that Dad had donated the flagstaff made me determined to win the Empire Day race and carry the shield home. But fate conspired against me, using my own mother's thrift and ingenuity as its involuntary tool.

Back in the depths of winter, one of my older sisters had brought home a woman's magazine that sometimes sported free dressmaking patterns. This particular copy included instructions and tissue-paper patterns for *Madam's Dream Trousseau*, complete with knickers, chemise and petticoat.

Studying the magazine carefully, Mum said she could see no reason why the pattern could not be adapted to make summer undies for my sister Nora and me. The book gave several alternative materials as being suitable. Lovely names like *nainsook, cambric, dimity, nun's veiling* or *angel skin crepe-de-chine*, but my Mum had some cotton sheets that had only worn thin in places, and she saw no reason why the stronger parts could not be utilised. A snag arose when someone used a small bit of the pattern to test the heat of their hair waving irons, having decided that it was just a small square of tissue and of no account, but Mum went on sewing, undaunted.

These then were the underclothes I wore on that Empire Day when I was so determined I would win the shield. I had realised there was something not quite right with the shape of my knickers as I hurried to school that morning. By the time we were lined up for the start of our minor marathon, I knew something was sadly amiss. I crouched down with the rest of my peers. Hampered or not, I had to run.

The inevitable happened before I had even negotiated the first corner. With two cotton legs and a buttonless waist band flapping round my ankles, I took refuge amongst the shrubs, hoping that some 1914–18 hero had no objections to my shedding my breeches behind his memorial bush.

"Ah, yes!" said my mother when I returned wearing a pair of the schoolmaster's wife's chaff sack bloomers that she insisted I used to cover my shame on my journey home. "I'll bet that little bit of spare pattern was a gusset fitting in there somewhere, I'll mend them up and stick a patch in the middle, and they will do for you this year."

Now Dad's flagstaff has crumbled to dust along with any reason to celebrate a glorious empire, but little girls still make daisy chains out in School Field and the tall flowering trees that surrounded it blaze with blossom in May.

The Crosscut Saw

Standing selfconsciously beside his mother, Tom watched the village shopkeeper rummaging amongst crumpled, yellowing tissue paper in a couple of dusty cardboard boxes. Having established that the large sized black cloth cap was the only item of mourning headgear that he had in stock, the shopkeeper adopted a take-it-or-leave-it attitude. He handed the cap to Tom's mother, saying she could please herself as to whether or not Tom should try it on for size.

Tom, a gangling, thirteen year old, studied his scuffed boots for a few embarrassed moments, then reluctantly balanced the wide peaked 'cheese cutter' black cloth cap on the side of his head. A grimy mirror behind the counter reflected his blushing image between the peeling, tarnished gilt lettering that advertised Peerless Erasmic Soap. The cap seemed to give him added height and maturity, making him keen to wear it. From his one experience of a talking picture show, Tom knew that the American city of Chicago swarmed with gangsters carrying guns in violin cases and wearing caps identical to this. He tilted it lower over one eye, surveying the effect until his mother clipped him smartly round the ears to remind him why the cap needed to be bought.

As she readjusted it to a less flippant angle, engulfing Tom's right ear and obscuring his forward vision, she noticed the price tag dangling at the back. Any possessive aspirations Tom had nurtured evaporated as his mother snatched the cap from his head.

"Five shillings and elevenpence?" Her voice was shrill with incredulity. "If I let young Tom follow his poor Grandfather wearing that thing, I'd half expect the old chap to lift the lid and sit upright in his coffin berating me for indulging in such wicked extravagant waste. It's a lad's cap I am willing to pay for, not the tithe rates on your shop!"

As she slammed the offending cap down on the counter, a piled up platter of stale doughnuts quivered in anguish. The top few, slipping and sliding, started a small sad avalanche, spreading snail trails of damp sugar across the unswept shop floor.

Glad to avoid the unpleasant atmosphere above counter level, Tom busied himself dusting dried mud and fluff from the retrieved doughnuts, and piling them up again almost as good as new.

Watching the abortive transaction with avid interest, was Alfie Pearce's Mum who lived in an adjoining cottage. She made sympathetic clucking noises in the direction of Tom's mother and added fuel to the fires of female indignation by observing that the selfsame type of cap could be purchased from the stall of the town market place for one shilling and sixpence, or one shilling and elevenpence if there was real rubber in the peak. Her Alfie had a cap Tom could wear for the funeral and all Tom's mother would need to purchase was a twopenny black Dolly tub dye.

Alfie Pearce's donated cap completely engulfed Tom's head. He loathed it. Black dye failed to shrink it and stuffing the headband with folded newspaper only heightened the illusion that his neck was a stalk supporting a monstrous mushroom of gigantic size.

For two days in succession his mother had indulged in a frenzy of baking, then early on the morning of his grandfather's funeral Tom helped his father carefully load baskets of crockery and trays of food on a home-built four wheeled truck. As they hauled it towards his grandfather's cottage on the far side of the village, it was difficult for Tom to realise that behind the drawn curtains of the front parlour, stiff, cold and unmoving, was the gentle old man who had always found time to tell Tom tales about his own boyhood. The one person in the world in whom Tom could confide his troubles, hopes and fears.

Alfie Pearce had regaled Tom with some horrific stories about dead people, ghosts and hauntings, so he was extremely apprehensive when his father suggested that they say their last goodbyes to Grandad before the other relatives arrived.

Unashamedly clutching his father's hand, Tom entered the airless gloomy parlour and wondered aloud about the nightlights standing in saucers of salt that surrounded the coffin trestles. There was little comfort in his father's explanation that it helped to keep evil spirits away.

It seemed totally incomprehensible to Tom that his grandfather would never open his eyes and joke with him again, for he looked so naturally asleep that Tom walked on tip-toe to avoid disturbing his dreams.

Several unknown aunts and uncles arrived, speaking softly at first as they made excuses for not visiting the old man more often, but their voices became more strident as they crowded into the tiny house.

Tom's father was determined that the tenancy of the cottage should be relinquished in a tidy state, so while his relatives were staking their claims to various items as they awaited the arrival of the village undertaker, he took a pair of garden shears out to trim the front privet hedge. He knew he would invoke conjugal wrath by pottering around the muddy garden in his new white shirt and best blue serge suit, but an intolerable atmosphere of tension was developing among his older brothers and sisters that made him want to be by himself.

Tom cast envious glances through a gap in the drawn curtains but did not dare to defy his mother's orders that he stay clean and tidy, seen but not heard. He seemed to be in everyone's way, an unwilling listener to long standing family arguments that were being aired. Relatives that had not been near the place for years catalogued all the help they had supposedly given Grandad in secret, knowing that none could refute their claims now the old man was dead. Elbows were nudged, quietly spoken words fell like small stones rippling muddy puddles of innuendo. Smiling lips that could not mask the glaring looks cast in Tom's direction, murmured cautious observations about little pigs standing around and staying quiet because they were using their big ears.

It was beyond his comprehension that they could be bickering while Grandad lay peacefully asleep in his oak coffin in the middle of the room. If only the old man would wake from his dreaming, Tom knew that the arguing would stop in an instant.

A sudden impulse made him want to shout and use all the swear words that he knew to make his elders stop it, but the resinous woody smell of the coffin combining with the stuffy atmosphere of the crowded room, made him feel as if he was choking. A sharp prickling sensation overwhelmed him, as if a bed of stinging nettles had suddenly sprung up behind his eyes. He ran through to the back scullery where his mother was setting out trays of borrowed cups and saucers, trying to express an unhappiness for which he had no words, but she was too preoccupied with her own problems to show any reaction beyond observing that she was well aware that while the rest of her in-laws were jostling with each other to divide the spoils between them, Tom's father was skulking in the garden letting them take first pickings of what by any sort of justice, should be his. She was upset, hot, and flustered, and irritated at Tom's interruption.

"Do get out from under my feet boy. Busy yourself by finding some nice dry kindling wood from the shed. The weather is so damp and dreary, everyone will be thankful to hear a kettle singing for the teapot when we get back from the church."

The windowless wooden garden shed seemed colder and darker, steeped in a listening silence, as if it might be waiting to hear Grandad's hand upon the door latch. This place had been Tom's childhood refuge from his well meaning but sharp tongued mother.

Here he had listened to the harvest of yarns and stories that Grandad had gathered during the sixty years he had worked at the timber yard. His youthful days spent as an under-dog in a saw pit, getting covered in sawdust as he pulled a huge ripsaw through the tree trunks, provided many oft repeated tales. Later, of course, Grandad became a 'top-dog', guiding the ripsaw from above, and when the whole process became mechanised Grandad was made foreman of the yard.

All his tools were hung on nails and pegs around the shed walls. The iron-runnered wooden sledge, which he had made for Tom's Christmas present one snowy winter, still stood in the corner. Tom could recall every moment of that moonlit, freezing cold, white winter night when both Grandad and his father took him over to Banky Meadows to try it out. All three of them had laughed together, skimmed down the slopes together, tumbled in the snow together. His mother, coming with a lantern to find them because it was long past bed-time, was sure it would do Grandad's arthritis no good at all.

Tom and his father often helped the old chap cut logs for his fire, with Grandad for ever teasing Tom about having muscles no bigger than sparrow's kneecaps, and saying he would need a lot more meat pudding inside him before he would be man enough to use Grandad's huge crosscut saw.

Filmy with cart grease, and resonant as a church bell, the eight foot long saw still hung behind the shed door. Touching the cold steel that had been the old man's pride and joy somehow gave Tom comfort. Lifting it from the hook, Tom recalled Grandad's judgement that a man who owned such a tool need never go cold or hungry, as long as there were trees to be felled.

"Tom. Where are you? Get that wood and hurry up about it. We are just leaving for the church, so do come on!"

Suddenly aware that his mother was calling, Tom tried to replace the saw, but it bowed and bent back and forth. His mother was becoming more angry, so Tom hurriedly lowered the crosscut and let it slip down behind some old planks of timber, putting his sledge in front of it to prevent anyone getting too near to the sharp blade.

Running into the cottage, he found everyone silent and sombre, watching the coffin lid being screwed into place. Only in that moment did the finality of death hit Tom's senses. His mother gave him a clean handkerchief, jammed Alfie Pearce's borrowed cap down over his forehead, and straightened the sagging crepe armband on his sleeve.

The village undertaker, leading the procession, had forgotten to remove his cycle clips, but it did not seem to matter. Tom clutched a bunch of flowers that had been thrust in his hand, and walked along behind the six men who carried Grandfather's casket shoulder high. His father was one of the bearers. Tom could have sworn that he was weeping, but for the fact that grown men never cry. As if the heavens wept for Grandad's passing, rain fell steadily, making the dye from Tom's borrowed cap trickle black streaks down his face to mingle with tears. He watched the burial service through a mist of sobbing misery, then trooped back to the cottage with all the other mourners, hurrying to get out of the wet.

Enlisted into the task of handing round hot tea and piled up food plates, he was amazed to see the assembled relatives eating as if they had not been fed for a fortnight, before they started systematically sorting through Grandad's possessions. Raised voices discussed everything they touched, and he watched two staid lady aunts stage a tug of war on the narrow stairs, pulling at each end of a feather bolster like two thrushes fighting over a worm.

Taking advantage of his mother's absence in the scullery, Grandad's tin box was turned upside down on the kitchen table. Tom watched the group crowding round, discarding the medals Grandad had earned for attending Sunday School regularly, scrabbling for the few golden sovereigns they found in a small wash-leather bag. In their mourning clothes, they gave him the same feeling of nauseous revulsion that he had felt when he once saw a flock of rooks swoop on the carcase of a still warm dead lamb.

Attempting to find refuge in the shed, he found his oldest uncle piling a barrow full of Grandad's tools.

'Nothing much left in here boy, except that old sledge and those rough bits of timber,' he said sheepishly. The shed door swung back and forth in the wind. During this time, Tom's father had said little and eaten nothing, slipping away to clear up the clippings from the hedge. The rest of the mourners departed, with their loaded barrows, pony traps, and hand carts. Tom helped his father sweep out one empty room after another, the echoing silence broken only by his mother's complaining voice listing various household items that should by rights have been hers.

"Woman," Tom's father said sternly, "the whole darned lot would have scarcely raised ten pound in an auction. My family came here greedy, grabbing, making excuses for staying away from my old Dad when they could have carried their guilty consciences back with all the stuff they grabbed. We did our best, and the old chap knew it. We had his love and no one can take that away, so we'll hear no more about it. Today has been about as much as I can stand!"

For a brief moment the red, raw weal of his father's private grief and anguish was so painful to witness that Tom hurried out to add a couple of old door mats and a broken windsor chair to the borrowed crockery already loaded on the four wheeled cart. Looking back at the windows as they left the cottage, Tom heard the shed door swinging back and forth in the wind. As his father went back to help him secure it, both saw the old sledge and knew they could not leave it behind. Tom suddenly remembered that he had left the crosscut saw down behind the planks of timber, and was delighted to find it still there.

Carefully wrapping it round with the mats, they put it on the cart, and in the gathering gloom of twilight, trundled their load back home.

The moon rose and the rain abated early that evening. Restless and unhappy, Tom's father suggested that they take the crosscut saw out and try cutting up logs from the felled tree in the fruit plantation behind the house.

Muffled against the dampness of the evening, they hauled the handcart across the sodden grass by the light of a hurricane lamp that reflected the wet branches as gleaming tinsel all around. Standing each side of the tree trunk, they made little progress, and the saw seemed to jerk and jump as if it had a will of its own. Then Tom learned the art of knowing when to pull the saw toward him, never actually pushing, and within a few minutes found a steady rhythm that made his toes and fingers tingle with warmth, and set the saw singing as it sliced through the wood. Using a beadle mallet and wedges, Tom's father split the sawn lengths into logs for the kitchen fire. In helping to load them, Tom's borrowed cap fell off and was trampled in the mud.

"For God's sake let the blooming thing lie there," his father told him. "I don't reckon your Grandad would want to see you dripping black dye and running around like a kid advertising gravy powder. If what the parson say be true, the old chap will be resting peaceful, knowing that the pair of us are out here thinking of him, and you man enough to handle his old crosscut saw."

A sudden chill gust of wind set the lamp flame flickering, Tom remembered Alfie Pearce's assertion that the spirits of dead people stay earthbound for about a fortnight, as something dark and shadowy swept across the wet grass. But if one is considered man enough to take the handle of an eight foot crosscut saw, he should not frighten easily. Tom turned defiantly to face whatever was moving behind him. It was just the shadow of a swaying branch.

May-time

Still wallowing in the trough of an agricultural depression, few villagers could afford the luxury of benevolence. Nevertheless, everyone in our rural community regarded King George V and Queen Mary's Silver Jubilee as a once in a lifetime opportunity to outdo Lockley and the other neighbouring villages with the extent of our celebrations, thus establishing our natural superiority once and for all. Every inhabitant became involved in the frantic preparations.

With committees springing up like mushrooms in a wet autumn, old enmities and unsettled scores were set aside in the welter of patriotic fervour. Folk who had previously ignored the existence of their next door neighbours, now combined forces to decorate the front elevation of their properties with red, white and blue favours, their new found friendliness as tenuous as the pennants of paper thin cotton that fluttered on thin string.

By virtue of his being an ex bunting tosser in the Royal Navy, old Jim Puddington took on the task of ensuring that even the most remote and isolated cottage sported some sort of patriotic emblem to honour King George V and his Queen.

Scratching hens had spoiled the effect my mother had hoped for when she planted white candytuft and blue aubrietia around the clumps of peony flowers in our old farmhouse garden. It did nothing for her nervous system when, to prove that we were patriots, I scrambled up to place a flag on a stick high up in the massive copper beech tree that spread its mighty arms to shield our home from the worst of the easterly winds. It hung there until the gales of the following winter shredded it to ragged ribbons, with few to notice that it was upside down. Those who did accepted it as just another example of my being born awkward, having the unfortunate habit of tackling every straightforward task *widdershins* or the wrong way round.

Just thirteen, this failing had caused me more than a few low spirited moments of rejection amid all the rush and bustle of preparations for the big day. Enthusiastically as the rest, I had bound cane hoops with silver paper, adding dozens of painstakingly made, crepe paper, red, white and blue roses, ready for our spectacular display.

Soon after our first rehearsal had begun, the long suffering soul who had volunteered to attempt to transform thirty lumpkin country children into flower wielding elemental sprites ducked out of allowing me to remain among those performing.

Her reasons were specific. My unfortunate tendency to take off in the opposite direction to everyone else was totally disruptive. I was so gauche, so completely left handed, I caused instant confusion to all around me. It was her expressed opinion that inside my drooping socks I blundered along on two left feet.

Appreciating my disappointment, she explained that at 5ft 9in, my height alone could ruin the sensational effect of her highly original finale, wherein the flower festooned hoops became one massive floral tribute of loyalty. Behind this the performers lined up, holding and completely hidden by a sheeting banner bearing the legend, *Long Live His Lordship And Her Ladyship. God Save Our King and Queen.*

It was vital that this production should go well, for we had competition. Because His Lordship's son and heir was once a day scholar at an august, exclusive and ludicrously expensive college for the sons of gentry, situated in the next parish, a group of the illustrious young gentlemen were going to honour our celebrations by presenting excerpts from a comedy. This was to be their contribution to the happiness of the day. This I knew, for on the previous evening an impromptu parish meeting had convened around my Mum's kitchen table.

In retrospect it seemed that the main items on the agenda were to munch away at still warm bread and cheese and sample Dad's home made beer. At the same time everyone was trying to co-ordinate the many and varied activities into some sort of order so that a Jubilee programme could be formed.

The parson's sister, being the only lady committee member present, looked askance at such rough fare, but declined Mum's offer of a seed cake and a cup of tea. She would not say no to a sip of fruit cordial, if Mum had any to offer. Mum gave her a full tumbler of cherry ale to keep her quiet.

From the fireside stool where I sat, supposedly reading, I watched her face assume the same colour as the contents of her glass. Slurring slightly, Parson's sister put forward the proposal that, since various farmers were contributing barrels of cider and beer for the men of the parish to drink the loyal toast to Their Majesties, Mum could provide a few bottles of home made fruit cordials to enable the distaff side of the village to pledge their loyalty too.

The motion was carried unanimously. Old Charlie Cartwright sitting near me, stage whispered to my Dad that he "bet the old gal would make sure she was put in charge of the bottles and come with a corkscrew in her hand."

Old Charlie confirmed that His Lordship had personally telephoned him about "Them college lads giving a bit of a comedy performance." He had jotted it down somewhere, but could not put a hand to the note just at that moment. He knew it was by one of their masters who taught Greek, or some other high flown lingo. A Mr. Risto-Fanies or some such double barrelled name. No matter what, the committee could thank him for a good laugh after the sketch.

The timing of the two entertainments hinged on the arrival of His Lordship and his party. With Her Ladyship, he was to attend the Service of Thanksgiving in Westminster Abbey, and at the conclusion hurry back to our celebration. He would then graciously give us a first hand account of this auspicious occasion, and present every child in the parish with a Jubilee medal and a mug. The village children would then present their patriotic spectacular, followed by the college's comedy play. Until our noble patron arrived, the main item in the day long festivities was a cricket match, the ladies of the village versus the men.

The rules of the match allowed one innings only, men to bowl underarm, batting with a hedge stake, women to bat or bowl by any method they chose.

Originally, twelve slightly daring or downright defiant souls had volunteered for the ladies team, but two dropped out. One was keeping a low profile, having got herself married with what was then regarded as shameful swiftness, while the other non starter admitted that she had the choice of respecting her husband's disapproving viewpoint or being thumped. All this I heard, ear-wigging at the meeting in our kitchen. Listening to my elders discussing the advisability of asking the parson to supplement the ladies team, since he was nought but an old woman, I longed to volunteer to fill the vacancy. With three older brothers, I learned early how to hit a ball and run. Rejection from the dancing display gave me the chance.

Most housewives produced their best cookery in readiness for the early hours of Jubilee morning, when Dave's milk float and our covered cart did the rounds of the parish, collecting all edible contributions to take them to the various tents and the huge marquee erected in Glebe Meadow. Jim Puddington's flags and bunting fluttered like lines of coloured washing as the black-smith's wife stacked row on row of Jubilee mugs on a sheet covered table by the tent flap entrance. There was an excited, chaotic kind of rush and bustle all around.

Alighting from three parked cars, a troop of white clad college lads, wearing effeminate looked pleated tunics, followed their dismal looking master. Presuming him to be the Mr. Risto-Fanies that had been noted down for Charlie Cartwright's attention, Charlie greeted him by name. The perplexed, pale face crumbled into a semblance of a smile, like creased tissue paper.

"How droll. Risto-Fanies indeed. Your ready wit will no doubt savour our excerpt from The Archarnians by the Athenian classical genius Aristophanes.'

Old Charlie nodded uncertainly.

Out on the field, the toss of a new Jubilee penny decided that the ladies cricket team were batting first. I was opening bat. Stifling my stage fright I walked out toward the wicket, watching the warm southerly breeze flutter the canvas of the marquee.

The ladies team had met with many cross currents of opposition and disapproval, caused by strait laced individuals who believed that any female flaunting herself by cavorting around Glebe Meadow with eleven leery and agile men must degrade and disgrace all womanhood.

The relevant Jubilee committee tactfully asked lady cricketers to "act with decorum and play soberly and suitably dressed." In no way could our ladies team captain have been accused of flaunting or attempting to arouse baser male passions. Inappropriately named Violet, she was totally lacking in feminine attributes. Heftily built, hearty voiced and clad in the washed-out looking shirts and breeches that seemed to be the entire content of her wardrobe, any stranger might well have believed her to be one of the more lusty members of the opposing team.

Her interpretation of the committee's advice on dress was to keep any part of the anatomy inclined to flop or wobble crepe bandaged or tightly corseted. Glimpses of bare flesh between suspendered stockingtops and bloomer elastic were taboo, and the fashionable, lace trimmed, wide-legged french knickers were definitely out.

Our team were conservatively clad for the occasion. Most wore hats, either straw or floppy, wide-brimmed floral cotton, while some favoured head bands or hair nets. With tall spiky dead grass in the outfield few risked wearing their best silk stockings. Instead they displayed thick cotton lisles and flat heeled shoes. Even the more sprightly chose calf length skirts and severe blouses or subdued summer frocks.

Conforming to the prevailing proprieties, some wore white cotton gloves. In what had seemed at the time to be an inspirational moment, I had borrowed the outfit my older, fashion conscious sister had made for her Saturday afternoon tennis sessions. It was a blue, linen garment, with a bloused bodice and knee-length divided skirt. Skinnier than the garment's owner, I pulled in the waist with a wide, red, patent leather belt. In conjunction with my white socks, white gym shoes and the red bow that was supposed to hold back my long hair, I thought I had struck the right Jubilee effect.

Others whittled away my self confidence. Parson's sister, who held herself to be above such low class frivolity, said that for an almost grown girl I was dressed flightily, and exhibiting far too much bare leg. Granny Gammon asked what sort of contraption I was supposed to be wearing. With that red belt around my middle I looked like six pennyworth of long stalked rhubarb tied together with string. There was no time to run home and change.

The scorekeepers, male of course, chose the side of the refreshment tent as the best place to chart the match as it progressed. From the line of empty tankards set before them, they already viewed the state of the pitch through the amber glow of farmhouse brewed cider and ale. Albert Parsley, still spry then, was our opponent's choice of umpire. They grouped around him, listening as he ran through the rules of the game. Our chosen umpire, Big Bertha Pye, allayed any fears that our opponents might try doubtful tactics. This truly liberated and muscular lady advised my batting partner and I to imagine that we were "clumping them fools around the yud with a copper stick." She promised that any of them inclined to argufying would feel the back of her hand around their ears.

Nervously aware of a small, sporadic burst of clapping, I took guard with my bat. Old and unoiled, it had lain in the toolshed since the days when my brothers and sisters could have formed a cricket team of their own. Now the bat's infrequent use was for driving hazel spars into the straw of loosened thatch.

Bowling the first ball of the game, Slippy Springer sent down a spinning snorter. With a muck shovelling kind of stroke I helped it on its way.

"Run," I yelled, scuttling up the pitch towards my batting partner. She paused in her attempt to straighten the brim of her hat, looked vaguely surprised to see me, and in answer to my loudly repeated entreaty said, "Run Jo? Do you mean me? Which way?"

I tore back to the safety of the crease, while Bertha explained the finer points of run scoring, but this made the poor soul more confused. She set off to meet me before Slippy bowled the second ball. There were loud appeals. "Howzat?"

Still out there batting, with six wickets down in as many

overs and only fourteen runs on the scoreboard. I was joined by the doughty Violet. The grinning fielders who had gathered like flies around a jam jar, moved well back from the wickets. Two or three of her swiping agricultural strokes followed in every successive over, with myself scoring an occasional single, but mostly tearing up and down to keep my end up. When the limited overs of our innings ended we had scored fifty seven runs.

There was a slight altercation before the men started their innings, due to Big Bertha's refusal to accept the sawn-off posts they intended to use for batting. She would only settle for hedge stakes, literally taken from the hedge. That the young bullocks in the adjoining pasture took advantage of the gap in the hedge seemed to her to help make for more jollifications. Heaven knew there were enough idle folk standing around to drive them back. Time and again the makeshift bats broke and splintered.

The men's run rate rose, but wickets fell, thanks to some highly doubtful umpiring decisions. They needed three more runs in four more overs when Lordy's limousine was sighted turning in along Church Lane. Adhering strictly, and in our case thankfully, to the prearranged plan, stumps were drawn and our game came to an end.

Having attended the Royal Service of Thanksgiving in London, His Lordship was too tired to make long speeches. A rearrangment of the programme gave him the opportunity to watch the children's patriotic spectacular before he presented the medals and mugs.

Grass stained and windswept I watched the display from the back of the tent, then had to push my way through the assembled adults to collect a Jubilee medal and mug from the hands of Her Ladyship. She scowled at my untidy appearance. The handle of the mug she held towards me was, and still is, cracked.

The young college scholars then presented their Greek Comedy, but this left everyone slightly baffled, since it entailed two dozen pimply boys chanting and speaking a strange language. Everyone clapped politely, taking their cue from Lordy and the parson, who, in his speech of thanks, pronounced it "most enlightening, witty and extremely droll."

At the freely given village tea party Grace was said and this was followed by the first of many loyal toasts. For children this meant powdery lemonade, but for their elders the choice was tea, farm brewed ale or cider, or home made wine. Granny Gammon had put down a special five gallon crock of wine the previous summer, and among all the other prized and coveted recipes there was nothing to touch her wild strawberry wine. It matched the flame of the beacon fire of that happy evening, a magical ingredient of a celebration long remembered and long past.

Rats Castle

Perhaps our more affluent forbears believed it to be wrong that those requiring their charity should enjoy receiving it. There seems to be no other explanation for building Butchers Row, a terrace of four alms cottages a mile out from the village at the end of a woodside track. The Butchers Bequest, was a phrase that those who had their roots in the village often heard, but rarely understood. We only knew that someone in the 18th century, a Butcher by name or trade, had bequeathed the money to build and maintain the four houses.

Generations of trustees must have taxed their brains, fairly allocating the cottages at either end to *men abiding in lawful wedlock, who by bad favour or an act of God have no habitation for themselves Their Kin or Kine.* Beneficiaries for the two centre cottages were only eligible providing that they were *righteous, sober-minded bachelors, in no way blasphemous, clean in manner and of good repute*, or *industrious spinsters of honest birth and proven virtue*. How this was to be proved was not defined.

By the time my generation came along the fabric of the cottages and the trust fund were both in an advanced state of decay and their official name of Butchers Row was seldom used.

We called them Rats Castle and anyone who lived there did so as a last resort. Grubby Jack, who lived in one of the centre cottages, must have had his application for tenancy granted by trustees in a very liberal frame of mind. Far from being sober, clean and in no way blasphemous, Jack was frequently as tight as a tick, rejected soap and water since it washed one's natteral iles away, and had a vocabulary of oaths and swear words colourful enough to curl the devil's horns.

Maybe his unsociable habits encouraged the trustees to bend the rules in his favour, since this would remove him from the close vicinity of the village. If his uncouthness caused his neighbours at Rats Castle inconvenience, beggars could not be choosers, and they were in no situation to complain. Next to Jack lived Miss Minnie Wood, a timid woman of uncertain age, struggling to exist in a state of half starved gentility. If there were but dry bread to offer, Miss Minnie would slice it thinly, place it on one of *dear Mama's* china plates and serve it on a tray complete with starched white cloth.

Her history was one of devotedly nursing a bedridden, domineering, dear Mama, until ultimately Miss Minnie was left to face the fact that when Mama expired Mama's Army widow's pension expired too, leaving her daughter penniless, untrained, and without a soul in the world to care about her plight. The cottage at Rats Castle was her only refuge, and somehow she existed as church organist and part time librarian, stamping our library tickets every Tuesday afternoon.

She made beautifully patterned pillow lace, which she sent off to the city once or twice a month, but so quiet and unassuming was she that to most of the parishioners little Miss Wood was affectionately known as Minnie Mouse.

When old Zekey Dodds fell from the top of a corn rick the chances were that he would never walk again. The farmer who employed him needed his tied cottage for his replacement, so of necessity Zekey and his wife Hester moved into the end cottage at Butchers Row. Slowly Zekey became more mobile and with

Hester's help transformed the large end plot into a productive cottage garden.

This demanded constant vigilance against marauding rabbits, pheasants and pigeons that raided his vegetables from the safety of the nearby wood. The contest was not one sided. Many a pheasant was tempted by the currants Zekey placed under a tilted bushel basket, balanced by a stick of kindling wood. His skill with a catapult thinned out the rabbit population and provided many a main course for themselves and Minnie Mouse.

A farm worker's tied cottage could be either a blessing or a curse. The minimal rent, if rent was paid at all, cushioned the lowness of his wage, but there was the ever present threat of dismissal. That could mean instant eviction should the employer's displeasure be invoked. From the farmer's point of view, a good reliable farmhand was someone to be shown every consideration, and a free cottage near to hand was essential if they were to settle down and be content.

In the last years that it was inhabited the remaining cottage at Rats Castle constantly supplied the need for temporary accommodation for homeless farmhands searching for new jobs, and seemed to change occupants as frequently as most country people changed their winter sheets.

Hester Dodds and Minnie made the best of their surroundings, and had Jack not lived between them, with his filthy windows curtained by old sacks, the cottages would have been the picture of rustic charm. Minnie's one up two down home was packed full of dear Mama's heavy furniture, with scarce a space between the pictures on the walls. The doorstep was hearth stoned, the door knob polished, and the rambling Dorothy Perkins roses disguised the fact that damp beneath the flaking limewash was eroding the wattle and daub walls.

Apart from seeing Miss Minnie scuttling back and forth on her village duties, no one gave much thought to Rats Castle until a new cowman came to Oak Farm. Although his family increased the school roll by eight, besides those that his wife pushed around in a tattered pram, he seemed determined to get the sack from the day he started. Inevitably he did, and straight away demanded to be housed by the Butcher's Bequest. He moved into the first cottage of the row, his kin and kine being twelve children, two goats, a dog and a scattering of fowl.

He bullied Miss Minnie and Hester, knowing that Zekey being crippled, was unable to retaliate. The goats played havoc with their garden crops and were liable to butt them as they pegged out their washing.

There were frequent swearing matches with Jack, who for once came second best. The day that he went to his little house at the end of the garden path and found it occupied by a nanny goat and two hens Jack decided that he must act. The vicarage study was foreign ground to Jack, but as chairman of the Butcher's trustees the vicar was the man he went to see.

"That poor dear lady next to me daren't step out of her door between choir practice and early communion. There's been such a hammering and yammering going on that the pictures have fallen off the walls," he complained.

The vicar suggested he should go and try sweet reason, but Jack took a poor view of that. As his next line of attack he held consultation with the group of men who usually foregathered on the forge wall on Saturday afternoons. That night, soon after dark, several people carrying tins, rook scarers, rattles and iron frying pans, made their way along the track to Rats Castle. Gathering silently in front of the first cottage they began to beat, bang or rattle a steady cacophony of contempt.

By the time Miss Minnie came home from matins the next morning her neighbours had gone. Jack and Zekey looked inside the swinging open door.

Every piece of burnable wood had been torn or sawn out. Staircase, bedroom floors, roof rafters and even the purlins of the house.

"Strewth," said Jack, "the whole damned lot is liable to fall down."

One by one the tenants of Rats Castle were found new accommodation and it stood empty, dropping into roofless decay. Inaccessible, but visible from the grand new trunk road, Rats Castle ruins still remains as four broken chimney breasts that in spring provide nesting places for jackdaws and in summer are clothed with wild clematis and an old pink rambling rose.

The Trees of Time

During the 1880's young Robert Packman persuaded his employer to let him convert a large acreage of old pasture land on the estate into fruit orchards. Neighbouring farmers were unanimous in their belief that to have appointed young Robert as a farm bailiff was a rash decision and encouraging his hare brained radical notions was the fastest route to a failed farm and the bankruptcy court.

The farmers who worked alongside their men through summer drought and the mud of winter knew the land too well to indulge in daft experiments. Grassland fed sheep and cattle, and arable soil could make a profit from potato crops and grain. Only a city bred landowner with more wealth than agricultural wisdom would indulge an inexperienced bailiff's whim, and wait around watching his pastures being ruined for the sake of fruit trees that might or might not grow.

Unperturbed, young Robert set six horse teams to pull the heavy ploughs tearing up rough grassland and cultivating until the tilth of the soil was fine enough to trickle like sand through Robert's hands. Then he planted his trees.

They were sapling thin, bending wherever the whim of the wind took them until Robert drove in sturdy stakes to support them, binding live and dead wood together with straw ropes. The rabbits gnawed through the bark of the young trees, killing them by the dozen, but Robert replanted, protecting each scion with a wire netting shield. Under sown with fine grass and white Dutch clover, the orchards grew lush with the greenness of early summer. Mown with scythes they yielded fodder and when the sheep flocks were brought into shelter for the winter it was the new orchard that they grazed.

If Robert's employer was only a part time farmer, having more interest in the city than in his country estate, his son was different. Cared for by nursemaids, taught by a tutor and kept far from the social whirl of his parents' high society town life, the young boy spent his formative years in the country, having more contact with Robert Packman and the estate staff than with his own parents. Only on rare or great occasions did he reluctantly enter the other circles his parents moved in. Then he would thankfully return to the country and report what he had seen.

Soon after Robert's orchards were established the boy accompanied his parents to London for Queen Victoria's Diamond Jubilee. One of the Royal Princes had asked for his impression of the royal procession and the marching of the soldiers. The Young Master replied that "they were all in straight rows, whichever way one looked at them. Just like Robert's cherry trees." The Royal Prince, indulging a young boy's interest on a day when the pomp and ceremony of Empire was at its peak, commanded that when the young master became a fruit growing farmer the pick of his first crops should be sent to grace the table of the royal household. This too was excitedly reported to Robert.

"By God, boy. Then we'll grow fruit that is fit for a king."

By the time the trees were really starting to bear fruit the boy had become a young man, foregoing his rural interests to follow the family tradition of serving in the Army, much against his will. He came home on leave late one evening when the trees were all in full blossom to find the orchards under a pall of smoke haze from innumerable bonfires lit beneath the trees. With frost in the air Robert was taking no chances.

Equally determined that there would be fruit fit to offer the royal household that year, the young man stayed in the orchards, helping Robert stoke the fires all that night. Both Robert and he looked like smoke blackened scarecrows by daylight the next morning. Ice film coated the yard pond, but in the orchards not one spray of cherry blossom had been singed by the tell tale brown of frost.

The Young Master gave instructions that Robert send him a wire when the Black Heart and Napoleon cherries were ready. But the year was 1914 and along with the rest of his regiment he was mobilised for war. By the next fruit-picking season he had become a name on the casualty lists, posted as "Missing."

Robert went on tending his orchards, determined that if his employer's son should ever return there would still be fruit fit to offer a king.

When the autumn leaves from the cherry trees formed a red carpet, word came that the young man had been found. Shell shocked and with one leg amputated he was in a Belgian hospital, neither comprehending nor caring whether he was alive or dead.

Surrounded by attendants and nurses, he was brought back to the country to recuperate. This failed to bring the slightest improvement to his blank indifference. His scarred mind was imprisoned behind a high encircling wall. Robert's employer instructed him to report to the sick room each day to talk about the orchards in the hope that this might rekindle some of the interest in fruit growing that the young man had previously shown. It was a useless exercise achieving nothing but blank stares. Back stairs gossip among the servants spoke of him being moved to a hospital for brain damaged heroes, but Robert Packman was convinced there must be a way to set him free.

A silent bedroom with servants standing around like paid mutes at a funeral seemed a highly ineffective method. Asking no one's permission Robert carried the invalid downstairs then took him out to the orchards, wheeling him in a basketwork bath chair. As soon as he had made sure that the young man was safely settled, Robert resumed his tree pruning, talking as he worked.

"Your father can fire me just as easily as he hired me," he called down. "But I've brought you here out of everyone else's way to tell you privately that you make me puking sick. These ruddy trees have more sense than you, for all that you are supposed to be an educated gentleman. When a gale comes tearing in amongst them, they bend with it, letting it sweep past them. They don't curl up their roots and wither because the roar of the wind has been too loud for them to stand. Trees understand that a lost limb or a broken branch doesn't mean they are finished. It makes them more determined to sprout fresh wood, put down deeper roots and grow. When the storms and gales have passed they stand up straight like rows of soldiers, lifting their arms to the sky.

"Once you were keen to keep a promise and offer fruit from here fit for a king. You were the pick of the crop old son. You were the best we could offer. Your bark took a bit of a tanning and you lost a branch on the way. Now you can either stay in that bloody chair like a log of rotten wood, with the wood lice of self pity gnawing you into a heap of nothing or get off your backside, shore up what is left of your lopped limb, then let the rest of your branches reach up for the sun to make them grow straight again."

From beneath the trees Robert heard a harrowing howl, like a trapped vixen baying. Rushing down the ladder he saw the young man sitting with his arms raised upwards, all his soul's agony imprinted on his uplifted face. The torment and anguish were expurgated in one screamed phrase, "Oh Christ. Help me Robert."

Robert held him close like a father comforting a frightened child, till his tears were done.

The orchards flourished and so did the Young Master. Fruit from the estate graced many a royal banquet and Robert's authoritative advice became sought after and well known. As his trees grew taller he became more bent and round shouldered, until one day he decided that he and the orchards he had planted were long past their prime. It was time they were both rooted out to make way for new growth.

"An orchard needs a life-time of tending," he told his

employer. "You must find some young keen man to tend the replanting."

Knowing that his own days were numbered, old Robert Packman deliberately took up his axe and started to cut the old trees down.

The Ranks of the Elite

Hidden by the thick hawthorn hedge that used to grow along the twisting steep gradient of Folly Hill was a small secluded hollow, shaped as if some giant hand had scooped it from the steep grassy bank. When sheer accident caused me to discover its existence I was unappreciative of the wild violets and primroses that grew there. I was flat on my face, vaguely conscious of a fern frond probing one nostril, and a wet tongued collie dog licking my face. My forward vision was totally obscured by a pair of farm boots and corduroy trouser legs tied just below the knees.

"What in tarnation be you a-doing here Jo? You fair put the wind up me, for I thought I'd found a dead 'un! I only came up here because old Patch was yapping about as if he had found an old ewe on her back, and here you be looking as if you have been pole axed."

I recognised Shup Woolley's voice long before his face would stay in focus. As he helped me to sit up he continued, "My stars! You look fair mazed and muzzy! How did you get here?"

I had no idea what had happened, yet irrationally I was glad that it was the old shepherd who had found me, and not one of my tut tutting aunts.

They were always imploring me to behave in a more lady like manner, and my Aunt Flo had predicted that when I stood before the pearly gates of paradise on the day of Judgement I would hitch up my skirts and try to climb them. She had no doubts that I would find them closed! At fifteen, I showed no sign of becoming elegant, or refined, which seemed to worry my older and more distant relatives a good deal.

Patch, the collie, continued to lick my face with his long wet tongue, while I tried to marshal my confused thoughts in a brain that had suddenly become as retentive as a wide meshed sieve. I was convinced that my plight was somehow connected with being lady like, yet Shup said that I had been rambling on about the day that Harry Applethorn, our old waggoner, tried to teach me to ride a horse.

As I explained to Shup, that incident occurred long before my fifth birthday, when Harry lifted me onto the bare back of a placid old shire mare. All four of the mare's legs seemed to be moving in different directions to its bony spine, so I bawled and hollered that I was slipping and would be trampled underfoot. Harry was equally adamant that I stayed where I was.

"You've got elbows and knees, ain't you?" Old Harry said sharply. "Just you use them to stay on and ride, young 'un. This world is divided between Haves and Have nots. The Haves ride, while the rest plod through life on their own flat feet. Stay put unless you want to be a Have not and never walk when you can ride."

Taking Harry's advice, I spent much of my childhood cadging lifts on farm carts, timber tugs, milk floats, even dust carts, or the rear carrier of my brother Stan's old bike. Even so, it was unlikely that I would be riding a horse through one of Shup's lambing pastures. As Shup said, there were no hoof prints on the turf. My breathing was making odd wheezy noises reminiscent of the chapel harmonium on Sunday nights. A baby rabbit, defying Patch and scudding to a burrow under the hedge, seemed to be a jumbled part of my present state, but that made no sense at all. With does in kindle and bucks too rank tasting to eat in springtime, this was the close season for rabbiting, so there was no way that I could have been out in the steep banked pasture poaching other people's rabbits by setting hingles or wire snares.

I drew no formal wages for helping my parents with the farm so rabbit catching provided a source of income, making my finances at their lowest ebb each spring. My addled brain registered the fact that I had needed cash for some urgent reason, but all Shup's attentive prompting could not make me remember why. Sufficient for that moment that I attempt to get vertical instead of horizontal. All the time Harry Applethorn's remarks about being a lady and riding kept repeating like a cracked gramophone record in my mind.

As I sat up, an oast house across the valley seemed to sway from side to side, like the pendulum of Elsie Dalton's grandfather clock. Mrs. Dalton was somehow part of the confusion. She was real enough, so I concentrated all my thoughts on her.

She was so houseproud that Shup was sure that she dusted and polished her husband, Wally, each night before she would allow him to go to bed. Her zeal extended beyond household possessions. Wally's must have been the only chicken farm where the hen houses had their windows polished every week. Wally owned an old motor bike and side car, and no royal coach could have had more wax polish lavished on it. Elsie covered it with a dust sheet in the shed when it was not in use.

My Dad used to sell the Daltons the tail corn for chicken food and every time I called there, I cast envious glances at the ladies bicycle that was suspended by two hooks on their corn store wall. It was wrong to covet other folks property, but I could have found so much use for the bike that Elsie, as a prim and proper young matron, felt too dignified to ride. When I approached Wally about the chances of her selling it he promised that I would have first refusal if she did.

Inordinately proud of his fastidious wife, Wally was very conscious of the fact that he had taken her away from her city world of service in genteel households, where piped water was taken for granted. Just as I would have given much to own Elsie's bike, so did Wally wish he could offer her some of the modern facilities she had sacrificed to become a chicken farmer's wife.

With the prospect of a happy event impending, Wally informed me that Elsie was now willing to sell her bicycle, but this came when my prospect of buying it seemed almost nil.

Aunt Flo would have looked upon it as a case of the devil helping the wicked, but a series of happy coincidences gave me a chance. The selling price was thirty shillings, fifteen of which my more affluent older sister lent as a long term loan. The opportunity to raise the rest presented itself when my Dad bought a sundry collection of drinking troughs at a farm sale. Among them was a huge cast iron bath tub, the sort of which Elsie Dalton still dreamed. Saltpetre worked wonders on restoring the enamel, and green oxide paint gave the exterior a new lease of life. Having hammered wooden barrel spigots into the bung hole and overflow opening, I took the bath tub round to the delighted Daltons on a cart.

Thus did I become the proud owner of a high framed bicycle with a wicker basket on the handle bars. Instructing me on how to ride and keep my balance, Wally suggested it would come easier if I headed downhill. Folly Hill was one of the steepest in the district, so in my ignorance it seemed the best place to try.

Sitting beside Shup and Patch, my clearing brain recalled the thrill of travelling downhill ever faster toward the bend of the road, then the breathless panic of being airborne as I sailed clean over the hedge. Still shaky on my feet and with a dull thudding headache I followed Shup as he cut a passage through the thorny hedge. My newly acquired bike lay bent and buckled and as Patch lifted his leg against it Shup reckoned the old dog was simply expressing an opinion on its sorry state.

"This old heap of junk will need more than a touch of the blacksmith's magic hammer and you need to have your head looked at, so I'll see you safely home. You and me are Havenots like old Harry said, and by the looks of this scrap iron it will be a long time before you join the ranks of the elite and ride."

Kubla Khan

Perhaps the supper time discussion about the amount of work involved in preparing our Christmas poultry orders invoked the nightmare. I dreamed I was plucking feathers from penguins on an ice floe, and woke up shivering with the cold.

Too drowsy to differentiate between fact and fantasy, I wondered why my bare feet were still on a frozen surface when the rest of me was snuggled under the blankets of my bed. Lighting the bedside candle meant moving my feet from the metal bed-warmer that spent each winter day in the kitchen range oven and each night in the nether regions of my bed. Never before had it gone cold before morning, but my bedroom felt as cosy as an ice box. Had I been spartan enough to consider a cold water wash in the basin on the marble topped washstand, it would have been impossible, for the jug was filled with solid ice. I dressed quickly, piling on layers of warm clothing, but nothing seemed to stop the cold that seeped into my bones.

To be the first one up in the morning was an unusual experience. The eerie silence enveloping the old house was accentuated by the plodding pendulum of the clock on the kitchen mantel-shelf counting time.

Relying on the open fire of the old wood burning stove for heating, cooking, and boiling water, we always made sure that there was a good supply of dry kindling sticks left in the kitchen overnight. The dry twigs flaring under the kettle soon provided boiling water to wash with, and to brew tea in the brown earthenware pot. By the time Mum and Dad came downstairs, I was warming my hands round a half pint mug of hot tea.

Our early routine never varied, no one sitting down to breakfast until all the farm animals had been watered and fed. Dad's first task was to see to the horses in the stable, while I fed and milked Dolly, the shorthorn cow. We then combined forces to mix pig meal, cut chaff, and carry fodder to the young bullocks fattening in the stockyard, opening up the chicken-houses to feed Mum's free ranging hens on our way back to the kitchen and our morning meal.

Pleased with my early start that morning, I put on a thick old coat, and pulled my boots on. Despite their overnight drying by the hearth, and the coat of greasy dubbin, they still struck damp and stiff to my chilblained feet. My storm lantern was a feeble glow-worm wavering along the passageway. The massive bolt and latch on the back door was frozen fast.

Dad helped me heave and tug to force it open, spilling a heap of snow on the doormat, seeping in the top of my boots. A coal shovel from Mum's brass companion set and a tin lid tacked on a broom handle were inadequate tools to tackle the five foot drift blocking the doorway, then dig a path to get garden spades and shovels from the shed. After an hour of hard work we were still floundering around trying to get to the farm buildings where the animals were loudly demanding to be fed. My stomach rumbled persistently, thinking of our warm breakfast spoiling in the oven while we wondered how to water the stock.

The yard pump was covered in icicles, like grease from a snuffed candle. The rope around the well's winding roller was glazed with thick ice, a coiled snake in aspic jelly, and with the winding handle set fast, as if in concrete, there was no means of getting water. The horses began chuntering for their drinking buckets, the bullocks lowed beside their frozen trough, porkers squealed insistently, and the old boar, Genghis Khan, heaved his great bulk up to rest his front trotters on the top rail of his sty. His ultimatum was as plain as if he had spoken. His bucket of pig meal would be delivered immediately, or he would break down his fence.

Even in his more contented moments, Genghis had the savage look of an overweight mongolian warrior with six inches of impacted snow raising the level of his sty floor, he needed little aggravation to bring him blundering over the top. We knew that a bad tempered boar could be the most dangerous of all farm animals, and did not relish the prospect of rounding him up in the snow and ice.

We could think of only one way to get water quickly, and this meant taking a sledgehammer and an iron spike to break a hole in the ice on the pond. This involved walking out on the slippery jetty to squat like a pair of Laplanders hammering and hacking to make a hole in the ice. With only a flimsy frozen hand-rail to hold while one scooped up water in an iron bucket, walking that glassy plank was a downright dangerous operation and by the time we had watered the horses and cattle, then mixed up pig meal, I was sick with the cold and very close to tears.

We followed the cleared track across the slippery yard to the sound of mournful hens, and old Kubla Khan, the rooster, complaining that the ladies of his harem were being neglected and unfed.

"Breakfast first Jo," Dad decided, seeing that it was almost noon, instead of our usual time of a quarter to seven. Mum had stoked up the fire under her stock pot, and doled out enormous basins of thick, hot soup.

With snow falling from a sky the colour of an old floor cloth, we knew that our flock of ewes in lamb needed to be brought into the shelter of the barn, but first Dad had to dig a way to the fowl houses, while I continued to water the stock before the hole in the icy pond froze again.

Realising that the chicken's mash pail would be lighter for me to haul up from the pond, Dad had mixed the chicken food in the iron water bucket. I watched from the jetty as the hens took one look at the arctic conditions outside their warm fowl house, then retired back inside. Kubla Khan was much braver, but as roosters go, Kubla had a personality of his own.

Of Rhode Island Red stock, his mother must have mixed in some fine feathered company, for his colouring ranged from midnight blue and peacock green to all shades of brownish reds, black, white, and cream. He ruled his harem ruthlessly, and chased mice, rats, cats, and dogs. I watched him crow his defiance of the weather, then got on with my work, the chicken feed pail clattering as it hit the ice then went down into the pond.

Kubla Khan came rushing towards me, half flying, half running, wings flapping, hitting the frozen surface of the pond at speed. One moment there was a very surprised rooster skidding on his parsons nose, with his legs thrust inelegantly forward, then he simply vanished down the hole. I put out a hand to grab him but he disappeared, fluttering beneath the ice.

I slithered to the tool shed, grabbing an old sheep crook to puddle around in the water, but this proved futile. Dad brought a long ladder, crawling out along it as it lay across the pond. Elbow deep in the icy water, he tried to hook the crook round Kubla's neck or legs, and just when he was unable to bear the cold any longer, a few tail feathers came into sight. He hauled out the limp, wet, lifeless Kubla. Mum tried artificial respiration by the kitchen fire, but to no avail. She left the old bird lying in a state on the kitchen side table, saying that he might be as tough as old door hinges, but in this wintry weather, his carcase would work wonders for her stock pot.

With the snow storm assuming the proportions of a blizzard, we rounded up the sheep to safety, gave all our livestock double rations, littered them in deep straw, milked the cow early, and brought a plentiful supply of firewood inside the house.

The lamp was lit and the evening meal cooking before Mum had a chance to think about preparing Kubla Khan for cooking. She sat by the fire with the old rooster on her lap. As she tugged at the first few bedraggled feathers, one doleful eye opened, then slowly closed. Mum hesitated, knowing that fowls can run round flapping long after their necks are broken, but Kubla's eye blinked balefully again, then one sharp spurred claw twitched.

It was as if Mum was watching an old friend's resurrection.

She wrapped him in warm flannel, put him in a basket on the fender, poured neat brandy down his gullet and, by bedtime, we were sharing the hearthrug with an unsteady inebriated bird.

He was strutting around, chasing the cats from the kitchen first thing the next morning, so we took him to the fowl house for a frantically amorous reunion with his wives.

The bitter weather held, making caring for our livestock a nightmare, with every spare moment taken up with clearing snow. Unbelievably, the village postman struggled along the snow bound lanes to bring some Christmas mail. Pausing from pounding hot boiled potatoes into a warm oatmeal mash, Mum read a wistful message from a city dwelling friend.

"How happy you must be, making preparations for a white Christmas in the enchanting beauty of the snow covered countryside."

Mum chuckled as she read it. Applying dubbin to my snow saturated boots, I suggested that the word ecstatic more or less summed up my feelings on the subject.

"Humph!" my father grunted, shaking the paraffin drum to estimate if our supply of lighting fuel would hold out until road conditions allowed the oilman's van to get through to our cut off farmstead. "You can say that again!"

Miss Letty and the Sergeant

Shimmering through a mid-summer heat haze, the early morning sun infiltrated the closed upper window of Gunwanda Villa. Vaguely restless in her unruffled, virginal bed, Miss Letitia Pinke hesitated to get up and dress until "Matty Dear", her elder sister, called her. Matty Dear could get so irritable if anything disrupted the set pattern of their daily routine.

On bed-socked feet, creeping quietly to avoid the creaking of the uncovered floorboards, Miss Letty pulled back the long dark curtains and opened the windows. With her crocheted bed-shawl drawn close around her shoulders, she stood listening to the blackbird that, as chief chorister, was leading a chorus of birdsong in an anthem to the dawn. She knew he would be perched among the top branches of the garden elms that kept the South side of the house in shade all summer, and that during winter, when the gales made the high boughs creak and groan in protest, threatened to smash Gunwanda Villa.

In her interminable, eventless adult years Miss Letty had spent what seemed to have been a lifetime of hours watching the constantly changing country landscape framed by the full depth window. It was the one place in the house where she could call her dreams her own.

Dear Papa and Matty Dear had such dominant personalities that she sometimes felt like an insignificant daisy growing in the shade of two large sunflowers, folding her petals and sheltering in the sanctuary of this tiny bedroom in any domestic storm. For Dear Papa the "Last Post" had long since sounded. With his demise, Matty Dear seemed to have added most of his idiosyncrasies and military foibles to the ever-increasing number of her own.

In Miss Letty's boarding school days, when Dear Papa first bought this old country cottage, he named it Gunwanda Villa to commemorate some far-flung outpost of the Empire where he professed to have served as an army officer. The place was still full of foreign trophies and mementoes that Matty Dear insisted should not be moved. During the last months of Dear Papa's life, the entire household routine had hinged around a massive jigsaw puzzle the size of his study table.

Dear Papa assured his daughters that when all of the several thousand pieces were completed the finished picture of *The Royal Durbar At Delhi* would reveal him in full dress uniform standing close to the King and Queen.

Still as he left it, the unfinished puzzle stayed scattered on his table. Each day it was Lettie's task to dust it. After Dear Papa's death she would sometimes add a piece if she noticed where it would fit while she was dusting, but Matty Dear seemed to know if any piece had been moved. Matty Dear's moods of irritability had increased noticeably from the day they faced the distressing task of going through Dear Papa's personal papers after his funeral.

It was then that they realised that Dear Papa had journeyed abroad only in his imagination, for his military travels had taken him no farthest than Aldershot, and this as the lowliest grade of army clerk. They learned, too, that the mother neither remembered had not in fact been careless enough to become a

Bengal tiger's breakfast. She had obviously died in an influenza epidemic, and it was the money she left in trust for her daughters that gave them the meagre financial allotment on which they still lived. Matty Dear insisted that the truth must be their secret. They must keep up appearances at any cost.

Their frugal standard of living grew more spartan and, as the two women struggled to exist in the decaying old dwelling, anything that could not be mended without cost or paid assistance was left alone.

A damp patch, shaped like a map of Greenland, marred the whitewash of Miss Letty's bedroom ceiling. It extended its territory with every rain shower, but maiden lady daughters of a military gentleman could not lower their dignity to clamber up on the roof to mend the sagging roof timbers and slipping peg tiles, it was simply not *done*. Assured by her elder sister that the roof would outlast their lives, Miss Letty kept a bucket on her bedside rug, ready to catch the drips each time it rained.

But on a sunbright morning such as this Miss Letty could forget the draughty, damp discomfort of Gunwanda Villa in winter. Bees were working in the full-blooming honeysuckle covering the porch below her. Clematis and the pink Albertine roses that climbed unrestricted up to the bricks of the crumbling chimneys were heavy with flowers. Still wet with dew, they filled the air with a sweet-scented, almost tangible presence, and for one of the few times in her life Miss Letty felt happy with her existence in the rose-infested slum.

Across the lane, so close that she felt she could almost pick them, wild dog roses blossomed in the high hedge of the hayfield that a few days ago was a knee-high carpet of ox-eye daisies, mauve vetch, red sorrel and tall flowering grass.

All week long the field had echoed to the sound of agricultural activities. First, the clattering mowing machine drawn by two perspiring Shire horses cutting the grass and leaving it neat in patterned rows. There were old men with scythes, then women wielding wooden hayrakes and pitchforks, turning the drying hay and piling it into lumps. And all the time the happiness of their laughter seemed to taunt Letty, shut in as she was behind the bottlegreen roller blinds that Matty Dear insisted must be drawn to prevent dust and sunlight ruining the furnishings and all the valuable trophies Dear Papa had brought home.

The sun was gaining warmth with every moment and, knowing that Matty Dear would still be sleeping until the alarm clock Dear Papa had used throughout his military career woke her, Miss Letty let the woollen bed shawl drop from her shoulders, undid the top buttons of her high-necked nightdress, rolled up the sleeves and let the sunshine soak into her chest and arms. Warm and happy with this one small gesture of uninhibited freedom, she watched men from the farm across the meadows lead their Shire horse teams to pull the loaded haycarts that had stood overnight at the far side of the hayfield.

Someone was singing in a strong baritone voice that kept in rhythm with the lurching cart being hauled across the field. Unaware that she could be observed, Letty listened to the sound of the shod hooves in the lane, then watched the approaching cart slow and stop while the waggoner mended the trace horse's leading rein. The top of the load drew up directly in front of her bedroom window. And there, stretched out full-length, khaki-shirted, with a highly polished brass-buckled leather belt holding up his extremely scruffy grey flannel trousers, was a man. Not young, not old, but bronzed as if he made a habit of sunshine, and with a lot of crinkly lines around his eyes.

If he was surprised to see Miss Letty standing at her window with her hair loose around her shoulders and her white cotton nightie undone to the third button, Miss Letty was transfixed.

"And aren't you the most lovely sight in all this beautiful morning?"

For one moment Miss Letty thought he intended to leap across to the bedroom window, instead he leaned over and reached among the green foliage close by her, then handed her a half-open bud of a perfect Albertine rose.

Afraid to look into mocking eyes that must surely go with so cruel a jest, she held the rose as if it might shatter like a cobweb and thanked him for the gift. As the cart jolted into movement, she looked at the man on the hay load. There was nothing but gentleness and an inexplicable awe in his expressive eyes. "I'll be back," he called as the cart moved off.

At that moment she realised that Matty Dear was standing in the room. Matty marched across, hurled Miss Letty back on the bed, slammed the window and pulled the curtains to shut out the sun as if it were a *man*. For the next half-hour her behaviour and language were obscene.

Letty hid the rose under her mattress, and through the sameness of the day was forced to listen to a diatribe of hatred for a fool of thirty exposing herself to a common soldier who was home on leave farm labouring by day and carousing in the village inn by night.

The last of Miss Letty's evening tasks was to lock the back garden gate. That night she saw the sergeant standing waiting under the elms. He explained that his leave was almost ended, but he would like to write. For the first time it took a long time for Letty to lock the gate and, when she went indoors, her long hair hung around her shoulders like a girl's.

Matty Dear's barrage of sarcasm did not diminish with the passing weeks. Then one day, while Miss Letty was dusting Dear Papa's jigsaw puzzle, a letter arrived for her. It bore a foreign stamp. She read it, smiling, then deliberately swept every last piece of the jigsaw off the table and into the dustpan. Ignoring her sister's protests, she quietly went around the house raising the dark blinds, opening the windows and letting in the sun.

The Chinese Ghost

Like children enjoying the last game before bedtime, a gambol of lively lambs jumped and skipped, playing follow my leader around and over the trunk of a fallen elm that had lain uprooted since gales of winter flung it, groaning to the ground. Impatient, as all parents are when children remain energetically wakeful while their own eyelids feel lead-heavy, the old ewes ran towards them, calling, and stamping irritated hooves. One by one the romping lambs abandoned their game for their suppers, milk frothing around their mouths as they sucked noisily, their tails wriggling furiously, until, contented, they settled down to sleep.

Smaller lambs snuggled close to their thick-fleeced mothers, still overwhelmed by the wonder of being born. Their infantile bleating was answered with deep-throated maternal reassurances, and ruminating in-lamb ewes around them watched like well-meaning aunties offering advice.

Celandines, handfuls of small bright buttons made from pure sunlight at noontime, folded their petals as tendrils of cool mist haze, scented with wood smoke from some distant cottage chimney, drifted across the valley. In the duskiness of a still March evening a lone blackbird sang his requiem to the dying day.

One last look to make sure that no births were imminent then I could go home to the luxury of a book by the fireside.

A restless ewe, well away from the others and clearly in some discomfort, banished all hopes of such a pleasant hour or so. There were times when I envied those with the kind of nine to five occupations that allowed them to wear dancing slippers in the evenings instead of heavy farm shoes. Yet I knew that I could go to the ends of the earth searching and still find no place offering the peace of mind and contentment I had found in the few acres where, in grouchier moments, I could swear that I recognised every blade of grass.

I had no lantern with me and although the ewe had returned to her grazing I knew her lamb would arrive before daybreak, so I decided to go home for an hour then come back. During that hour ground mist had spread across the grass like a downy grey blanket, deadening the yellow light from the hurricane lantern I carried and making it difficult to count the slumbering flock. The ewe that I had specifically gone back to check on was close to where I had left her and was now the proud mother of a lamb. She stood licking it, encouraging it to rise on unsteady legs and stand beside her, but its first attempts to feed were rebuffed in her efforts to help its twin make a feet-first entry into the world.

This required assistance. Putting the first lamb close to the ewe's head to occupy her attention while I engaged in elementary obstetrics, I concentrated on the job of getting the second twin born. As soon as it began to breathe I laid it close to its mother's head, to join its brother, but the first lamb was not there. A new-born lamb cannot wander far of its own volition, and if it is lost it cries. The lantern was still where I first placed it, with the ewe well within the radius of its light. Convinced that I would still hear or see it, I searched in ever widening circles without finding a sign of the missing lamb.

I wandered around and around for what seemed like hours,

and by then another pair of twins and a single lamb had been born. These, carefully watched by their calling mothers, I shepherded into the warmth of the thatched shelters close by the gate. Watching the eddying mist rise and swirl like rippling waves at the ebb tide, I listened for the sound of a stray lamb crying, but all was silent, until I decided to do one more circuit of the field and began walking close by the hedge. At first I could hear a rustling behind me and was conscious of an unpleasant smell. I stopped. The noise stopped. I walked slowly, the rustling continued, and to my straining ears seemed to be coming from the far side of the hedge.

Reason tried to tell me it was one of Charlie Cartwright's grazing farm stock, attracted by the light. That theory leaked as surely as a rusty kettle, for I knew that the field had been sown with clover and had not had cattle on it since last year. If the unknown thing that was stalking me came through the hedge into Ten Acres I only had to turn round to find out what it was. I headed across the field toward the gateway, my imagination filling our quiet countryside with prowling leopards and wolves. Trying to lift my courage with the lantern, I turned around and where the bush of blackthorn makes the hedge lower saw the vague outline of something with hunched shoulders, standing six to seven feet tall, and with glowing eyes in a thin, pale, bearded face. The hurricane lantern flared, then dimmed, so I knew it was almost empty. I took to my heels and ran.

My father was coming across the orchard to see what had delayed me, and never was I more pleased to see the glow of his pipe. I told him about the lamb's disappearance and mentioned the rustlings in the hedge. The apparition was something different. Could you convince your father that you had just seen a seven foot ancient Chinese with amber eyes?

Dad thought that the lamb may have snuggled up to another ewe, and would be back with its mother by daylight, by which time I would be back out in Ten Acres acting midwife to the sheep. It was not there and one of the other twins that had been born the previous evening had disappeared as well. We realised then that any surviving pairs of lambs in our flock had been born during the daytime. If, as Dad suspected, a fox was lurking near the lamb pens, the ewes could defend one lamb but not two.

A couple of old doors, making a platform to stand on, were wedged into the branches of the fallen elm and the following evening we were both installed in a look-out made of straw bales. Dad had his double-barrelled shotgun with him and the loan of the village policeman's long-beamed torch. Windows across the valley darkened, a dog barked, someone cursed it, and a goat's incessant bleating suddenly stopped. A flight of lapwing, calling as they flew over, were invisible against the stars playing hide-and-seek among high clouds in the dark sky.

"There," said my father, pointing. The beam of the torch I was holding found what to me was just a shadow. My ears sang with the blast of a double report.

Scrambling down through the branches, we ran toward the thatched hurdles. There lay a very dead, very large dog fox. We walked around the startled flock until they settled, then went home to take the night chill from our bones with a warm fire and a bowl of Mum's thick soup.

A late caller arrived just as we started eating. The village policeman, having heard Dad fire, asked what he had shot. We told him and thanked him for the loan of the torch that had made it possible, but he brushed our thanks aside.

"Seems we've both had a successful evening, Harry. I caught that gippo chap from Pork Green tethering his old Billy for a bit of illicit night grazing on Cartwright's clover field."

Suddenly I could tell Dad about seeing the apparition. The *Thing* that had stood on its hind legs to glare at me over the hedge-top the previous evening was a smelly old goat.

Daily Deliveries Guaranteed

The Hare and Hounds marked the half-way stage of Dave's milk round so a midday pint for himself and a nosebag for his plodding pony were part of his normal routine. Each day the same old regulars congregated, sitting in their customary places, never varying in their habits until the day they greeted him with a handful of printed notices, each of them eagerly asking, "Ere, boy what do you think of these?"

Not too good at reading, Dave made the excuse that he had not brought his wife's glasses with him, and asked if the publican would mind reading the notice aloud: "Starting soon. Fresh milk twopence halfpenny a pint. Speedily delivered to your doorstep. Daily deliveries guaranteed."

While the landlord read the text of the notice twice for good measure, Dave pondered the implications of opposition that intended undercutting his prices by a halfpenny a pint. Anyone "speedily delivering" milk around the houses faster than his old pony would need to have a racehorse between the milk float shafts. No-one that the present company could think of had such an animal, but the publican was of the opinion that whoever was setting up in opposition to Dave intended to deliver milk by motor van or car.

Dave did not think that feasible. On our rough country roads milk shaken and bounced around in one of those infernal motors would be buttery and curdy by the time the churns were low and the milk round nearly done. Besides, who around here had a motor and the inclination to start up an opposition dairy round? At that time one could have counted all the car owners in the village on the fingers of one hand.

With the sense of hearing not then dulled by incessant noise and the ever increasing volume of traffic it was easy to differentiate between the individual sounds of local cars, and everyone would have known if a stranger was driving along our still quiet country lanes. The district nurse and the parson both drove venerable old Austin Sevens, yet their cars sounded completely different. The nurse subjected hers to the same hearty treatment she administered to hypochondriac patients, jollying it along with a stout-clad, accelerating foot.

The parson extended the same scant fervour to his driving as he did to his professed religion. The steepness of Lockley Hill invariably crept up on him like a sudden, unpleasant revelation.

No-one within a mile radius could fail to recognise the agonised, tooth-grinding groan of his car's gearbox undergoing torture. Neither nurse nor parson would be likely to start a pirate milk round. 'Nearly' Nigh, the publican's son, ran an old Vauxhall taxi, but he never reckoned to surface from bed before midday, so a milk round was the last thing he would want to own.

The gamekeeper's Trojan van pottered along like a rather breathless old spinster, unless it was chasing a gang of poachers, when it would snort along in pursuit, steamed up with indignation as if its modesty had been outraged. As His Lordship's employee, the gamekeeper was out of the running as a milkman. The only other car owner in the village was Jimmy Trott, a farmer. Dave knew that Jimmy's old bullnosed Morris had spent the early months of the summer out of action because Jimmy's barnyard geese had chosen to hatch out a clutch of eggs in it.

There was always the possibility that Jimmy might be considering milk production, but Dubber Walls vouched that the old Morris was greased and jacked up on old roof beams for the winter, its cylinder block and radiator guarded against freezing by the fact that it was buried under a ton of straw.

The only other regulars driving through our village were the paraffin chandler, the travelling draper and the vet. There were still those who believed that the 16 horsepower engine of the vet's Jowett had, in some mysterious way, retained an equine instinct that could find its way to any pub forecourt just as the bar doors were opening, and, by the same token, take its owner home safely at night. The Jowett's powers didn't run to doing a milk round without the cooperation of its owner, and milk was the last thing on earth he had any interest in.

The old men who watched the world go by from their perch on the forge yard wall were the first to notice the disreputable, rusty, overloaded tourer of mixed pedigree pass through the village, and by the time it had made its fourth return journey they were able to inform Dave that his rival intended to lodge with some smallholders over by Marsh Side, a hamlet eight miles distant. His plan was to collect surplus milk from farmers in the surrounding district and sell it in all the outlying hamlets on the way. He seemed a personable, cheerful young chap, dressed untidily, but with a touch of college learning about him, answering to the name of Miles. That was all we were ever to find out about him.

Dave, listening to the rattles, clanks and knocking of the rusty old car, decided he had nothing to fear. If the young man intended to try carrying full milk churns in that it would never get far from Marsh Side. It did though. Next morning Miles drove into the forge yard with ominous hammering noises coming from the car's internal regions. He asked Bert, the blacksmith, to strengthen it and put it right. Bert, inspecting the rusted running board and battered mudguards, said that it had restored his belief in miracles. It was not oil and petrol that had kept it running, but faith.

Enlisting the help of various bystanders, Bert put the car on its side, as if it were a thrown and hobbled mule, then fixed the loose and almost sheared couplings of its propshaft with four solid bolts. By the time he had strengthened the chassis and the bodywork, replaced rusted bonnet, mudguards and door panels with sheet metal and rust-protected it with green oxide, it looked more like a miniature Roman chariot than a car.

Bert even got the hood to move up and down, but that was a wasted effort, because within a few days of Miles starting his milk round it blew away and sank in Miller's Pond.

Miles's old car kept going, summer and winter, and even when our village was supposedly cut off by snow drifts Miles lived up to his original promise: 'Daily deliveries guaranteed.'

He had a ready wit, never lost for a reply to some tormenting old granny, but with a touch of chivalry about him, as witness his remark of "Sorry, mister," when he opened Tom Grommet's wash-house door to stand the milk out of the sunshine and caught Tom's wife taking a quick dip in the warm copper water suds. He kept his milk round going all through the middle and late 1930's, then just after the time of Dunkirk his customers found that one day their milk had been delivered long before they were up. Bert, whose forge was open at 6.30 every morning, was just in time to see Miles drive his old car into the forge yard. An Army jeep waited by Plough Lane corner.

Bert, as a World War 1 veteran, knew a military policeman when he saw one. Miles was being escorted away by two. Miles had left as mysteriously as he had arrived. Rumours ran riot. Some had him branded as a deserter from the regular army. Others were sure he was a secret agent for the allies, the enemy, or both. The folk he lodged with over at Marsh Side could throw no light on the subject.

One vague and uncertain clue came in the form of a newspaper photo which showed a group of commandoes embarking on a landing craft. With one exception all were grinning at the camera. The profile of this one soldier's face was remarkably like Miles.

Bert was sure that if he came through alive he would be back to claim the old car when the war was over, but it stood where he left it, enshrouded in bindweed and tall grasses until Bert and the forge itself had gone.

Shockodolly's Drains

It was the nearest Harry Applethorn had ever been to striking,
but no self-respecting waggoner could be expected to enjoy
falling face-down in sticky clay twice in an hour, when he
was supposed to be planting spring barley. He came stumping
down the stable yard, looking like an unkilned toby jug, with
both horses plastered to the hocks in mud. "The man ain't born
as could make a fair old job of planting on the far side of
Mockbeggar Field," he complained to my father. "'Tis like walking on half-cooked suet pudd'n when the water's gone off the
boil in the pot. I ain't wasting my breath or breaking the horses'
spirits stodging around up there."

"If you want it planted I reckon you'd better set to training
they old crows to scratch around and sow a bit of seed. 'Tis
certain sure they're the only things that won't sink in, for you'll
not get it sown by anything with legs or wheels until it is
properly drained."

Mockbeggar Field lies at the top of quite a steep bank, yet one half was always wet and extremely heavy to work. Given a warm dry spring, with planting conditions so good that we managed to get all the field sown at once, the seed on that side was always reluctant to germinate, remaining a month's growth behind the rest of the field, right through to reaping time.

It was one thing to recognise that it needed new drainage – finding the money to get it done was something else. Dad stood silent for a moment, as if he were weighing up the problem, then, serious-faced, replied. "If you think that rooks and crows are our only hope of planting Mockbeggar this year, Harry, how would it be if you helped me train 'em? With a bit of luck we might be able to teach them to line their nests with five pound notes. Doubtless we would both shin up the elm trees like schoolboys after eggs. That's the only way I can see me having cash to spare for miles of pipes, unless we're able to gather three harvests in one year."

The two men, friends as well as employer and employee, stood on opposite sides of the horse trough. Harry Applethorn grinned first. "You girt lummox," was all he answered, but both men understood that any anger had evaporated. "Reckon you could hand sow her, given a dry weekend, and if it's still too sticky for a horse harrow I could follow behind draggin' a hawthorn bough to cover it in."

A few days later I was dispatched in a hurry up to Mockbeggar Field with a jug of hot cocoa and two 'plate-pie-vittals' wrapped in tea towels for the two men's midday 'bait.' It was like stepping back into history, for men have sown and harrowed seed in the same way for at least two thousand years. My father, walking with easy strides, scattered seed from a hod hung around his neck to balance on one hip, while Harry Applethorn used a pair of crossed leather straps on his shoulders as a harness to haul a branch of a hawthorn tree to harrow in the corn.

The kidney-shaped seed hod, lip or maund, depending on the name each locality gives it, has remained unaltered through the years and some historians believe that the Maundy Money distributed by the reigning monarch on the day before Good Friday get its name from the maund, or pouch, used by the medieval kings to carry their largesse.

Promptly at noon both men stopped work. As I sat down with

them, waiting to take the empty jug and plates back home, three men who had been hedge cutting and ditching on Foxley Banks came across to join us. Each followed Dad's and Harry's example, folding an empty sack cornerwise to make a hood and protect their backs from the chill wind. What conversation there was centred on the sad and soggy condition of the tilth that side of Mockbeggar Field, although the hedge cutters were pretty monosyllabic, as if it cost them money to spare a word. The three bachelor Dann brothers were known as Ben, Treacle and Shockodolly.

In a family where thrift was a religion carried to fanatical extreme, Shockodolly's mop of snow-white hair grew far bushier than most before he would consider a fourpenny haircut to be financially worth while. A tall tale in the village held that Shockodolly's hair changed colour when he was young enough to enjoy Harvest Home. On such occasions it was the custom to pass around the hat for those who were sick or needing help.

Filled with free and unaccustomed beer, Shockodolly had recklessly put what he thought to be a penny in the hat, until the vicar made special mention of his philanthropy in so far as he had generously given a half-crown.

The story went that the thought of giving away almost half a day's wages turned his hair white with shock. True or not, the Dann family gave such junketings a wide berth after that year. In fact, they mixed with very few people at all, so that both Harry Applethorn and Dad were surprised when they came across Mockbeggar Field to spend their half hour dinner break. The hot bacon, onion and potato pasties were finished and the last of the cocoa generously shared between all five before Ben Dann got round to voicing the object of their visit.

"We did a bit of drain laying with our old chap when we were boys and we don't see why we couldn't get this 'ere water soaked away. It'd have a downhill fall. If its all right with you, we'll start on it first chance we get when the crop is off." Dad said he didn't think he could afford to pay for their labour and buy the pipes too.

"Pipes?" Shockodolly lifted the aged cap that lay on his head like a loose, mossy tile and scratched his scalp. "What'll we want pipes for when we can cut a hedge? We'll be over and make a start by the back end of the year."

They all stood up to go, but as Dad lit his pipe for a quiet smoke before he started work again Treacle took a clay pipe from his pocket and asked Dad for a match.

His tobacco smelled like nothing I had ever encountered before, and I said so. When they left, Harry Applethorn told me that the unique aroma was accountable to the fact that Treacle made his own smoking mixture of dried plantain, sainfoin leaves and a plant that grows on stagnant ponds.

That year went by, and so did the next. Mockbeggar Field still stayed muddy, although its draining was always going to be the Dann's next job. Ben Dann died suddenly, and that, Dad thought, was that, until Ada Dann met me in the village. At first glance she was a nondescript little woman with as much meat on her as a yard of pump water, and was about as colourful in character and dress. She only told me to have a load of straw bales ready in Mockbeggar Field the following morning, yet I could see why her brothers were loath to upset her.

Treacle and Shockodolly arrived at dawn with their new partner, a cousin who introduced himself as Nipper. As he made yards of straw rope with a hook and ratchet he said; "Poor old Ben, scrimping, saving, to put some money under the mattress, and all he got was a lumpy bed.

"Old Ada is so mean we only have one newspaper a week it's used as a table cloth, then torn into squares. She rations it out and gives us a piece at a time to take to the privy. If we don't need it we're supposed to bring it back. I saves mine up though, that fools 'er."

The Danns dug trenches, lining them with straw ropes and bundles of ash and hazel twigs. By the following spring Mockbeggar Field was drained enough for sowing to be over in time for Dad to plant potatoes before midday on Good Friday, thus adhering to an old country tradition known as planting at the foot of the cross. Nipper survived the Danns and had a whale of a time spending their hard-saved money. Now they have all become part of village history. But the straw rope drains they laid in Mockbeggar Field work on.

A Cushti Day

With the early-morning sun transforming the dew-damp grass into scintillating diamonds, I crushed a king's ransom of beauty with every step I took. From the encampment fire beneath the ripening cherry trees in the orchard, a tenuous wisp of blue smoke drifted lazily up into a sky as clear blue as a starling's egg. A broad-hipped Romany woman carrying a painted bucket to fill at the yard pump, acknowledged my "Good morning" with the prediction that the chance of riches would cross my path, and that for all of us it would be a *cushti* (good) day.

Lockley church clock striking half-past-six came clear across the still air as I walked to Barn Field to bring in the grazing horses; the sound of metal hammering metal echoed across the wooded valley from the village street. Bert, the blacksmith, was 'chiming the anvil' to announce the forge was open for business

84

at the start of another country working day. Reluctant to leave their lush and shady pasture to be harnessed for working, the four horses continued munching, but Jim, the chestnut gelding, always inquisitive, every-ready for tit-bits and affection, ambled over to see what he could forage from my pocket. Cold bread pudding, carrots, apples, these were among his favourites, top rating being, without doubt a handful of potato crisps.

Happily quiescent as a contented baby, he stood with his chin resting on my shoulder as I slipped the rope halter over his head. Punch, the grey, was inclined to petulance, using heels and teeth if anyone upset him. The sight of Jim nuzzling around my pockets brought him at a full gallop toward me, a habit of his that looked terrifying to an onlooker, but I knew he would come to a sudden halt a few yards in front of me and stand whinnying, plainly asking for his share. Two haltered, two to catch.

Prince was a Suffolk Punch of doubtful ancestry, since he was a full 17½ hands high, had feet as big as meat plates, enormous strength and the obstinacy of a mule. He seemed to possess a fiendish sense of humour, taking the attitude; "So you think you will harness me for work when I could be grazing? Right then – first catch your horse." His one weakness was toffee, and if after a preliminary chase around the pasture I had still not managed to grab his mane and get him haltered a lump of toffee was my last resort.

Not that I dispensed these freely. At two old-fashioned pennies for a quarter pound they were too dear to lavish on a mule-headed, obstinate old horse.

Turpin was a different proposition altogether. A much later acquisition, this barrel-chested bay Welsh cob ignored all the undignified chasing, seemed impervious to blandishments and would continue grazing until the other three were haltered and heading for the gate. With an expression on his face as clear as words, he would trot over and fall in behind the others as if to say "You three off to work then? Wait for me."

That we always seemed to muster a motley crew of haymakers was really understandable when the more agile local casual workers could earn far more money with less effort picking fruit. This meant our labour force consisted of helpers too old, nervous or otherwise decrepit to climb ladders or work aloft. Surprisingly, five helpers were mustered in the yard to start work at seven that morning. One was old Jimmy Spit, whose predilection for chewing tobacco had brought expectoration to so fine an art that he had the reputation of being able to engulf a flying gnat in sudden death. Apart from this one failing and his disconcerting tendency to nod off into a deep sleep at the most inopportune moments, Jimmy's willingness to help was pure gold.

With twelve acres of hay fit to carry, Dad considered it unbelievably good fortune to be faced with the other four eager volunteers. Tolly Budd and his three hefty sons were thatchers and hay trussers, wielding the enormous hay-knives to cut the compressed hay out of the stacks during the winter months, in the days before all mowing grass was baled. They lived on a cold comfort kind of smallholding, neither Tolly nor any of his sons having been wed. Of late Tolly had let it be known that they were not averse to having a bit of female influence at their homestead. Not that they wanted the place to be lumbered up with a "passel of scritching and gossiping wimmin," but if a hard-working young woman would choose any one of them she would require no wages, but could look after them all.

This to Tolly was a serious proposition, and as they stood there eyeing me in much the same way as they would any livestock that might be available for purchase I had began to realise just why they had come. Dad knew my thoughts without my having to voice them, but he grinned back the unspoken reassurance that he would keep a careful watch on the situation. A shrug of his shoulders told me that with four chaps eager to show off their muscular charm for my benefit in our hayfield, this was far too good an opportunity to miss.

Luckily my first job was to drive Turpin to and fro with the lumbering hay rake, gathering the rows of dried grass into lumps. Jogging along with scented honeysuckle and sweet briar in the hedgerows, the air filled with bird song and the sun-warmed, sweet-smelling hay piling up behind me seemed to me to be as near to living in paradise as I could wish for. It was as the gipsy woman predicted, a cushti day. I had finished the raking by eleven, and joined the others loading the waggons or working on the stack. Jimmy Spit seemed quite agitated and at our midday break called me for a word in private on the far side of the stack.

"Can't think what Harry is up to. There's Tolly Budd saying

that Harry ought to begin thinking about getting you wed and off his hands, and Harry hinting that you had ideas along that road yourself. Don't you get mixed up in that rum lot, gal." For all that he chewed tobacco and was scruffy, Jimmy was a true friend, so I let him into a secret that the Budds did not know. Chuckling, he sat down under the ladder on the shady side of the haystack and promptly fell asleep. Although Dad and I had a packed meal with us I didn't fancy spending an hour being watched by a bevy of Budds, so I made an excuse that I was going to slip home.

Instead, I took my sandwiches to eat under the shade of the walnut tree on the edge of New Take orchard. The tree was loaded with green walnuts the size of pullet's eggs, just the right size for pickling. I asked one of the gipsy men if I could borrow a picking basket, and he volunteered to bring over a sixty stale ladder to put up into the tree. One of the gipsies, seeing the ladder empty took it away. For once I was glad to see Tolly and the youngest Budd approaching. I called down that I was stuck. Tolly summed up the situation. "Try walking about up there and you'll soon come down, gal," was all he said.

His son brought a ladder and stood at the bottom as I scrambled down. Paws, green teeth and perspiration, he attempted a passing peck, muttering in a fervour of thwarted passion: "Gor. You dun arf taste good." I ran.

Time to start work, I went around the stack to wake Jimmy. He lay snoring, his hat over his eyes, and just above him on the stale of the ladder a hanging, humming, heaving swarm of bees. Tolly thought we might shake them into one of the horses nosebags, but it seemed too risky. I was dispatched to find the lady bee-keeper over at Penny Pot Lane.

The Budds and Dad would continue to load the waggons, leaving Jimmy to sleep on if he could. It so happened that the lady apiarist was out chasing the swarm. Jimmy woke to find her hooded and netted bending over him. He thought his end had come, but saw nothing remarkable in not being stung. "You chew tobacco, girl, and nothing'll pester you." That I could well believe.

The hayfield was cleared and stacked by evening. When the Budds collected their pay Tolly again raised the question of my getting married and off Dad's hands. Only then did Dad inform him that my banns of marriage to the blacksmith's son had been called in church that week.

As we turned the tired horses out to graze, the gipsy woman called: "Cushti evening, Guv." "Cushti," we replied – and meant it, too.

The Conservationists

Conservation was not a word much used in the days when Jack helped us with sheep dipping, cleaning cattle yards, muck spreading and the more disagreeable jobs that took more muscle power than Dad and I could muster on our own. If anyone had called Jack a supreme conservationist, his denial would have been forthright and probably unprintable, him having no inclination for fancy phrases or long words.

Despite his obvious willingness and ability, the local landowners were reluctant to employ him. His dishevelled appearance and aversion to soap and water put them off. We could not afford to be so fussy, and in accepting Jack's enthusiastic help we had to accept his shortcomings as well.

True, we did try to nudge him into more hygienic standards, but tactful hints that his social habits left much to be desired were as effective as trying to break up concrete with a pin.

Dad spoke plainly. "Good God, Jack. The last time I whiffed anything to equal you was when that old ewe went missing for a fortnight and I found her drowned and rotting in the dyke."

Such pointed insults scarcely scratched the surface of Jack's finer feelings beyond the instant retort of "Yus. And wouldn't the silly old mutton head 'ave still been alive and kicking if 'er 'adn't ventured to put her hooves in water. Didn't do 'er no good. Nor would it me."

In a village where mains water was still a council election promise, where sink and bath tub taps only functioned in those households affluent enough to engage someone to pump well-water up into overhead tanks, we learned young the true value of the wells and springs around us. Every dwelling had its water butt for catching rain.

There were advantages since there was, and still is, nothing to match rain water for making hair soft, silky and shining, with the minimum of fuss and shampoo. It was the one concession to beautifying that the most straitlaced and narrow-minded matrons would allow, and the clear smooth complexions for which country girls were once noted owed much to the old water butt by every back door.

Water snails and fat yellow-bellied slugs that were sometimes hauled up from the depths of the well in the huge elm-wood buckets were regarded as proof that the water was pure and proud we were, too, of its clear clean taste. All of us except Jack. He reckoned that if we had been meant to drink water from buckets we would have come on this earth equipped with necks the same shape as a horse.

Of course, he drank it indirectly, keeping a battered enamel teapot constantly brewing on the hob of his cottage range. Lined with a thick coat of tannin that would have stiffened leather, this was topped up each morning with water and a fresh pinch of tea.

By the weekend there were more leaves than liquid, but each Sunday morning Jack would empty the pot, carefully straining off the leaves to dry them on an old tin tray in the oven. Mixed together with the contents of his tobacco tin, Jack knew how to make half an ounce of shag last a very long time indeed.

As I said, Jack was a model conservationist after his own fashion, so thrifty that he would transform the roadside nettles into a passable home-brewed beer to supplement tea. For years he lived a solitary bachelor existence but when his cousin died, leaving a widow penniless in a tied farm cottage, Jack offered her the shelter of his home.

Old Lou's arrival as Jack's housekeeper gave those who were intrigued by his way of life the opportunity to seek verification as to whether he did, or did not, wear his wellies in bed.

He made no secret of the fact that, come winter or summer, he never shed shirt, pants or hat at bedtime, saying that, "When horses, cattle and rabbits take their coats off at night, so will I."

Timorous as a skinny, ageing squirrel, old Lou was too grateful that Jack had let her retain some measure of independence to have discussed his sleeping habits with anyone. She asked little except that she be allowed to rest on the broken-springed old sofa in the kitchen when her day's work was done.

Simple, economically minded, her standard of living was as frugal as Jack's, although she was somewhat more hygienic, and nothing that went into that cottage was wasted, nothing was thrown away.

Jack would never leave a piece of wood that would feed his kitchen stove and, in turn, the wood ash was emptied on the garden to fine down the soil. He grew some marvellous crops that never wilted in dry weather, because the well water that Lou used went, via the dish pan, back into the soil.

Table scraps, peelings and wild seeds helped to feed the chicken at the bottom of Jack's garden. Even the few tins that were used were cut open, flattened and nailed like slates or tiles around the hen house walls to keep it snug and dry.

Jack collected or cadged any garden seeds he noticed, and these would be hung up in unlabelled paper bags on the innumerable nails and hooks that covered the ceiling of the kitchen. This could sometimes lead to slight misunderstandings and mistakes, such as the time that Lou, acting on the kindest of intentions, administered a brew of the silvery dried 'Honesty' seeds instead of Senna pods when Jack's stomach was upset.

Lou collected sheep wool from the hedgerows, washing it and making it into the padding for warm patchwork quilts. She would collect the bundles of binder twine that used to clutter up the farm barns after threshing time, plaiting and stitching it into mats. Despite her ministrations, Jack continued to resemble a walking straw stack. It took desperate situations to make him even consider replacing his worn-out clothes. I remember the year that the seat of his trousers was so threadbare that total disintegration was simply a matter of time. Dad and I had private wagers on the limit of their survival. "Tomorrow, the weekend, next week—," but we had not reckoned on Lou's ingenuity. Just when Jack was obviously due for an embarrassing predicament, he came to work with the hole in his trousers cobbled together with massive stitches that had been sewn with a sacking needle threaded with binder twine.

That day Jack was pulling mangolds, taking the leaves off and piling them up in lumps. I was loading them on to the trailer of my old tractor and hauling them into the frostfree shelter of the barn. I noticed that each time I passed by that morning he looked discomforted and purple faced beneath the top dirt and the stubble of his beard. At last he came trotting over and asked where Dad was. He had to see him "confidential-like and quick." I knew that Dad was with a sow that was farrowing in the pigsties. "For pity's sake then, gal, drive me up there quick."

I didn't hang about. Nor would you with Jack close beside you on the tractor, and his face looking more pained and purple all the time. Dad, hearing the tractor, came out to see what was the matter. Jack leapt down and dashed toward him. "Quick, Harry, get out your shut-knife and come into the barn to help me." Dad stood still, more than a mite puzzled. "Don't stand there asking fool questions. I'm desperate. There I was, quietly behind the hedge and settling down nicely to drop my tailboard to answer a call of nature when I realised that Lou, silly old besom, stitched up more than she ought when she mended up my breeches. The blamed things won't part company with my shirt!"

Dad emerged from the barn, Jack following some minutes later. He clutched a corn sack coyly around his middle. I was despatched to ask Mum for an old pair of my father's trousers. We rummaged around in the old wooden box known as our hope chest, since we dumped discarded garments in it, hoping that they would prove useful later on. We found a rough pair of old corduroys with more patch than leg to them. Dad was much taller than Jack, but this worried Jack not a bit. Standing in the middle of the yard, he put them on over his worn ones, tucking the spare into his wellies and commenting that they would keep him warm a treat.

Now when every section of the media entreats us to save water, energy and fuel, I remember Jack. If that true master of conservation could have been around to lecture folk on the subject he would have earned a lot more money than he got by dipping sheep or pulling mangold-wurzels with us.

Someone's Pet

Sunshine and drying March winds made planting conditions perfect for me to tractor harrow the ploughed furrows to let Dad sow barley with his old-fashioned two horse drill. We worked until it grew too dark for Dad to follow the line of the drill marks, then he led his tired team back to the stables while I sheeted up the old tractor under the larch row fringing Parsons Wood. A chill dampness had descended with twilight, and an unfelt breeze that sighed among the tree tops made me shiver as I walked along the edge of the lambing pasture on my way back home. The cracking of twigs and a movement in the wood startled me until I recognised one of the estate game-keepers emerging through the trees. He called out, warning me that a couple of sheep worrying dogs had attacked his foster hens raising clutches of young pheasants in his rearing pens just beyond our boundary fence. The local policeman had given him the description of the dogs as being a black and tan collie and a smaller black mongrel, along with permission to shoot either dog on sight.

Our lambing season was almost at an end, the fine weather working wonders for the mothers and their babies, and as I walked home in the deepening gloom, all the ewes were placidly chewing the cud, with their lambs snuggled close to their fleece for the night.

Mum was anxious to get breakfast cleared early the next morning, for Spring to Mum meant chick rearing, and with several of her hens already going broody, she intended to transform apple boxes and chicken wire into maternity coops for fowls. Leaving Dad to tackle the essential farm chores, before he brought a load of seed corn down the field to start drilling, I went on ahead to count the sheep and see if the last few barren ewes had achieved unlikely motherhood, then start harrowing to get the soil ready for the seed drill.

Watching rooks and pigeons clustering around our fields in anticipation of an easy breakfast, I took the old single barrel shot gun and bird scaring cartridges to persuade them to move on. My footsteps left a distinct trail in the dewy grass, but other tracks criss-crossed them and when I reached the lambing pasture, the flock was in one corner, panting and wild-eyed.

I stayed to calm them, but there was ploughed land waiting to be planted, so all I could do was keep an eye on them each time I took the tractor and harrow to the top end of the field.

'Florrie Fordson' was sometimes temperamental when I tried to overwork her. That morning she sulked, coughed and spluttered every time she met rough going and, soon after Dad began drilling, she misfired and stopped. As I took a spanner to her filter, I heard a commotion coming from the direction of our yard. A dog was barking, chickens squawking, then I heard the unmistakable sound of the stableyard bell. This was Mum's recognised emergency signal, only rung when she needed urgent help.

Dad could not quickly leave his horses so, grabbing the rook gun and a few cartridges, I raced across the field. As I ran I saw two dogs running in the lambing pasture, advancing on the terrified sheep. Ears flat to his head and half crouching, the collie circled the flock, but the little black mongrel tore in among them snapping at the fleeing lambs. He caught one by the back legs the collie coming to join him, grabbing the lamb's head in a macabre tug of war. I had been midwife to the flock, knowing each by sight and name.

Trembling with fury, I loaded the gun as I scrambled through the hedge, oblivious to the thorns that lacerated my clothes and arms. By that time the lamb had been decapitated, the collie seeking further sport, but the black mongrel lingered to play with the headless body, heaving it in the air like a rag doll. Knowing that the cartridges were only powder and wadding, I was so raging angry that I aimed for the mongrel's head. The old gun had a kick like a stallion thumping my shoulder and seemed to make a double report.

The collie had vanished by the time my eyes would focus properly, but the mongrel lay inert beside its victim. I ran over to it, wondering how a badly aimed blank cartridge fired at a distance could knock it out cold, then realised that it had been shot in the head. Another shot reverberated across the fields, but I was in no state to recognise if it was Dad's twelve bore. I only knew that I had actually killed in anger for the first time in my life. A tag on the dog's collar gave it the name of 'Blackie', and I realised that I had probably shot someone's pet.

The persistent ringing of the stableyard bell brought me to my senses so I left the dog lying, counting three dead lambs and a savaged ewe as I ran.

I found Mum hysterically tugging at the bell rope, blood pouring from her arm. Sobbing, she said that she had been collecting a broody hen from the nest boxes in the fowl run when the two dogs dashed through the unlatched gate. They had killed and savaged several hens before she could drive them off, but the collie had turned on her, flying for her throat. Protecting herself by covering her face with her hands, it had bitten her arm instead. She was in a state of shock, needing more than iodine to treat her injuries. Dad brought the two horses into the yard at the trot, we harnessed one to a tip cart and I drove Mum to the casualty department of the hospital in town.

The overwhelming anger I had felt in the lambing pasture welled up again, watching my trembling mother, I wished that the owners of the dogs could have the carcases of our tortured animals dumped in their own back yards. While I waited for Mum outside the hospital, for there were no facilities to park a tip cart, I realised that the address on the dead mongrel's collar was a side turning off that street.

Leading the horse down a narrow entry that was sunless, drab and smelly, I hammered on the appropriate door, determined to say my piece. There were sounds of movement behind the paint-starved panels, but whoever was answering my knock was taking their time. All my anger evaporated as the door slowly opened to reveal a tiny, shrunken old lady, crippled with arthritis, supporting herself with a stick. She smiled a quavering welcome, thinking I was the daughter of a man who went round the streets selling bundles of logs. I tried to explain, but she continued talking in a confused fashion, saying that she could not afford more than a tanner's worth if I was charging sixpence a bundle. She spoke so quickly, I could only stand and listen to her saying that I was the first soul she had spoken to for days. Praying I had come to the wrong house, I eventually managed to ask her if she had a dog called Blackie.

"Blackie?" Her face lit up with the warmth of affection. "He's my little baby! Has he been showing off his tricks to you then, bless him? My late husband taught him to do all manner of nonsense like playing hide and seek with dog biscuits, or pretending to die for the king. He knows every word I say, does Blackie. Now I'm alone and so tottery that I can't get out of the house, he's all I have left."

She looked so frail, so unloved, so poverty-stricken, I could not bring myself to tell her that I had shot her dog. All I could do was burst into stupid snivelling tears and break the news that Blackie was lying dead in a country meadow. At this point Mum came along. She had seen the horse and cart in the entry and, taking immediate grasp of the situation, backed me in my white lie.

"An accident?" the old lady sobbed, tears coursing down her grey cheeks. "My poor little boy did so love a run in the park, he would have loved being in the country. Did he follow someone out there? Will you see he is properly buried there?" We left her with the illusions about her dear little pet and headed for home.

On the way back, we met the village policeman. He looked

with concern at Mum's bandaged arm. Before I could admit to him that I had shot the black mongrel, he said, "You know the game keeper has killed both of the sheep killers, don't you? He said he was afraid you would fire that old rook gun before he could get a shot at the small black dog, but he beat you to it by a fraction of a second. The collie he got at point blank range. That pair accounted for at least sixty head of stock between them. Your evidence will get us a couple of convictions when we put the owners in court."

Thinking of that sad, housebound old cripple, Mum said there was no point in threatening a prosecution. Putting the poor old soul in court would not bring sheep, lambs, or chicken back to life. All she wanted to do was to get home and get on with making hen coops for the baby chicks that would soon be hatching. I had an appointment with a temperamental tractor, trying to make up for lost time to help Dad plant seed barley.

The Antagonists

A skilled craftsman, making ashwood fruit-picking ladders all winter, Joe Sprockett's summer inclination was to work in various farm orchards, moving ladders from tree to tree for those who picked the apples, cherries, pears and plums. Happily content to set up a makeshift warm-weather home in some disused chicken ark or cattle shed, bachelor Joe's mode of life was regarded as a family disgrace by his sister-in-law, Emma, who lost no opportunity to air her vituperative views.

No love was lost between Joe, nearly sixty, and his brother's widow, a lady of uncertain age. Waging continuous verbal battle, Joe did nothing to disprove the village stories circulating after the Monday morning when his brother, Sam Sprockett, breathed his last.

Sam made an unfortunate, unexpected exit from this vale of

trouble beneath an overturned manure cart. That a carelessly replaced cotter-bar of a dung cart would change her status from wife to widow seemed to Emma typical of Sam's contrariness. It irritated her that Sam should create a crisis when her copper chimney was drawing well and heating water quickly, and this on the first fine warm Monday washing morning there had been for months.

Joe Sprockett's antagonism towards his sister-in-law rose to explosive proportions when, in company with three other shocked and white-faced farmhands, he carried the victim home. To have taken Sam to the parish mortuary involved a two-mile trudge, notwithstanding the fact that the small stone building by the churchyard had long served as the grave-diggers' tool shed and a store for the parson's logwood supply of winter fuel, so there would have been no room to lay Sam out. In any case poor Sam was smelling none to pleasant, so the perspiring quartet took him to his cottage to clean him up.

Emma refused to let them carry the hurdle-gate borne load over the threshold, peremptorily ordering them to lug their pathetic burden down-wind of her washing line. Given time to finish her laundering properly, she offered to provide a copper full of hot soapy suds for Joe and his helper to wash her late and less than sweet scented husband in the back yard, suggesting that while they were busy with bass brooms and buckets they could well scrub the yard. She thought it a terrible pity to let good hot water go to waste. Joe complained that after all the muck and manure his late brother has succumbed to, this was the last straw.

Harsh words and insults flew like missiles between Sam's two sole surviving family mourners and for all Emma's caustic tongue, interested onlookers thought Joe's observations at the funeral won him the contest of words, game set and match. To the parson, commiserating on the sad loss of his brother, Joe said:

"I don't think old Sam would reckon much on me a-grieving on him when he be tucked in down there snug, quiet and peaceful, out of old Emma's earshot. He had a smile on his face, and I ain't seen him look so happy since before the day she told 'un she'd decided they must get wed."

Regarded by most as being middling uppity and having ideas above her husband's wage packet, village curiosity questioned how Emma would react to having no income at all. Joe's offer of financial assistance was met with icy rejection as Emma chose to retire behind the drawn blinds of Woodbine Cottage.

Apart from Short-foot Price, the travelling draper bringing mourning clothes on approval, and a smartly dressed insurance man from the city, there were few to whom Emma's door was open.

Bothered by a sense of brotherly duty, Joe Sprockett wondered if Sam's widow might be penniless but too proud to admit it. The situation was not improved when he heard that she had somehow found the money to buy her house. Woodbine Cottage became Wood Villa, and an advertisement in the local weekly paper announced that Mrs. Sam Sprockett was offering the hospitality of her country residence to suitable and impeccably referenced guests.

Puzzling aloud how Emma had achieved such a financial miracle, Joe was enlightened by the post-mistress who informed him that for several years Emma had paid hefty insurance premiums on both Sam's life and his own. The news gave Joe an uneasy, cold sensation that ran from the region of his back collar stud down to his twitching toes.

Emma's only guest proved to be the smooth-talking insurance man from the city. The downstairs front room became his bedsit-office, complete with typewriter and filing cabinet. It did wonders for Emma's ego to tell callers clutching insurance books, "My guest is in his office. I will ascertain if he can be disturbed."

It was a thought to treasure that she alone in all the village sat down to meals with a shaven, shiny-shoed man wearing a clean celluloid collar and a blue serge suit. Joe, who still kept the hedges clipped and the garden tidy, called her a daft old besom to make sheep's eyes and act dotty over some rent-paying tame insurance man.

Short-foot Price was allowed to take a cup of tea in the kitchen when he called every Thursday, and while Emma Sprockett could hardly have been said to encourage visitors, it seemed for a while that her caustic temperament had begun to lose some of its sting. This state of affairs faded when her lodger started rushing through his tea to don cycle clips and bowler hat, then go pedalling down the lane. He was reticent about these nightly excursions, frequently returning with cement dust, paint and distemper on his boots.

Emma confided he suspicions to Short-foot. With every local birth, wedding or death providing his drapery round with potential profit, Short-foot made it his business to investigate. It sounded as if old Emma's lodger was setting up home elsewhere, probably needing household linens. It was in his own interest to find out.

On his next drapery round day, Short-foot imparted the news that the insurance man was courting a kennelmaid from Foxley and renovating an old cottage out that way.

"Of course," said Short-foot astutely, "these young women wear different clothes that make them look slimmer and more attractive than more matronly ladies."

With a sour expression, Emma asked him to explain.

Fetching a box from his van he held up a type of corsetry she had always favoured. Strong sludge grey cotton, supported by fearsomely stiff whale boning, it was beset with eyelet holes and yards of stay lace, looking less like a garment than a barricade. Short-foot then offered a small tubular garment for her inspection, but taking it for some sort of elasticated stocking, Emma said she wasn't fretted over the shape of her knees.

"Dear Lady," said Short-foot, the super salesman. "These are the height of fashion in upper-class circles, guaranteed to hold upward and inward all that has sagged or spread. It is called a roll-on corselette."

He suggested he might leave the garment for Emma to try on in the privacy of her bedroom, then she could pay for it when he came round again.

After a tea of cold kippers and icy disdain, Emma's lodger went to his room to get ready to meet his loved one as his landlady stalked haughtily up the stairs, some moments later he heard strange bumping sounds coming from her bedroom, followed by a strangled kind of groan. He went up the stairs, knocked on the door, but found it locked. Cycling off for help, he met Joe Sprockett who collected one of his fruit-picking ladders and leaned it against Emma's bedroom window sill.

Wasting no time with formalities, Joe clambered up and into Emma's bedroom to find her clad only in sleeved vest and knee-length fleecy-lined bloomers. The roll-on girdle like an updated strait-jacket was imprisoning her chest, upstretched arm and head. On the top of the ladder, the lodger leaned on the window sill, laughing loudly, saying that his girl friend always put her feet into a similar garment, then hauled it up. Joe dispatched him to the kitchen to fetch a carving knife to cut Emma free.

Almost hysterical she called out. "Who is to pay for this Joe Sprockett? How can I explain to Short-foot Price that you have climbed into my bedroom and hacked his elastic corset to pieces while I was trying it on!"

"Me, I reckon!" Joe said, trying to calm her. "Get yourself dressed decent. We could both do with a cup of tea."

Emma sat in the kitchen, flushed and embarrassed by her ordeal.

"What did you want to squeeze into that thing for, you silly old besom?" Joe said, smiling. "If its company you want, I need someone to look after me a bit during the winter. I know that folk reckon you take a rasp to your tongue to keep it so sharp, but you ain't bad looking under your burrs and prickles, and I do enjoy a good old argufying fight."

Emma Sprockett, sitting beside him drank her tea, uttering not one word.

Queen Ethel Who?

The Parsonage Garden Party had always been a select affair, patronised by the more affluent parishioners who were too refined to expect anything more from the price of entry than to have the right to take stewed tea and stale scones on the ant infested lawn beneath the cedar, or browse among the articles for sale on a flag draped table on the terrace in front of the house. Penny glasses of powdery lemonade were provided for small fry brought unwillingly by mind-your-manners mothers, as were tuppenny dips in tubs of bran.

It was always hinted that a golden sovereign was hidden among the paper wrapped gobstoppers, marbles, liquorice bootlaces and penny whistles, but no one ever found it, and the Doubting Thomas element in the village questioned the existence of such mythical wealth. At an exorbitant half a crown to get past the Parsonage gate posts, those who knew their place in the social pecking order of the parish, regarded 'parson's party' as an uppity annual non-event.

That year the parson was forced to the conclusion that while he deplored the lowering of social barriers, he must widen the scope of the occasion to ease a pressing financial need.

All due respects to the ladies of the Busy Bee's Sewing Circle, but if every knitted egg cosy, embroidered chair back and stitched hot bottle cover was snatched up, there was no hope that their price would raise one fiftieth of the filthy lucre he must find.

The church roof timbers were plagued with an infestation of beetles and, closer home, wet rot was crumbling the floorboards in the parsonage scullery and bathroom, causing an embarrassing situation he hesitated to discuss publicly.

Shunning pleasures of the flesh, he favoured the early morning cold water scrub routine of bathing, but his spinster sister was made of weaker stuff. She tended to stoke the kitchen back boiler until the pipes vibrated then indulge herself in a twice weekly soak, chin deep in a decadent, huge, hot bath. Her weight, combined with that of the brimming iron bath tub, had eventually proved too much for the floor joists. Hearing her screams from behind the locked bathroom door, he had been obliged to enlist the blacksmith's help to get in and help her out. The spectacle that had confronted them after the blacksmith had forced the door with a crowbar, was one he would have difficulty in eradicating from his mind.

While the bung hole of the bath had stayed firm, the top end had fallen through the floorboards, lodging at an angle. Head down, feet threshing the air, his solidly-built sister was trapped, made more hysterical by the fact that a cold water pipe had fractured and was showering her with spray. Eyes averted, using the bath mat to cover the victim's confusion, it had taken all of the blacksmith's muscular effort and the parson's own words of encouragement to haul her out.

In beseeching the blacksmith to maintain a discreet silence about the incident, the parson stressed how urgent a new and massive repair fund had become and how few were his hopes of success. Never one to mince his words, the blacksmith suggested that the garden party be enlarged and made more attractive to ordinary village folk. Democratically the parson put up several notices asking for suggestions. Any ideas thus offered would be discussed at a village meeting. No workable scheme would be refused.

The notice began: "Our village church has seen a thousand years of history . . ." Of such words are inspirations made. If this was so, why did we not stage a celebratory gala instead of the usual garden party? We could perform a pageant or some similar spectacle.

This idea was backed up by the new and still enthusiastic schoolmaster who had found some ancient local history books. It was agreed that this could be planned and the scenario written, subject to the parson's approval. Suggestions poured in, some feasible, some not.

One so approved was grass-track cycling, or even motor-cycle races around the parsonage paddock, the proviso being that the four acres of waist-high docks, thistles and couch-grass be mown and cleared without charge to the parson. There were to be bookstalls, white elephants and the less dignified rummage. Prompted by his privately-tippling sister, the parson even consented to a bring-and-buy bottle stall, as long as she was in sole charge.

At one time, before it was hauled off to the city as tourist bait, there was a ducking stool at a village along the river in which scolds and nagging shrews were dunked in the water. Someone suggested that Old Humph, the wheelwright, make a replica, for there were several men who would gladly pay to see it used. Old Amos, the horse-dealer and a betting man, offered to put a subscribed stake on a dead-cert dark horse he was backing, thus dispensing with any need for a gala, but this the parson overruled.

Meanwhile, the process of delving into local history made it plain that the village forbears were a pretty rough unpatriotic lot. Admitted, when Queen Ethelburga's horse dropped dead beneath her as she travelled along the wooded terrain on the edge of our parish, the locals made a rough litter and carried her on her way. That was an episode easily enacted, except that we could foresee problems in trying to find a co-operative horse. Seeing that our local Lordship and his Lady always patronised the Parson's Garden Party with a donation rather than their presence, we wondered if a scene depicting the first of the noble line earning his title might bring them to grace our gala day.

Research showed that the personal services to the Monarch that brought such grace and favour had been rendered by his illustrious ancestor's lady wife. In the circumstances we thought it better to leave that dusty bit of history unstirred.

Working in conjunction with the coastal marsh villages, running an escape route for French prisoners of war incarcerated in the hulk ships out in the estuary, was a remunerative source of income around abut the 1800's. There had to be a story there.

A villager had once been hanged for sheep rustling; then there was the girl who swore that visions and unseen voices had asked her to send messages to some very affluent people. The proof of her integrity was that she became instantly bed-bound and turned black. She fooled folk for years, too. Long before the Tolpuddle farmhands raised their voices our local lads were marching from farm to farm in protest at the new threshing machines that had robbed them of their winter task of flailing corn in the barns. Faced with starvation, they made their pathetic gesture, their banner being a loaf impaled on the prongs of a pitchfork, their cry of battle being, "Give us bread."

All in all, we were proud to hand our finished script to the parson. "Ah yes," he said. "There might be one or two small alterations, but I do see the stature of Queen Ethelburga in the blacksmith's wife." "Queen Ethel who?" was that lady's immediate reaction but she consented, and that scene alone was all that was regarded as suitable from our script. Considered far too radical and reactionary in outlook, 'The Enduring Forest' became 'Our Glorious Land.'

Drake played bowls on the parsonage lawn, Stanley met Livingstone, but somehow it was not the same. The funds raised just about patched the floor in the parsonage bathroom, and Old Amos added the final touch to the futility of the effort. As he told the parson, it was a pity that no one would listen to his offer. His dark horse had romped home, first past the post at odds of 100–1.

The Leaning Post

For years the latch post of Barn Field gate had rocked back and forth like a loose tooth every time the gate was opened. Replacing it was a task Dad always planned to do, "come the slack time after harvest," but time, like money, always seemed to be in short supply.

On the day that I misjudged the width of the trailer I was towing behind the cleat wheeled old tractor, thus flattening the gate post, Dad and Jimmy Spit were riding along deep in agricultural conversation, their legs dangling over the back of the trailer, until its iron banded wheel nave hit the gate post. Simultaneously both shot off and sat down hard on the ground.

"Bloody speed crazy, these young 'uns," Jimmy swore, complaining that he had just swallowed a whole new plug of chewing tobacco. I tried to explain that with a light load and a downhill gradient, I had been trying to alleviate 'Florrie Fordson's' sluggish performance which always affected her like chronic constipation if she had been subjected to a long period of slow heavy field work. In top gear, with the hand throttle pulled out to the last notch, this had seemed an ideal opportunity to give old Florrie her head.

This may have helped her internal workings but did nothing to diminish Dad's dislike of a mechanical contrivance incapable of being halted with a hollered "Whoa!" To be hurtled along by a speed-mad daughter at ten miles an hour could be stoically endured, but to clumsily clobber the gate post was something else. His dignity had collected as many bruises as his backside, so he was scathing in his comments.

"I teach you all I know, and you still know nothing! How many times have you been told you will never hit a gate post if your horse's nose is pointing straight down the middle of the track."

I pointed out that Florrie Fordson was without a nasal organ, but this remark collected all the contempt it deserved. I acknowledged that I had been distracted by the clusters of bright orange rowan berries covering the tree by the gateway, for they bore a remarkable resemblance to the decorations on my mother's refurbished felt hat. That too was adored with innumerable droplets of coloured sealing wax, in defiance of war time drabness.

Like Mum's hat the rowan tree was old, but provided a wide canopy of shade. Long years before someone had hung an iron 'S' hook in a low branch. The tree's defiant bark had all but engulfed the top half, but time-honoured custom decreed this to be the place to hang our dinner baskets and bags of food. Our food had come through the jolting undamaged but Jimmy Spit was more concerned about the two-gallon stone jar he had been holding steady in the back of the trailer. Like him, it had landed in the dust.

A protecting worm-eaten wickerwork basket had kept it unbroken, and I said so when Jimmy started to complain about good beer being spoilt.

"Book learning don't teach young 'uns that home-brewed beer needs to be kept quiet if it is to put starch in a working man's backbone. Mad beer, shook up like this, will just tie my chitterlings up in knots.'

We put the stone jar in the deep green shade beneath the rowan tree, piling corn sheaves around it to keep it cool and settle itself to rights. A few hefty stones rammed down into the post hole made the latch post straighter than it had been before.

With the two men opting to walk rather than ride up the field to start loading wheat, I drove along the field edge, wondering what good-intentioned soul had planted all the wild fruit in the hedgerow. There were wild damsons, codlin apples and yellow bullace plums along with the rowans. Strict wartime sugar rationing prevented jam-making, but my Mum preserved them just the same. When all preserving jars were full she used jam jars, topping each one with a thick layer of melted mutton fat.

Swarms of wasps and hornets were gorging themselves on the ripe damsons and hollowing out the codlin apples. They were more ready for picking, but being so short-handed, all we wanted was time. The trees were old and spindly, liable to snap under the weight of a ladder, while the busy wasps made me wary of shinning up the trees.

Few of the imbecilic government slogans that the authorities delighted in sending farmers made much sense, but we agreed with the one advising that corn ricks should be made small and spaced well apart in case enemy air raids set them alight. Our corn stacks stood like circular tea cosies dotted along the farm track.

Dad always built our stacks, making them beautifully symmetrical. That day Jimmy Spit pitched from the load, tossing the sheaves across to me, while I in turn pitched them from the stack edge across to Dad. This was fine all the time the stack was not up to roof level, but once it was as high as Jimmy could comfortably reach with a six foot pitchfork, I took up station on the sloping roof side, where a few sheaves missed out from a couple of layers provided a precarious ledge just large enough for a pair of feet and a sheaf of corn, this being in farming parlance the 'lubber's hole'. To work in this was sheer hard labour, but infinitely safer than changing places with tobacco chewing Jimmy on the load.

By the time we were topping out the roof of the stack, both Dad and Spitting Jimmy were vaguely apologetic for being grumpy, making the excuse that everyone was getting edgy since the Nazi doodle-bugs began buzzing about. We had cheered when the first flying bombs passed overhead earlier that summer, believing that their jet flame meant they had all been set on fire by some marvellous secret weapon.

We soon learned differently, and by the time we were gathering the wheat harvest a line of heavy anti-aircraft guns was positioned across our quiet countryside, the object being to bring down the V1's in the areas of low population or deflect their course and turn them back out to sea.

We finished one wheat stack about midday and went over to the rowan tree to eat our food in its shade. We sat munching, with Jimmy contemplating a good swig from the stone bottle and cursing wasps, horse-flies and every other kind of flying bug, with good cause.

As the guns two fields away began to fire we heard a V1's engine cut out. Heads down, we counted to seven, then experienced a weird sensation as if we were caught in a loud surging current, breathlessly struggling in the surf of an invisible sea.

When the shock wave subsided we took stock of the situation. Jimmy was sure that the doodle-bug had been specifically sent by Hitler to spoil his harvest beer. It had solved the problem of picking the wild fruit: damsons, codlins and bullaces lay like a carpet on the stubbled field. The stack we had just finished had a definite list to port and the gate post I had knocked earlier in the morning now lay horizontal in the field.

"I reckon we ought to charge the government for fixing that, come the slack time this winter," said my father.

"I'd let that bloody post bide where it be, mate," Jimmy said, pausing from cutting chunks off an onion to eat with his bread and cheese ration. "There be too many mad tractor drivers and other awkward cusses about."

The Hop Picking Lark

Transcending all the familiar sounds of the waking city, young Barney Shilling heard his mother's early morning voice hoarse and rasping. She called him to get up. He had long learned the wisdom of keeping on the right side of her temper on mornings after both parents had spent a convivial evening in the 'Capstan and Compass', then staggered home to fight like cat and dog.

Barney and his four younger brothers had spent the previous evening picking berries on a bombed site. Consequently little Billy, who shared the bottom half of the bed with Barney, had disturbed his brother's slumbers by being spectacularly sick. Volcanoes of rage would have erupted had Barney called his mother out of the pub to deal with the crisis, just as they would when she eventually found the revolting mess on the unsheeted mattress and blanket coverings.

Scrambling over Burt, Bruce and Bob, all feigning sleep at the top end of the bed, Barney's bare toes explored the inside of his sandshoes. He hauled up his threadbare shorts to meet the T-shirt he had slept in, then ran down the dark uncarpeted stairway, which always reeked of kippers and next-door's tom cat. His mother stood by the ash-heaped kitchen hearth, rolling the bleached ends of her hair into curlers, coughing spasmodically as she lifted her arms above her head. Barney watched her haggard reflection in the fly-spotted mirror.

"Don't stand there gawping, unless you want a touch of your father's belt behind you. He's left me without so much as a fagend, so nip along to Ma Slavinsky and say you want five Woodbine on the book."

Sorting among the clutter on the sideboard Barney found the little red sixpenny note-book that served as an unofficial passport, giving the Shilling family access to the goods in Mrs. Slavinsky's corner shop.

The complete antithesis to his mother, Mrs. Slavinsky was enormous, every bulge and spare tyre of fat quivering whenever she moved or laughed. Few of her smiles were aimed in the Shillings' direction, although she was always kind to Barney, offering him titbits of dried raisins or broken liquorice bootlaces when there were no other customers about. On the credit sale of five Woodbines she was adamant. "My life. Are Hymie Rothschild and Abe Rockerfeller my cousins by marriage, ask your mother? Do I lay awake at night worrying how much you Shillings owe me already? Am I finding a gold mine shaft beneath my cellar that I can watch my capital go up in your mother's Woodbine smoke. Tell her there'll be no fags, no tick and no welcome in my shop until she pays off what she owes."

Daunted by the prospect of returning home empty handed, Barney hesitated. The old shopkeeper gave him a stale cake and a Shalom. Still stalling for time, Barney dragged his feet along the gutter, then sat down on the edge of the pavement to share his cake with Widow Mutton's mongrel dog.

The miserable little back street was not yet wide awake behind its drab, dusty curtains; the paving stones were wet with morning dew. At the street end, down toward the river, the dockyard cranes, the factory chimneys and the gas-holder at the reeking gas works were all shrouded in sulphurous, phlegm-foul fog, yet above his head was a patch of blue sky, and the first glimpse of watery September sunshine.

Perched high on the cowl of Widow Mutton's front room chimney, a speckled brown bird began to sing. Suddenly Barney experienced a great upsurge of his spirits that could only be expressed by bursting into song. Down the street the postman was delivering buff envelopes to first one house then another. Here was Barney's shield from his mother's anger. He ran home to tell her: "Mum, Mum the hop picking letters have come. I saw Mrs. Jenkins run across to Widow Mutton. They've both got theirs."

"Where's ours, then?" his mother retorted, following him back out into the street. Barney ran after the postman and asked if the Shilling's letter had been overlooked.

"Shilling," said the postman, as if the name rang bells in his memory. "Isn't Shilling the name where any bill or invoice we deliver gets sent back to the sorting office, 'Address unknown'? You're the kid that was singing in the street back there, aren't you? Tell your mother that I'll see if there is any mail lying around before the midday delivery starts, and say I told you that if she's hard up she ought to put you to singing in the halls."

Morning in the Shilling household passed by in a succession of tea-drinking neighbours offering commiserations that the Shilling's four-week holiday in the country seemed so uncertain, when their own arrangements were all signed and sealed. One or two hinted that the hop grower might have seen more than enough of the five Shilling boys. It was not only because they shared the same initial that made some folk refer to them as those five little B's.

Too unsettled to play on the bomb sites when neighbouring hop-garden bound children were helping collect and paint identification marks on every old tin bath, basket or substantial box they could muster, Barney, Bruce, Burt, Bob and the still queasy-stomached Billy punched a few heads, then formed a deputation to meet the postman on his rounds.

It was there. Notification that Mrs. Shilling and family had been allocated sleeping accommodation at King's Court Farm. Pickers to arrive not later than 11 a.m. on Saturday. Tally basket numbering and hop picking to begin on Monday at seven sharp. Transport to the hop gardens was to be provided by the coalman driving his big new lorry, him being Widow Mutton's nephew and doing the thirty mile journey cheap. Widow Mutton was regarded as being somewhat aristocratic, having a regular order of a half-pint bottle of cow's milk every morning from the milkman, while any milk the Shilling family used came from tins. She was definitely someone to be cultivated at hop picking time because she took along a spirit stove, and while Mrs. Shilling needed to coax a kindling wood open fire to boil a kettle of water, Widow Mutton had the means of making a quick cup of tea.

Barney and Bert were sent to collect all the goods and chattels that their grandmother would be taking to the hop picking, wheeling it to their home on a soap box cart. Gran lived half-a-mile away so they did not see her very often.

She was tiny, her frame twisted with arthritis, her hands like chicken claws, her nose and chin almost meeting when she dispensed with wearing her false teeth. Tap-tapping along, shouting and waving her walking stick in her effort to restrain her high spirited grandsons, she was quite exhausted by the time they were passing the Capstan And Compass, so she popped in for a rest and to get a 'little something' for their mum.

Mrs. Slavinsky was someone else Barney was sent to deal with. He took two pound notes and a message from his mother to the effect that the backlog of debt would be reduced, if not cleared, by the Shilling's hop picking money. Barney cajoled the old shopkeeper into giving credit for some groceries and five assorted pairs of the special line she was offering in cheap and substantial Wellington boots.

Even with boxes, baskets, baths and backless chairs piled up over the cab of the lorry, Barney was sure there would never be room for all the goods and people trying to cram together on almost new coal sacks spread across the back. Nevertheless, with Billy on his lap, squeezed in with the other children leaning against the tailgate, Barney watched the scenery change as the lorry climbed up and out of the city.

With the sun on his face and the air rushing past he felt that same indefinable uplift of spirit that always forced him to lift his head and sing. ·

"Voice of an angel, your Barney," said the woman whose

elbows were prodding Barney's mother. "Little devil, more likely," Mrs. Shilling replied, dismissing her son's gift.

They arrived at the hopper's huts in a welter of lost baggage, wet-bottomed children and excitement, finding their allotted number in the rows of wooden hutments, each with less living space than most right-minded country cottagers would have deemed adequate to house a couple of fattening backyard pigs.

Puzzled by the noisy invasion, farm horses stamped their enormous hooves and nervously pricked their ears as they stood in the shafts of waggons loaded with wood faggots for cooking fires and oat straw and oat chaff 'flights' to fill makeshift mattresses. Some pickers managed to instil a semblance of homeliness in their huts, but Mrs. Shilling had no such houseproud inclinations. Despite this, Barney knew that by sandwiching themselves between a couple of 'chaffies', huge clean hop-pocket sacks filled with oat flights, they slept warmer, cleaner, and in greater comfort within the confines of their hopping hut than in the bed all five boys shared at home.

In a cluster of tents, the hop gardens mission workers brewed field coppers of tea as a Christian gesture of welcome. After dark they built a huge camp fire, encouraging the pickers to gather around for a friendly singsong. Nicknamed 'Holy Joe' by the irreverent pickers, the young missioner in charge of the proceedings called out, "Is there anyone here who can sing?" Barney found himself being pushed forward toward the fire. His heart and his voice rose with the sparks ascending skyward. The circle of pickers fell silent, listening to an urchin singing like a lark.

Ragged, thin and all too conscious of the shortcomings of his background, any childhood illusions Barney might have once cherished had long since been nullified by an indolent mother's disinterest and a pub-crawling father's leather belt. He knew happiness as an infrequent will-o-the-wisp sensation, but for those few glorious weeks of September magic in Kings Court Farm hop gardens, his sheer exhilaration induced the familiar compulsive feeling that he must either sing or burst.

Encouraged by 'Holy Joe', Barney sang solo after solo. Unaware of the impact he was having on what was his first real audience, he stood by the camp fire, warm, watching a round September moon rising, pouring out the elation of his heart. Except for the clear young voice there was absolute stillness until a brushwood faggot, placed on the fire's depleted embers, sent a volcano of sparks erupting into the night sky, then settled into a flaring flame that somehow broke the spell of Barney's voice.

A murmur of approval surged into spontaneous clapping, then Barney heard the chink of coins being thrown around his feet. As he stooped to collect his unexpected bonus his face turned crimson with family shame.

"He's the eldest of the Shilling tribe," a woman close to him was explaining to her neighbour. "How the poor little devil can sing like a bird when he gets more back-handers and bashings than breakfasts is beyond me. I'd be ashamed for my kid to stand there with legs like broomsticks and no backside to his breeches. Don't chuck your money to him, love. He won't see none of it, and I for one am not buying beer to pour down that Shilling woman's neck, or her old mother's."

Sick with humiliation, Barney tried to creep away from the circle of the fire, but Holy Joe saw him. Hot baked potatoes were to be passed around and in Holy Joe's estimation, Barney had earned his share.

As Barney's mother took his collection of coppers his Gran, chumbling on a baked potato, suddenly became aware of a personal crisis. "Oh, my gawd," she cackled, "I've gone and left me teeth at home." His mother's reference to the wizened old woman as a "daft old faggot," contributed nothing to family harmony. Gran countered with the ultimatum that she would neither pick hops nor set foot in The Fox And Duck down in the village minus her false teeth. Mrs. Shilling seemed to regard both contingencies as catastrophic. Listening to the arguing women, Holy Joe asked how long a journey of recovery might take.

Too dim-witted to appreciate the distance a fast lorry can cover in 90 minutes, Barney's mother estimated it would take a young man like himself some three hours walk. "No problem then," said Holy Joe, trying to be helpful. "Barney can borrow the mission bike and slip back for the dentures tomorrow morning.

"In return I would like him to sing a solo at the Festival of Harvest Thanksgiving we are sharing with all denominations of the local people in the village church tomorrow night."

"You hear that, Barney?" said his mother. "Just you mind that you do what 'the reverent' says."

Barney had no time to speculate on the deficiencies of the mission bike when he left on the following morning. Oil starved, rattling, cursed with a wobbling saddle, it was too high for Barney to ride in safety or comfort. Marco Polo, orientating eastward, could have endured no more qualms than Barney venturing in unknown country.

Putting his stamina in unequal contest with an uphill climb by standing on the pedals, he felt his knees give way beneath him and fell off into the hedge. As he paused to rest he heard a vehicle climbing the hill behind him. A blue van passed, then stopped. A police sergeant and a constable got out. Barney's immediate action was one of utter amazement that the narrow lane should merit police attention. With miles of nothing but empty corn fields, what could anyone steal?

"That your bike, son?" The sergeant was not unfriendly. Barney only wished he could claim the social status of being a bike owner, but explained about the mission worker and his grandmother's teeth. "Where would they be then?" the sergeant asked.

"With the knives and forks in her kitchen drawer," Barney answered, wondering why both policemen laughed. Looking around the bike they said that only mission prayers could account for the fact that the wheels were still turning. It needed a spanner and an oil can around it. They gave Barney a lift to the main police station in the city, put his bike right and sent him on his way.

With the saddle fixed and lowered he found it easier to keep the wheels turning once he had left the 'cop-shop'. It took only a few minutes to reach his grandmother's terraced home and collect the set of stained and yellowing teeth. His way back took him past his own home, but being Sunday morning he knew that his father and his hangover were always best left undisturbed.

Mrs. Slavinsky, outside her corner general shop that sold everything from arrowroot to second-hand coal shovels, waved to him, calling. "You became so rich with hop-picking that you're back, riding a bike already?"

Having explained his mission Barney said he had to hurry

back because Holy Joe wanted him to sing for a lot of country people at a church festival that night.

"This is a rabbi person, and he lets you ride sixty miles on that thing? So he heard you sing then. And does he find you some different clothes before you stand up singing to these fine people? Of course not. Without money what can you do?" Barney told her about the money he had collected round the camp fire. It would have helped his situation.

"Barney one day your voice will earn you pounds, not pennies, so here's what I'll do. Strictly business. I'll find you an almost new shirt and a pair of trousers, a bit big perhaps, but your tail end won't be showing. Then when you get rich you can pay me back. Soft in the head I must be getting, but to send you on a sixty mile journey then ask you to sing a solo? That I should have been given such a son."

A flat tyre delayed Barney so much that he could hear the village church bells ringing before he reached the hop-picking encampment. His brother, Bob, told him that Holy Joe had left him the message to get to the church as fast as he could.

His mother thought him clever to have got anything from Ma Slavinsky without cash or account book and, as a reward for getting Gran's teeth back, allowed him to dip both pieces of his bread and margarine into the sugar bag. Barney gobbled them down, anxious to get away.

"Gran, me and the kids are taking a stroll down the village, and I ain't having you get so high and mighty with this singing in church stunt that you can't walk down with us."

Mrs. Shilling suppressed his protests with the back of her hand. Bent almost double, Gran's pace of walking was snail-like. By the time they reached the village the churchgoers were leaving, and Barney realised that he was too late. The evening was suddenly cold.

"Never mind, Barney." His mother's voice was wheedling in tone, far different than usual. "You wouldn't have got any tips there, but if you give us a song or two outside the pub door I might find enough from what people give to buy you kids some crisps."

As if in response to Barney's utter desolation Holy Joe came striding up behind them. If he had overheard Mrs. Shilling's suggestion he gave no sign.

"Sorry you got back too late, Barney. I am sure you boys would not want to spoil the last chance of a bit of recreation your good mother and grandmother will have before picking starts tomorrow. Don't worry about them Mrs. Shilling. I will see them safely back to camp."

Tucked snugly between his chaffies Barney reviewed the day that was almost over. He had seen more of the countryside than he imagined to have existed. He had gained a new shirt and some trousers and had ridden in a police van. True he had missed singing at the festival, but Holy Joe seemed to understand the situation. Tomorrow hop picking would begin. A whole month of September magic stretched before him.

One day, when his singing made him rich, he would buy a house near the hop gardens, ordering groceries by the ton from Ma Slavinsky, strictly for cash.

The Sunday Paperman

The only way daily newspapers were delivered in the village was by getting the wholesale newsagent in the city to send them out by post. At a penny for the paper plus a halfpenny postage, this seemed expensive, many regarding it as absolute extravagance to spend money on reading about a lot of old 'furriners fighting' or 'them politicals talking out the back side of their heads', when the postman, scanning through the headlines in his post bag, would willingly impart the gist of yesterday's stale news. Giving the lie to their implied thriftlessness, those who indulged in buying daily papers made sure that no scraps went to waste.

Apart from being folded, cut into small squares and threaded on a string to hang on a nail in the 'out back', it served in various other ways. Apples, wrapped in newspaper and stored in cupboards or under the back room bed, kept firm until well past Christmas. Soaked to a pulp and sealing up draughty skirting boards or ill fitting windows, paper kept the winter winds at bay. Many a ploughman plodding the wintery furrows found comfort from a newspaper tucked under his jersey to keep his chest warm, with another couple of sheets keeping his kidneys cosy at the back.

Local weeklies came via the market day bus and the Post Office counter, but thanks to a lukewarm but longstanding romance between the saddler's daughter and a bald bachelor newsagent who had a small shop in the city, we collected a Sunday newspaper without fail. He always parked his motorcycle and boxed sidecare in the saddler's backyard shed. Spurred on by cups of cocoa, the newsagent spent too much time trying to persuade his prospective wife and future mother-in-law that a maiden of thirty five is not too young to marry.

Knowing that his regular customers were relatively honest, he trusted them to serve themselves and put the correct money in the enamel basin left on the motorbike seat.

Collecting the Sunday paper gave a cast iron excuse for the men who awaited high noon when the Hare and Hounds opened. Lady customers could exchange details of the latest village news while their Sunday dinner cooked. It made for friendliness and harmless gossip, but when I rode down for the paper one Michaelmas Sunday morning, I found that this atmosphere had entirely disappeared.

The village policeman was there with his pencil and notebook at the ready, asking if I could remember if anyone was in the shed when I had collected the paper on the previous Sunday, or if I had seen any strangers on my way home.

Glum faced at having to miss his cocoa and comfort, the bald newsagent said that in all the eighteen years he had courted the saddler's daughter, he had never been more than a couple of pence short in his newspaper money and never a foreign coin given as change. Now, when some light fingered sneak thief had pinched both money and basin, he was rapidly coming to the conclusion that it was not worth trailing out to the village for a measly cup of cocoa, and was seriously considering calling off his lacklustre love affair and his paper round.

The parson's sister and I had collected our papers at the same time the previous Sunday, and for once I welcomed her company, for the new under gamekeeper from The Hall was close behind. I had never felt the slightest apprehension about living and working in the depths of the country, but on several occasions during the few months he had been in the district, I had been aware of him watching behind bushes or standing around on the edge of Church Woods as I worked in the fields.

His swaggering attitude annoyed me so I gave him no encouragement realising that he had roving eyes and hands to match. He had followed me into the saddler's yard on the previous Sunday, but any suggestion that he might be the culprit was dismissed by our guardian of the law. The underkeeper had come to the Hall with excellent references from some of the highest aristocracy in the land. Only that week he had earned His Lordship's approbation in catching an estate hand trying to hide poached game.

I didn't care if the angels sang his praises, or if he had captured a gang of poachers single handed, every instinct warned me that he was trouble come amongst folk of honesty and mutual trust.

As I started back home, Slippy Springer the village poacher, chimney sweep and grave digger, came pedalling along on his rattling old bike, then rode along beside me, saying he wanted a quiet word with my Dad. Naturally our conversation centred on the stolen paper money and my suspicions. Slippy said quietly, "You're right to worry about that fly-by-night underkeeper. Just you be careful, Jo."

If Slippy came onto our land it was usually without our knowledge or permission, so Mum and Dad were intrigued to see him standing at the back door that Sunday morning and promptly asked him in.

"'Tis like this, Harry!" he began. "I don't need to tell you that this underkeeper bloke is a sly one. I've been telling your Jo that I've seen him standing prying and peering at her. She may be skinny as a bean pole stood up sideways, but he be after anything in skirts."

What little vanity I had evaporated with Slippy's evaluation of my beauty, but Mum thanked him for the warning.

"Well, missus!" Slippy answered. "That's not why I came! I've come up here to ask Harry's advice and borrow a tarpaulin stack cover. One of the estate hands is being evicted first thing on Michaelmas morning because he caught that slimy devil trying to maul his missus and gave him a fair old tousling before chucking him in the pond. Next thing he knew was that all three gamekeepers were in his cottage garden and peering down the well. They hauled up six brace of pheasants with rabbit snares round their necks."

Dad remarked that the estate worker might have been trying to make a bit of extra money by selling the birds to posh hotels which preferred game that was not peppered with shot.

"What!" Slippy grunted. "With the homemade snares the old keeper that left took off me last winter? That cunning snipe cut holes in the wire netting you set around Stony Field, and if he had been a few minutes later the other morning, I would have gained twelve pheasants and got my own rabbit snares back. Instead he used them to get revenge on that young couple. It troubles me badly, but I daren't shout the odds about it, because if I admitted I was trespassing in search of game I could be 'His Majesty's guest' for another twenty eight days. If you could drop a word in the right direction it might help them youngsters, or if they are evicted lend them the use of a waterproof cover to protect their furniture, for the only place they'll have for it is alongside the road."

Dad took a Sunday evening stroll through the woods to see the head gamekeeper, who promised to re-check his underling's credentials.

The underkeeper got wind of what was happening and by the next weekend he was gone. So was the saddler's daughter, taking her father's life savings with her.

The Sunday paperman drove off out of the saddler's yard in a roar of anger and exhaust fumes, and we villagers had to accept the fact that if we wanted to read the Sunday apers, we would have to wait for the following Tuesday morning's post.

Not Quite Cricket

This is the first home match of the cricket season. The white attired Lockley team, our traditional opponents, saunter around in nonchalant groups as if they are rehearsing a television commercial for a new detergent giving a whiter brighter wash. Making loud disparaging remarks about the condition of our sloping pitch, they calculate the probable tonnage per acre if the grass on outfield is ever mown for hay. This is sheer sarcasm designed to undermine the finer feelings of Popper Button and his band of stalwarts who have spent all morning driving Hugh's Friesian herd to temporary pastures, and clearing up the pitch.

Affectionately known as 'The Shovel and Pancake Brigade' to all our club supporters, the good hearted old volunteers have laboured hard and long.

Time was when the young men of the village would willingly

have forgone beer, skittles, overtime or courting, hoping that their presence at Tuesday and Thursday evening practice sessions behind Chappell's cowsheds, might persuade Popper Button, then the captain, to select them for our team to oppose Lockley in the yearly match.

It was then a matter of village pride, almost a bounden duty, that every able bodied person in the parish should go to cheer on Popper and his gallant cricket team. It is just another indication of declining standards to admit that today our team seems underpowered, scratched together with the help of an arthritic-inclined grandfather acting wicketkeeper, and two surprised but enthusiastic thirteen year old lads.

Despite all this, none of our club members seems despondent. We all share the secret that our newest member is so fast and furious a bowler that he runs the risk of launching himself into powered flight whenever he sends a sharp delivery up the pitch. Granted, he is a physical training college type given to jogging around the village each morning long before the ground is aired. Lockley-ites stare in disbelief to see him limbering up by sprinting round the pitch in a luminous yellow track suit.

In their day, Popper and his old stagers were content to defend the cricket honour of the village, fortified by belt and braces to support their corduroy trousers as they hurled down 'chinamen', 'bumpers' and 'yorkers', but this we overlook because the new man lives just over Lockley parish boundary and could well have been their secret weapon instead of ours.

This being so, he and his wife receive constant reassurance of the neighbourliness of our community by way of the odd sack of spuds, eggs, and occasional cabbage, when comparable supplies in Lockley shops are either dear or scarce.

Suspicious that we have once again resorted to some devious subterfuge he has not yet fathomed, the Lockley captain complains that fresh cow pats on the wicket were deliberately left there as a hazard to his players. For his part, no play will start until they are cleared. Popper trots across the pitch, shovel at the ready, marvelling aloud that Hugh's heifers would invade the batting area when there has been a single strand wire fence around it for the last week, and this with a clearly printed notice warning, 'Keep Off'.

Our captain makes the logical observation that our players

run as much risk of injury as any Lockley-ite, but the opposition seem to think that although Popper is a first-rate ambulance man at any other time of crisis, his cricketing loyalties might let him leave any injured Lockley player lying until stumps are drawn.

Lockley has experienced the same difficulties in finding enough players to field a full team as we have, so no one takes much notice of the shy willow-slim young stranger introduced as their eleventh man, hurriedly enlisted to make their number up.

Some misguided souls have fondly imagined this young player to be Lockley score-keeper's daughter, and as our captain walks over to win the toss with Hugh's double headed penny, he is heard to express the view that with Lockley being forced to field girlish characters with blow-waved blonde hair against our new demon bowler, the game should be a pushover. Determined to demoralize them from the start, he sends Lockley in to bat.

There is no nonsense about using the shine of a new ball for a fast bowler. Any shine disappeared while it stayed in the box after last season's matches. Nevertheless our new acquisition tears into Lockley batting until they are six down for twenty-four in the sixteenth over. Popper Button and the rest of his old cronies, sitting on the bench in front of our converted chicken house pavilion, express approval and the confident hope that it will all be over, bar the shouting before tea.

Popper's wife, Pearl, hearing this prediction, lights the flame under the tea urn. She had been a bit 'poorly-like' since her recent intricate and highly personal abdominal operation, so she calls for assistance from the watchers outside to help lift a plastic can of water to top up the tea urn.

At this instant our bowler, hurtling along his run up, slips and falls heavily on his shoulder just as he is raising his arm to bowl. The air seems to quiver with his screaming, then he passes out cold. His yells have the same effect on Popper and Pearl as distress flares to a lifeboat. They both scurry across the pitch to offer first aid. They make a cursory examination of our fallen idol who starts whimpering in an unmanly fashion.

"What do you reckon to it, Popper?" Pearl asks kneeling to place a tea towel under the young man's head because it is perilously close to a rather wet cow pat. This sets him yelling once again. "Obvious, old love!" says Popper. "Dislocation!" they remark in unison. It is pointless to ask if there is a doctor on the field.

Making reassuring noises, Popper tells our toppled hero that they will get a car across and take him to the casualty department of the city hospital. "Don't try to move me!" bawls the stricken athlete. Popper dispatches someone to fetch the first aid kit he never fails to bring on such occasions. He administers a quick slurp from the water bottle. Unappreciatively, the injured man complains that it tastes of warm rust, then faints again.

"Right!" says Popper authoritatively, realising that this gives him an opportunity to do the manipulative therapy he deems urgent and essential. Enlisting the help of the gawping players clustered round him, he tells them to hold the bowler down, and keep him perfectly still. Pearl, meanwhile, is clasping the patient round his neck as if she intends to pull his head off. Digging in his heels, Popper quickly grasps the arm attached to the injured shoulder, hauls on it as if he were practising to be the anchor man in a tug-of-war-team, then yanks it upwards. There is a sudden popping sound, like a cork coming out of a champagne bottle. It can be heard above the patient's curses and groans. Suddenly he sits up looking white and sheepish as Popper explains how the ball joint he had jolted out of its socket has been put into place again. He staggers into the pavilion to be given a cup of strong sweet tea. Pearl's sovereign remedy for shock.

The cricket fanatics who have lost interest in his welfare since he can no longer set Lockley wickets tumbling, are more concerned that we are fielding one man short in this needle game.

The rest is left to our more mundane bowlers and two leg before wicket decisions given by an umpire, not so much biased as having a due regard for his native village. With a hint of rain in the air and Lockley all out for forty in ninety minutes, the captains agree to continue with another hour of play before taking tea.

With his score nought, not out, having had no chance to face the bowling at the end of their innings, Lockley's effeminate looking eleventh man has done nothing to alter our team's opinion that he is a bit of a giggle. It comes as a surprise to our two opening batsmen to see Lockley team moving around to his instructions as he places his fielders in readiness to bowl. He tucks his long blonde tresses beneath a multicoloured headband, then proceeds to hurl down short pitched, high spinning fast deliveries that force our batsmen to play strokes more agricultural than authentic, or duck out of the way.

Molehills, sheep sent to stray across the pitch, a collie trained to catch and retrieve on the boundary, plus a few other minor diversions have all been recognised as legitimate strategems in our annual battle with Lockley, but Popper Button is not alone in his assertion that there has been nothing to match this in the last fifty years.

Popper's first reaction as the long haired bowler leaps down the pitch like a kangaroo with blisters, is that Lockley has imported one of them Australian fellows, but fair play to Australia, their breed of fast bowlers never pretend to be shy, simpering, long haired lilies who couldn't tell a leg-bye from a thigh pad. Only Lockley could dream up an underhand stunt like that.

It is misery to watch, and suffice it to say that we consider our team lucky to have made double figures by tea time. Tom Grommett's nose has almost stopped bleeding, and everyone applauds the bravery of a man who, rather than flinch in the face of danger, takes off his bi-focal glasses so as not to see it. Modest as ever, he admits that National Health or not, those glasses cost him a fair packet, so he doesn't dare to break them. All he could do was to close his eyes when he heard the ball whistling down the pitch, and hang out his bat to dry.

As tea and cucumber sandwiches are dispensed in the pavilion, Popper quietly agrees with our captain that we are on a good hiding to nothing. All that can be done now is to drag out the tea break to give our injured bowler as long as possible to recover from the pain in his right shoulder, then hope he can keep his end up as last man in.

Our captain issues his instructions. "Pass the word round. Give Lockley all the tea and cakes they can stuff, and keep them talking."

Popper ploughs straight in, asking the Lockley wicketkeeper if his mother's brother-in-law by her second marriage wasn't the driver of his ambulance back in his days in voluntary first aid. There is some discussion among the teams until this fact is established, village rivalry being momentarily suspended because both parishes shared the old subscription ambulance, making it permissable and even honourable for brigade members from either parish to work side by side.

"Where did you learn to put dislocated joints back into place then?" The Lockley captain asks Popper. Some heathen from the far side of Lockley boundary comments on the fact that Popper worked in a slaughterhouse before he retired, but his insinuating remarks are ignored. We know that when Popper Button starts talking about voluntary first aid work, it is like making a small hole in dam wall, and a torrent of anecdotes can easily be unleashed.

Popper reminisces about the days when Pearl and he were courting and saving so hard to get married, they had no money to spare on going out. Joining the ambulance corps presented them with the opportunity to gain free admission to shows and important happenings for miles around.

In the days of the silent movies, it was feared that such dramatic realism might cause patrons to faint, so volunteer first aiders were on duty for every performance. Pearl interjects that there has been nothing to match those old 'fillums' at the Electric Picture Theatre ever since. Minutes pass, Pearl and her helpers taking their time to top up tea cups as Popper repeats his oft-told story of the night Old Henery from the pig farm fell from a loft to land head first in his old sow's farrowing pen. Midwinter, knee-deep in mire, Popper and the ambulance driver from Lockley trudged along the rutted track with their stretcher to find their patient still lying in the muck, unconscious or dead drunk. Old Henery was heavy and took a lot of lifting. Plodding back through mud as thick as lumpy custard, Popper confessed that he was so near exhaustion, he feared he would drop his end of the stretcher before they reached the ambulance out on the hard road. Old Henery sat up cursing. "If you're going to rock the boat, mate, I'll carry your end of this contraption to the end of the track."

This he did, only climbing back onto the stretcher to be lifted into the ambulance, then they set off, covered in pig muck, all warning bells a-ringing. Popper's wry sense of humour as he spins his yarn inspires amusement in our injured player, reminding the Lockley-ites why they are here.

The Lockley captain sarcastically enquires if the fact that our lot are sitting around the pavilion like a consignment of mutton in a butchery cold store means that we concede defeat to a better team. If not, it is high time we got back on the pitch to take a thrashing. A sporadic patter of apprehensive clapping offers condolence to our batting pair returning to the fray.

Last man in, and leaving the pavilion with as much enthusiasm as a turkey feels for Christmas, our demon bowler bats left handed facing theirs. Suddenly there is a spot of rain. Then another. And another. Soon the pitch is waterlogged and we all gather in the pavilion, steaming around the tea urn. Both sides have tried their tricks and dishonour is satisfied.

Smudge

Red eyed with hatred for her owner, the wretched collie
bitch defied his attempts to approach the draughty barrel
to which she was chained. Wielding a long handled rake,
he had hauled out and destroyed all but one of her newborn
litter, so the abject creature guarded her surviving pup with
desperate, bare-fanged fury, lavishing on it an affection she had
never encountered during the years that she had been a chained
prisoner guarding the gateway to a few old sheds and the scrap
metal dump where her disreputable owner plied a dubious trade.

I first saw the fat little female pup when she was about a
fortnight old and no longer sightless waddling around on
unsteady legs to explore the world beyond the crumbling kennel.
Floundering in mud made viscid by her mother's dragging chain,
the pup lay whimpering until the collie patiently took her back
into the barrel and lovingly licked her clean. Seeing me

watching from the gate, the scrap metal dealer explained that he wanted to get the pup away because feeding their young made watchdogs lazy. His reactions to my outspoken comment on the old collie's lamentably thin condition was the observation that a bit of healthy hunger helped to keep a dog fit and alert.

I knew that any quixotic ideas about setting the old dog free would end disastrously for some farmer's sheep flock, so I saved scraps of our own poultry and pig food, and threw them to the hungry bitch whenever I went past. It came to the point where I felt guilty if I missed cycling over to the scrap yard, and the collie recognised the rattle of my old bike. The furious barking that warned off strangers, diminished to yaps and her mud-caked drooping tail responded as I approached the gate. Still wary for her infant's safety, she administered a sharp nip and a shove back into the kennel if the pup ventured out. As the pup grew rounder, her mother became more skeletal. If a totting expedition coincided with a drinking session, the dealer sometimes stayed away from the scrap yard for days, but I tried my best to see that the old dog had water and was fed.

The collie kept her baby safe for a month or so, but then one morning I heard a terrible commotion as I approached the scrap yard gate. Infuriated snarls rasped from the bitch's throat as it fought against the restraining collar. I saw the dealer standing between the straying pup and her mother with an axe shaft in his hand. As he saw me and told me to go away in extremely basic language, his hesitation gave the pup an opportunity to scuttle behind a pile of scrap metal, whimpering all the while.

The dealer cornered her in an old oil drum but space proved too restricted for him to wield his axe shaft. As he grabbed the small squirming animal and headed towards a shed, I went with him, threatening to get the police to make an unwelcome visit to his yard, and in return he promised me prosecution for trespass, plus the axeshaft round my head. Knowing that the pup would be slaughtered immediately I left, I offered to take it away. The dealer's attitude altered. He asked if I imagined he was daft enough to destroy a valuable puppy, explaining that he intended to start its sheepdog training early. Seeing that I had shown so much interest and appreciation of the fine points of a pure bred collie, he offered it for sale at the 'ridiculously' low price of one pound.

I was saving for some new winter shoes, but the sight of the axe shaft in his hairy hand made me accept his offer. It was only when I was safely outside the gate with the cowering little pup tucked under my coat that I realised that in passing I had stopped to stroke the old collie's head. She had not growled or snapped at me, but sat disconsolately on her haunches, watching me take away her pup with huge brown mournful eyes. Her misery haunted me, so later in the day, I rode back to feed her, but the barrel was empty, and her long rusting chain with the broken old collar lay in the mud. The dealer had by that time gone to the Cottage Hospital to get treatment for dog bites on his face and arms.

Taking the pup home was an exercise in diplomacy. Dad had always maintained that geese and peafowl gave better warning of strangers than any canine. The added advantage that they laid eggs and provided festive meals, meant that there were no dogs on our farm.

"You've bought what?" Mum raised her hands in horror, scattering a shower of flour from the pastry bowl into her hair. "You need a dog like I need toothache!" she grumbled. "I'll bet it is heaving with worms and fleas!"

Unmindful of these remarks, the pup found the unaccustomed luxury of the warm hearthrug, scratched itself lethargically, then went to sleep.

'Elgar' seemed a suitable name for the pup because the variations of her breed were a complete enigma, but when Dad saw her asleep on the hearthrug, he said she looked more like a smudge of dirty boot marks on the mat than twenty shillings worth of dog. In fact, he said, he would make it his business to see the dealer and demand nineteen and sixpence back.

It is hard to describe Smudge's shape or colour, for she resembled a frayed fluffy tangle of old grey and black mixtured sock wool as a puppy, developing a curly coated spaniel build, long floppy ears, and a miniscule tail like a short length of chewed string.

Mum still complained that a dog could be a nuisance as I explained the background story, but she gave Smudge a saucer of warm milk and suggested that she mix up some wormballs. These worm eradicating pellets of dough, laced with fennel and wild garlic, seemed a dubious kind of welcome, but I knew from that moment that Smudge was safely home.

As a house-dog she was useless, greeting strangers with the same enthusiasm that she offered guests. Farm cats and fowls completely over-awed her, and she tried to give the rooster a wide berth. She became my shadow from dawn until it was time for me to rack up the horses' mangers with hay in the evening, then she climbed an almost vertical ladder to sleep in the warmth of the stable loft. When I went ploughing with seagulls wheeling in a white winged cloud around me, Smudge plodded behind the rear wheel of the tractor, making friendly overtures to the screaming birds.

Rooks were a different proposition, a word to set her muzzle quivering with indignation, while an instruction to "See those rooks off then Smudge," transformed her into a supercharged mongrel racing over the ploughed furrows at such a pace that her mud-tipped long ears flapped up and down as if she might become airborne. She was often hampered by her short little forelegs treading on her ear tips, making her turn somersaults, but this never deterred her from scaring rooks, crows and jackdaws from the fields.

We made no attempt to train Smudge to work with sheep or cattle, but her intelligence saved miles of walking. If I suggested that she fetched a few straying ewes back, her chewed string rudder wiggled, and her ears bounced as she went eagerly about her task. She hated thunder and, during wartime air raids that were a fact of life in our corner of the country, some canine instinct warned her when we were in for a noisy time. Instead of trotting along behind the tractor, she ran ahead yapping, as if to say, "Do you want it in writing that there will be a raid?" If I ignored her, she soon set off home, only stopping when she was safely under Dad's old leather armchair. When she deemed it safe, she would appear again, greeting us effusively, all tongue and wiggling tail, as if to register her pleasure that such uncomprehending idiots had managed to survive.

Our 'farm-dog' was a standing joke among our friends and neighbours until a night just before one Christmas when Dad and I went out into the blackout to feed the horses and take Smudge to her stable loft. Some sound or movement attracted her attention and she crouched, whimpering, by my side. Carrying the dimmed lantern, Dad went toward the stable, but as I followed, I heard the rustle of boots on straw, then saw someone with a torch slip round the side of a rick to disappear into the shadows of the night.

Grabbing a pitchfork, I yelled to Dad, then ran in the direction of the fowl houses, Smudge staying close to my heels. Almost colliding with one intruder as I dodged round the straw rick. I prodded his behind with the business end of the pitchfork, but Smudge tore on ahead, displaying the same demented fury as her mother had shown on the day I bought her, snarling, barking by the chicken house door. Dad stood over the man I had floored, his lantern in one hand and a horse whip in the other. Amongst thumps, bumps, and a mêlée of squawking chickens, we heard our berserk dog and a screaming man imploring us to call the savage beast off. Smudge had never shown any sign of being savage before that night, nor did she again during the years of her short lifetime, and I have often wondered how she could have known that on the night two strangers came to steal our Christmas poultry, one of them had a loaded gun.

Room at the Inn

A single, smoke dried sprig of holly hanging above the dartboard acknowledged the Christmas season, but the bar of the Horse and Harrow was sparse comfort at any time of the year. The old fashioned 'spittoon and sawdust' country pub had wooden benches around walls darkened by tobacco smoke and brown paint, plus a few straight-backed chairs and beer stained tables on the bare quarry-tiled floor. The blackened oil lamp hanging from the ceiling cast a dim dispirited light that made the numbers on the dartboard in the far corner more a feat of memory than of observation. A sullen stove in a wide-hearthed fireplace emitted frequent billows of eye-smarting smoke, but gave out little heat.

Making desultory conversation with his first customer Jack Crookley, the shepherd, the landlord stood listening to the sound of singing coming from the village church and watching several adults and a horde of children hurrying up the church path.

"There's a fair old number turned out for tonight's rehearsal," the landlord remarked, "they tell me the only one who will take the part of Mary is Joe Gimble's missus."

"Good God," Jack exploded, "she sings sharp as lemons and wobbles her notes as if she's standing on a loose board."

When the old Christmas play was revived back in the nineteen thirties. Jack's own wife sang the part of Mary, sweet as a song thrush. It still made his eyes smart just thinking about her standing in blue and white crooning a lullaby to her own baby daughter asleep in the crib. Sometimes in the years that followed, a swaddling wrapped doll or a village baby was placed there, but never again could his wife play Mary, for when his daughter Ruth was less than a year old, the woman he adored fell from the top of a fruit-picking ladder and broke her back.

In the two years she lay bedridden before losing the battle for survival she was tended by friends and neighbourly women. These good hearted souls virtually adopted his daughter, making it possible for him to bring her up properly at home. Ruth had grown up with a strong resemblance to her mother, the way she walked, the way she laughed, the way she held her head.

She was clever too, passing exams and winning scholarships that took her away to college. For the last two years she had come home at the end of winter term to take the part of Mary in the village Christmas play. To hear Ruth singing to a doll in the nativity crib had made his soul weep, mumbling his lines as the first shepherd, thinking of his other Mary, and all the empty years.

Then last year in the tiny vestry of the church, with her blue and white robe still on her, his daughter had broken the news that she was expecting a child.

Sick with misery, disappointment, and a mixture of unfathomable feelings, Jack had voiced his strong beliefs and spoken harshly, ignoring Ruth's assertion that she and the child's father hoped to marry when their final exams were done. The upshot of this shattering incident was that Ruth caught the last bus out of the village on that Christmas Eve, leaving Jack to spend Christmas Day alone with the trappings of the holiday to mock him.

He knew it would not do to dwell now on the fact that no word had passed between them during the year, or that the letters he had written to her student lodgings had come back 'unknown'.

Jack had gone through the motions of living, this uncomfortable pub bar being the only companionable place for him to kill the empty hours after his working day was done.

Waiting for the landlady to take over behind the bar so that Tom, the landlord, and he could go to the play rehearsal together, Jack tried his hand at a practice round-the-clock game of darts. A remark of Tom's so distracted his concentration that the dart he was aiming at double top dislodged the holly above the board then flew back, flight downwards into his beer.

"Closing the pub on Christmas Day?" Jack could scarcely believe his ears. "I didn't think you publicans could shut up shop as if you were pork butchers or drapers, Tom! Are we regulars expected to spend all Christmas sitting at home and twiddling our thumbs?"

Tracing an intricate pattern in the spilt beer with one finger, Tom said, "Nothing in the licensing laws stops me having a quiet Christmas Day with my missus and friends if I want to. I'm supposed to offer sustenance, shelter and stabling to any bona fide traveller but if one should so happen to turn up this Christmas morning, he'll have to take pot luck with us.

"It's definite that this year I'm not propping up this ruddy bar waiting for regulars who always stay at home with their families on Christmas Day. Them that are so parched can get a bellyful of flat beer and wind across at the Felled Ox."

"Where do I stand in your line of reckoning then Tom?" Jack asked.

"You!" Tom managed to get a plethora of meaning into that single word. "There are some that say you have more good friends and better kinfolk than you merit, even if you have had more than your fair share of misery in the past. I see Joe Gimble is coming across, he reckons he can't bear to hear his old woman screeching, so before he gets here, I can only say that if you can't face Christmas without young Ruth, then you must come and have dinner with us."

No more was said: Jack's eyes began to smart and water so he went across and prodded the smouldering fire with the toecap of his boot. It was all very well for Tom to talk of good friends but how could anyone convey the utter desolation of existing in a house that was a void of echoing silence?

Did Tom have the slightest inkling that every second, minute and hour of work or leisure was just time to kill in a world that for him had been shattered twice?

"Come on, my mule-headed old matey." Tom called him back to the realities of the present. "Let's get over to the church and say our piece."

The rehearsal was utter chaos, the mouse-like organist having lost her music, the choirmaster his patience, and Joseph, trying to sing several unequal duets with his oversized, offkey partner, had simply lost his voice.

Jack heard someone whisper, "Look at Jack, the poor old devil, fancy having the guts to come back after last year." He ignored it, determined not to get himself upset about a plastic doll in the same old crib. Reminding the cast that this was their last rehearsal, the vicar said that he was sure that the actual performance would go swimmingly provided the gentlemen of the cast remembered that with all the ladies, angel children and choir trying to get dressed in the tiny vestry, they must follow the practice of other years, using the good offices of the Horse and Harrow porch and bar in which to wait or get into their costumes.

A small lad had been detailed as runner so that the performers could make their entries through the west door of the church on cue.

On Christmas Eve it seemed that the entire population of the village was heading for the church or the Horse and Harrow bar. Mixing with customers who had popped in for a quick one were black-faced kings in cretonne curtains, shepherds in striped dressing gown robes and bed-ticking headdresses. Scorning such make-believe, Jack wore the same outfit he had used to play the chief shepherd from the beginning, his father's billycock hat, his buckskin leggings and his old smock.

Rather than watch his wife's performance as Mary, Joe Gimble had volunteered to serve behind the bar, helped by a pleasant young chap who was acting barman and staying with Tom over Christmas.

As the church organ started the introduction to 'While Shepherds Watched', Jack knew it was his cue to go. Most of the others in the bar seemed to fall in behind him, pausing at the great west door as he walked slowly up the main aisle of the church.

Realising that this year the plump and none-too-youthful Mrs. Gimble and a plastic doll would be waiting by the wide steps of the chancel, he thought it would be easy to control his emotions, but somehow the familiar blue and white costume altered her appearance, making her look thinner. He told himself that it was just a trick of the lights. The routine had become so familiar that he paced his steps to the music almost automatically, the last notes dying as he stood before Joseph and the kneeling figure in blue and white.

"I, a simple shepherd. . . ." he began, saying his words and acting out his part by slowly draping a sheep fleece across one corner of the crib. As he did so, the baby stirred, snuffling as a tiny hand moved and a pair of dark brown eyes opened wide. Completely lost for words and oblivious of his surroundings, he gazed down at the face of his daughter as she had looked at six months old. He lifted the baby, cuddling it close to him as it chuckled and gurgled, knowing that in this strange other world he only had to brush away the unbidden tears and turn his head to see his own beloved wife. 'Mary' moved toward him, touching his arm tremulously and whispering, "Oh, my darling Dad!"

It was no part of the planned performance for 'Mary' to hug a shepherd, or for that shepherd to spend the rest of the evening with the babe cradled in his arms. Under the cover of carols being sung, Ruth and her father spoke of matters that were not in any script. The rest of the nativity play took on a dreamlike sequence and when it was all over, Tom and the young man Jack had seen behind the bar at the Horse and Harrow earlier that evening came over to where he sat with his daughter and grandson in a dim-lit pew.

"Well Jack, my old matey, you have your son-in-law to thank for this reunion. You would never believe the conniving and planning since he wrote to my missus. Joe Gimble's wife, the vicar and half the ruddy village have been in on the secret."

"You don't want to keep that youngster here all night," Tom continued. "Ruth and her husband are staying with us for Christmas. Seeing you won't have made any preparations I don't suppose you have to rush back home so you had better pitch in with us."

Walking back, cradling his sleeping grandson in the sheep fleece, Jack realized that from this moment his home would not have that awful echoing empty silence. As for tonight, he could find no adequate words to express his thanks that the world still contained caring kindly folk who could find room at the inn.

Liza

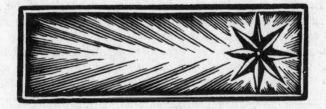

The proportions of Liza's sightless world had become reduced to the width of six painted bricks and encompassed by the cot rails round her hospital bed. Sickened with our own futile inability, we who loved her watched and wept the dry-eyed frozen tears that formed like lumps of ice to block one's throat. All the goblins of Hell seemed sometimes to conspire to torment her tired brain, but in her lucid moments she still retained the ability to create that atmosphere of love and tranquillity that had surrounded her all her life. She, so terribly afflicted, became our comforter, offering us solace in that small-windowed, dark ward that had witnessed the end of so many old dreams.

Knowing what part the hospital building had played in her long life, we were reluctant to leave her when the precious time for visiting was done, lingering at her bedside to clasp the hands that had spent a lifetime caring for our needs. Lifting her blind placid face for a benedictory farewell kiss, she offered comfort in her oft repeated phrase. "Don't fret so, love! Harry came to take me from this place before, and he will come again!"

Liza's Harry was born and raised in a sheep farming community on the coastal marshes, with everyone around him being related by marriage or by birth. At twenty years old, he was tall, dark haired, brown eyed, broad shouldered, and afraid of nothing, the obvious choice when it came to driving the two-horse waggon to the city wool chandler, and haggle the best price for the fleeces he had for sale.

Each year he undertook to deliver a wicker hamper of country produce to an aunt by marriage who had returned to the maze of city back streets to live out her widowed life. Since the journey involved staying in the city overnight, he lodged with this good lady, stabling his horses at a nearby inn, leaving early on the following morning to drive the thirty miles back home.

In the early summer of 1897, Harry set off on his annual journey leaving his home before daybreak, his horses wearing coloured worsted braids and burnished brasses, and he, smart dressed and striding out beside them, walking all the way.

Some two miles from his destination, he stopped at the top of a steep hill to rest his horses in the shade of tall laurels skirting a gravel drive. While the horses munched hay and oats from their nosebags, Harry put iron skidpans to the back wheels of the heavy waggon in preparation for the sharp descent. The city in the valley shimmered in a cauldron of heat haze and smoking chimneys, grey and uninviting. Close by, the shady long green drive framed the mock Gothic edifice of a boarding college for the sons of gentry. Harry imagined that to board there must be like living in a church.

A grey-dressed, thin young woman came limping along the drive as he hung the empty feed bags under the back axle of the waggon. He realised that she was one of the numerous daughters of his widowed aunt's neighbour, and asked if she would walk beside him down into the town. For a while he watched her hobbling along in boots that were plainly torture, then with scant ceremony hoisted Liza up to ride on the footboard of the waggon beside his aunt's wicker hamper. When he teased her that she was about as hefty as a hen robin in mid-winter, and crazy to wear crippling badly-made boots, she retorted that he might have been a few stone lighter if he had grown up knowing what it was like never to have quite enough to eat.

She was one of a family numbering thirteen, having seven younger brothers and sisters, and since her father had died of lockjaw when the youngest was still in swaddling binders, the wage of six pounds every Lady Day and Michaelmas was her contribution toward keeping her family from the workhouse door.

Cursing his bumpkin clumsiness, Harry plodded along in silence watching the pinched shadow of hunger on this pretty young girl's face. When he stopped the horses at the bottom of the hill to unhitch the skidpans, he opened his aunt's hamper to bring out a yeast cake wrapped in a white cloth.

"See if that will stop the mice gnawing at your innards!" he mumbled awkwardly then, as an afterthought, drew out the nosegay of lily of the valley that his grandmother had picked for his widowed aunt, and thrust it into Liza's hand.

Liza munched manfully, not caring now that her monthly half day off had started so late and must end at eight thirty that evening.

"Happen I could walk back here with you tonight then," Harry said, blushing.

"Happen I'll not let you!" Liza retorted, but she did. As Harry strolled with her that summer evening, he knew that he had met no girl to match her gentle beauty and irrepressible sense of humour in all his twenty years.

"Will you bring me a yeast cake and flowers when you come with the wool clip next year Harry?" she asked, smiling as they parted.

"You can't eat flowers!" Harry retorted. "Would a mutton 'fiddle' do instead? Next year when I come, we might do some serious talking." Harry watched her hurry down the drive.

Her thin face haunted him, waking or sleeping, all through the passing seasons. He wrote a letter to her, addressing it to the college, but had no reply. When he set out to take the next shearing to the city chandler, he was determined to find her and ask if he could court her. Again he stopped the horses by the college entrance but now there was no sheltering shade, for the laurels had been cut down. There was no Liza either, but Harry told himself that she only had one half day off every month and it was unlikely that he could be so lucky twice.

When the wool was sold, Harry stood awkwardly in his aunt's over-ornamented parlour and mentioned Liza's name.

"You won't give her my cake or flowers this year my lad! The poor dumb thing has been in the Workhouse since the start of last winter. What that poor girl endured left her witless and numbed her brain."

Stopping just long enough to hear of a timid girl waylaid, attacked and robbed of her half-yearly wages in the college shrubbery, Harry strode to the grim Poor Law Institution on the hill, demanding to see the master or matron of the place, and in a cell-like office the situation was explained. When Liza was found in a distressed state, bruised and bleeding, she dared to accuse some young college gentlemen without a shred of evidence to support her story. This earned her dismissal without references. Because she had no means of support, she could not be released to become a vagrant and an encumbrance on the parish rates.

No responsible citizen could be expected to employ a servant girl who existed in a dream world and had lost the power of speech so, although she was physically healed she had to work in the institution to help pay for her keep.

Demanding to see Liza, Harry found her wearing a drab union flannel smock and cap, and scrubbing a stone floor. If she was thin before, now she was pathetic. Only as he ran forward to lift her from her knees did he realise that he still had his aunt's country hamper on his arm. Her eyes were devoid of hope or expression as he called her name.

Frantic, Harry delved into the hamper trying to make her recall the yeast cake incident of the previous year. That failed to register, then he remembered the flowers that were intended for his aunt. As Liza pressed her face against the lily of the valley, their scent seemed to release some message to her brain. She looked at Harry in wonder and astonishment then, brushing away the tears that were streaming down his face, whispered hoarsely, "Harry love, don't cry." The matron suggested Harry apply to employ Liza formally so as to gain her release. "Employ her!" thundered Harry, "I want to marry her, Liza is going to be my wife! I'll take her out of here today!"

That was not possible. Formalities decreed that the banns of marriage be read for three consecutive Sundays, and only after the service could Harry claim her for his own. Some of his shearing money went to pay for Liza to be moved to the matron's private quarters and given extra nourishment.

Three weeks later Harry drove back to claim his bride, bringing with him a bunch of flowers and a grey silk wedding dress with an eighteen inch waist.

Their wedding was at noon, and by one o'clock Harry and his bride were out of the city, riding in a pony cart between hedgerows heavy with the scent of sweet briar and honeysuckle.

After eight long months of incarceration in a drab grey world, each roadside flower was to Liza a thing of wonder and delight. Good food, fresh air and Harry's gentle love worked wonders, and by harvest time Liza was sufficiently recovered to work beside her husband making bonds for the sheaves of corn he scythed.

They planted a bed of lily of the valley in their garden and thus the pattern of their life together was set. They met setbacks and heartaches, but with sheer hard work and a deep abiding love, built up a farm of their own.

They had a large family, but Liza made quite sure that none of her children ever knew the workhouse fears that had plagued her early life. For many golden years Harry and Liza created a quiet paradise, until men who saw the land as just so many acres of earth, brought their plans, their machines and their concrete mixers to tear the heart out of the fields, forcing Harry and Liza to leave the life they loved.

A few more autumnal years, then as Liza watched her Harry lose the battle against a cancerous scourge of sickness, something deep inside her soul died too. Sick in body, with the precious lamp of sight growing ever dimmer, Liza became so afflicted that she required constant medical attention. She was admitted to the geriatric hospital back in the refurbished old workhouse, and to her sightless muddled mind everything was as she remembered it before.

If the wheel had turned full circle, Liza steadfastly believed that Harry, who took her from this place before, would come for her again. We who loved her took her faith to be the ramblings of a senile brain, but we were utterly mistaken.

It was just an ordinary visit at the time of the year when the lily of the valley still bloomed beside her old back garden fence, and at visiting time one of her beloved children placed a bunch of them in her hands. She fingered the delicate flowers of the posy for a moment, then held them up to her face.

Full of wonderment, the eyes that had been dull and sightless for so long focussed in joyful recognition as an expression of sheer happiness came into her face. With a smile as radiant as a bride, she touched the flowers with her lips, sighing just one word of greeting in her deep contentment. Harry had taken his Liza home.

Liza

The returning dream took me home again
With the song of the years as yet unsung.
I walked by the side of the upright man,
As I did in the days when my heart was young.
Grazing sheep, placid cows, and an old white horse
All turned their heads as they passed him by.
A little black dog with long flapping ears
Looked at him with love and so did I.
We leaned on the gate and surveyed the land
That had known our laughter, toil, and tears,
Then Dad spoke of the bonds we had welded so strong
As we worked side by side in the golden years.
He talked of my Mum, and the ones that I love,
Of the echoing past, and of dreams to be
And he said that life changing and the mirage of death
Could never take this away from me.

Binder Twine &
Rabbit Stew

For My Grandchildren

Contents

Introduction

Confident that she had long since finished having babies, my middle aged mother gave the old iron rocking cot to gipsies picking fruit in the orchard. By the end of that summer she suspected she had been over-optimistic. The gipsies gave it back.

When I arrived one Primrose Day in the early nineteen-twenties Mum considered naming me after the flower, but Dad was determined that their 'afterthought' would not go through life labelled 'Primmy'. Even at the tiny bud stage I bore no resemblance to a rose.

'Home' was an old farmhouse set amid the patchwork of meadows, fields and orchards that lie between the wooded North Down hills and the marshes of East Kent.

A large family and a farmhouse made Mum's work neverending, so Dad and my three elder brothers often took me with them as they worked around the farm. A harvest wagon made a mobile playpen. Happiness was to sleep sun-warmed, wrapped in my father's coat.

Dad used his horses to haul timber from the nearby woodlands. As soon as I could manage the linen covered 'indestructable' buttons that prevented the 'tail-board' of my calico drawers from dropping, I was allowed to ride on the lumbering timber tugs with my brothers and spent day after day playing happily in the summer woods.

Winter-wrapped and snug beside a tree-feller's fire, I sat with the secretive silence of pine plantations whispering all around me, drinking down folk story superstitions and smoky, condensed-milk sweetened tea.

Blessed with parents rich in everything but money, I had a free, unfettered childhood. Mum, like a warm, soft fronted, bulgy bolster, cushioned the sharper corners of my small world with comfort, common sense and love.

The blind mare's colt was a favourite companion. Some of my best friends were sheep.

School was like chilblains, something to be endured; 'The Scholarship' a sword of doom hovering above my head. The written part was easy. The 'oral' assessment of my intelligence hinged on my ability to arrange toy furniture in a 'two up, two down' dolls' house. With all four rooms furnished, I had a miniature toilet suite to spare. A helpful adjudicator suggested one upper compartment could be a bathroom. Living where piped water was the dream of a slumberous rural council, and main drainage or indoor sanitation unheard of, I rejected that theory out of hand.

"Who would want to cart hot water jugs and lavatory buckets up and down stairs?" I queried. I did not pass. 'If, however, Dad cared to pay half fees, I was worthy of etc., etc.' Even at reduced rates, my school fees would buy enough pig meal to fatten a score of piglets into porkers. One could get mighty hungry trying to put text books between two hunks of bread.

The depression of the 'thirties' was a hungry rat nibbling Dad's capital away. He found safe city jobs for my brothers, my sisters who were still unmarried went away to work. The kitchen table that had always seemed short on elbow room developed areas of empty space.

I grew tall and spindly as a bean plant in a cellar. The ground had an increasing tendency to come up and hit me in the face. Pronounced 'a sick girl' by the village doctor, he prescribed fresh air, sunshine and rest. At thirteen I had spent my last days at school.

Since I spent hours reading in a sheltered corner of the orchard, it took no effort to keep an eye on the grazing sheep. By fourteen I had become chiropodist and midwife to a flock of Southdown ewes. I could not even contemplate leaving my hard-pressed parents. This was our land. My roots belonged there too.

Butcher's meat was a 'sometimes on Sunday' luxury. We ate rabbit instead. No small farmer would waste money getting farm equipment repaired if wire, or the twine that was used to bind sheaves of corn, would mend it. These then were the years when poverty and hard work were leavened with neighbourliness and laughter, the days of binder twine and rabbit stew.

I had been in love with the blacksmith's eldest son from my schooldays. We married on one of his wartime leaves from the R.A.F.

It is not everyone's idea of honeymoon bliss to go harvesting in company with land girls, ancient countrymen and a platoon of soldiers, but the weather was dry and the Germans were unloading incendiary bombs at night.

A few more leaves, then an overseas posting took Alan east of Suez for three and a half years. I continued helping Dad, awaiting his return.

One day I noticed a group of men out in Barn Field, and asked what they were doing.

"Just looking at likely post war housing sites," was their answer. For my parents it was the beginning of the end.

Demobbed, Alan embarked on a career 'in the public service'. This entailed much moving around the country. I have planted gardens from Devon to the Durham border, expressing a need to 'scratch about on the land'.

With steel-grey rain falling on the slate-grey roofs of a less salubrious area of Cardiff, I read an article in the local evening paper extolling the paradise of living in a prepackaged, plastic-tiled type world.

Watching a smoke pall drift over from the steel works, I realised that while I had been raising my own family, my country way of life had been swept away. Farming methods, unaltered for centuries, had been transformed into a mechanised industry. I scribbled down fragmentary memories of the little paradise I once knew.

Two days later, it was published in the South Wales Echo.

John Wiggins, then the editor, wrote suggesting that I sent more articles, and went to see his colleague, 'Geoff' Rich. Encouraged by the friendly, down to earth approachability of all the Editorial and Features staff at Thomson House, I started writing, and so a long and happy association with the South Wales Echo began.

We moved so often that the furniture creaked whenever a removal van went past, then, almost miraculously, we got a posting back to Kent, where we began.

We bought a little house with a wilderness of a garden, and wandered round the old haunts we had known. It was almost thirty years since I had last met one of my father's neighbours, but recognition was instantaneous.

"What are you doing dressed up like a Sunday tea-cake, and us just starting mowing hay?" he enquired. It was as if I had never been away.

JOAN KENT
Beam Ends

Hayforks and Blisters

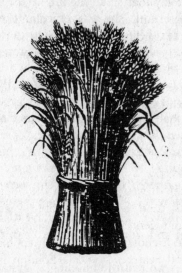

Recruiting extra labour for hay-making presented few problems for my father: he had a home grown work force of his own. Being a member of our family was like conscription into an army where no one was excused duties, and anyone feigning sickness ran the risk of being dosed with one of Mum's action-packed remedial brews. Instantly effective, these were far more tiring and painful than hard work.

My sisters were expected to muster to the hayfield soon after they got home from work, and like unsuspecting fish that swim too close to the engulfing tentacles of an octopus, any young man trying to make the running with one of 'Harry's girls' found himself red faced and perspiring, pitching hay.

The weaker, less interested lovers soon lost heart, while those who stayed the course were reckoned to have proved that they had honourable intentions. Three weeks of physically exhausting hay-making ensured that this was so.

My brothers were pretty luckless too. Disillusioned, one girl friend wrote to say that since she might just as well have got engaged to a pitchfork, she was returning the thirty shillings that my brother had given her to buy a ring. In future, the boy behind the bacon slicer in the Colonial Stores would provide the excitemnt and sparkle that her life had hitherto lacked. My brother, praying for rain and the chance of reconciliation, sang soulful songs of unrequited love that unsettled the horse in the wagon shafts and made the loaders curse.

The tentacles of family sometimes spread wider, and uncles, aunts and cousins from the town, thinking that they were being invited to spend idyllic summer days in rustic revelry, soon gathered blisters and sunburn as well as hay. Aunts who preferred cookery to boiling themselves in the sun found that there were mountains of food to contend with in Mum's kitchen and worked far harder than they ever did at home.

There was a definite art in building a haystack. First came a base of faggots of wood, topped by a layer of straw. As the stack was built up, the sides had to be straight, the corners square, and the centre packed in tight, layer after layer. This was called 'treading the stack', and providing that we could haul, shove, and push all sixteen stone of my Aunty Bet up the ladder, we had the best stack-treader in the business. Given half-an-hour just wandering around the top of the stack, Aunty Bet could compress the height of it by at least three rungs of the ladder.

By the time I was old enough to be on eye-ball level to a horse's nostrils, I was detailed to lead the horse in the wagon shafts from haycock to haycock and call out, "Stand hard above," to the chap on the load.

When my legs were long enough to reach the foot lever on

the horse-rake I was promoted and, perched on the rake behind a placid old mare, wandered across and across the new mown hay, raking it up into lines.

Phyl, the old mare, was replaced by a beautiful strawberry roan horse and, apart from a tendency to go around in circles, he seemed a docile beast. Plodding around a ten acre field with Gipsy in the shafts of the rake, I began to sing.

It had a traumatic effect on the horse. After circling on its hind legs, it did a spot of dressage, went into a waltz routine, took a bow, and attempted to lie prone. That is not easy with a hay-rake hitched on behind.

We concluded that Gipsy had been a circus horse, but it was ego-deflating to be continuously warned,

"For heaven's sake girl, don't sing."

Boy friends became husbands, girl friends became wives, and our kitchen table seemed to grow larger as our family shrank. In time there were only three places to set for meals. Dad's, Mum's and my own. Cushioning them against the farming depression, Dad found safe jobs for his sons and hay-making became a case of catch as catch can.

But if it was a time of poverty, it was the time of neighbourliness too.

War brought conscription and the younger men went away. We had to rely on casual labour for carrying crops and this was mostly old men who seemed to hibernate between threshing time and spring. There were some odd old characters among them too.

There was Captain Puddington, an eccentric ex-mariner, who hoisted and lowered the flag from a pole stuck up in his apple tree at dawn and sunset each day and kept his wife confined to ship, only allowing her shore leave to collect his rum ration from the Hare and Hounds.

Another stalwart was tobacco-chewing Jimmy Spit, who brought expectorating to so fine an art that he could be on target at twenty paces. His comrade, old Tommy Yellows, was willing enough to work, it was his bladder that was weak.

If possible we used to arrange it so that Captain Puddington loaded while the other men pitched. It was courting disaster to have them up aloft and if the necessity arose, one walked well clear or wore a wide brimmed hat.

By the next hay-making season, some of the farm buildings were providing temporary billets for troops evacuated from Dunkirk. Grey-faced, with eyes that had looked at hell, they had come back from a world that had gone berserk, while we continued gathering the hay harvest in the same old timeless way.

With food production vital, under-manned farmers could ask the army for seasonal help. Dad applied, stating his requirements as four or five men.

An enormous Matador transport, loaded with a platoon of soldiers in full battle order, trundled across the field.

They set up tents, field kitchen, and latrines under the trees and on the following morning, a sergeant, who could have used his larynx to crush gravel, bellowed his orders, "Get fell in there. Shoulder pitchforks. By numbers. Operation Hayseed, begin!"

Once it was clearly understood that I was there to gather hay and not roll in it, the soldiers became a bunch of homesick chaps with photos of wives and families to be admired, and by inviting their partners down for a visit Mum must have saved more than one or two marriages that were on the blink.

Captain Puddington was no longer helping us. He had constructed a crow's nest in his apple tree and spent his time on look-out with a spy glass and a marline spike, convinced that we were about to be subjugated by the German Fleet. He often reported the sighting of enemy cruisers, although the nearest deep water was a good day's march away.

It wasn't seaborne attack that bothered us, but the trigger-happy Luftwaffe pilot attempting to paralyse Britain's war effort by strafing a tractor-driving girl and two old men on a load of hay. This had a disastrous effect on Tommy Yellows, who worked in some discomfort for the rest of the day.

Relating his experiences to the soldiers who were surfacing from taking cover in the hedge, Jim Spit declared, "By gob, if it had been bullets I was chewing instead of baccy, I'd 'ave shot the booger down."

The soldiers were gone. The Land Army girls were a hard working, happy-go-lucky crowd, but neither they nor we were prepared for the additional labour force that helped us next. These were Italian prisoners of war and within an hour of arrival three Land Army girls had gone screaming indoors to show Mum where they had been pinched.

A pitchfork poised at the right angle has more uses than turning hay, and the language difficulty was soon overcome.

Efficient, methodical German prisoners, shell-shocked soldiers, each group in turn helped stack our hay in those grey years.

It seemed at first that we would go back to the traditional way of hay-making when peace returned but, walking around the implement section of the first post-war county show, we saw balers, rakes and lifts: monster machines that could mechanise the operation.

"Fine for prairie farmers," said my Dad, "but can you imagine any good farmer ruining his hay crop by packing it up in rolled square lumps. It will never catch on here."

The Miracle Kit

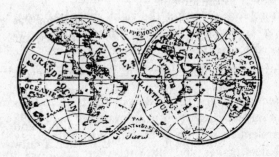

When mid-winter lethargy covers the countryside and the sun goes back to bed soon after it gets up, the daylight rarely sheds the last damp blanket of twilight. This makes life in the isolated cottages and farms dreary in the extreme.

Before the 'electric' came, winter was far worse.

The one link with the busy world beyond the dark, dank lanes, breaking the monotony of the long lamp-lit evenings, was the radio. It was called the wireless then, and regarded as little short of miraculous.

With the standard wage for a farm labourer at 32s. 6d. a week, the wireless was an extravagance not easily attained.

Although our family was in slightly easier circumstances,

the outlay of unnecessary expenditure was something to be churned and chewed over by my parents for months.

Then my brother saw an advertisement in a newspaper. 'Build your own wireless set', it read. 'Full instructions for easy assembly. Complete kit and cabinet. Success assured or money returned.'

To illustrate that it was child's play to construct the kit there was a picture of a curly-headed moppet clutching a soldering iron and surrounded by a group of adults transfixed in attitudes of astonishment.

Hardly surprising this, for in front of them was a wireless cabinet from which a volcano of crotchets, quavers, and treble clifs erupted across the page.

If a small girl could do it, surely it was not beyond the combined brain power of my three elder brothers to assemble a wireless and make it work.

Days extended into weeks as we waited, not knowing quite what to expect or how it would arrive; then a railway van delivered a crate the size of a tea chest.

Grand-daddy of all do-it-yourself construction kits, each part was lifted from a cocoon of wood shavings and laid out on the kitchen table.

Subdued into unusual silence I sat, a small, incredulous spectator, anxious to catch the first glimpse of the little black notes on stalks escaping from the bakelite chassis that my brother Harold was joining together.

No miracles occurred that night, or on the subsequent evenings either. For days we ate our meals crowded up together at one end of the kitchen table, since the wireless kit could not be cleared or disturbed.

Mum complained about the inconvenience incessantly, but four pounds worth of components, not to mention the seven shillings 'carriage paid home', was far too much to risk the loss of any pieces by moving them about.

Wallowing in strange-sounding phrases like 'tuning condenser', 'wave-change switch', 'high and low tension batteries' and 'rectifiers and transformers' made little sense to any of us.

Mum, trying to be helpful, bent close to study a diagram and a powerful magnet on the loudspeaker system pulled all the hairpins from her head, releasing the coils of her long hair to fall round her shoulders.

She distrusted the wireless after that and gave it a wide berth until all the pieces were safely inside the cabinet and the lid screwed shut.

At last six enormous valves were pushed into their holders, the batteries were connected, then faintly, but just discernable, we heard a low-pitched hum. Now all that it needed to make it work was an aerial, but this was not a matter to be undertaken lightly.

My brother Stan climbed to the top of the copper beech tree in the yard and, hauling up a long pole, lashed it to the top of the trunk.

There was a theory that the mysterious sound waves could dissipate themselves into the tree and kill off all the leaves, so a porcelain insulating cup was joined into the wire where it cleared the branches.

There was another insulator where the lead-in wire to the set entered the kitchen window, put there because without it sounds and signals from far-off places could infiltrate into the very walls of our home.

The aerial wire swung high above the washing line, announcing to our little world that we had joined the listening elite.

But any machine that could pluck music from the air and conjure up foreign-sounding voices must surely attract lightning and thunder-bolts or something worse, so a simple knife switch that earthed the aerial was fastened to the window frame. Each night the lightning conductor switch was religiously turned down, in much the same way as old-time horsemen hung hag-stones on stable doors to prevent witches hag-riding their horses in the church-yard still of the night.

There were those who were convinced that anything that could relay voices of people hundreds of miles away, must upset the cycle of the seasons, and our wireless was blamed for every storm or heavy shower that came.

Any attempt to explain electro-magnetic waves travelling across the ether only made it worse. Wasn't ether the stuff used in hospital operations? People who sat listening to the wireless obviously risked being put to sleep.

Nevertheless, Mum would kneel in front of the wireless cabinet, carefully trying to synchronise the two tuning dials to capture the signals from an elusive station.

"Fancy, Radio Hilversum! That accordian music is coming all the way from a country where everyone walks round in wooden clogs." I marvelled with her.

We would sit with our feet on the big brass fender, sharing the warmth of the huge old kitchen range in the chimney corner with two or three cats, a line of working boots and coats put round to dry and friends who had walked muddy fields to share in listening to the miracle of sound.

As time went on wireless sets became commonplace, but our old home-made set still worked and Mum became more expert at finding the Continental stations for our interest and entertainment.

I remember listening to a stirring military band, followed by a wild cheering and someone hysterically shouting in a harsh-sounding foreign language.

"That's coming from Hamburg. Must be that new Hitler chap that's taken over in Germany," Mum said, but Dad told her to change the station or turn it off.

"Sounds more like an underworked, excitable, penned bull looking at a passing herd of cows. That man sounds like trouble in anybody's language. He'll need watching, mark my words."

Mum shut the wireless off, but the shouts of 'Sieg Heil' that we heard that night in the nineteen-thirties was a sound the world would grow to fear.

The wireless was something to be savoured and not squandered by the womenfolk idling during the day. That would run down the high tension battery, heavy, awkward and big as a fair-sized roasting tin. The low-tension wet battery, or accumulator, needed recharging every ten to fourteen days.

These were cumbersome to carry and tipped over at the slightest provocation, making acid holes or staining anything the liquid touched.

The garage at the far side of Lockley Green, which was nothing more than a hand-cranked petrol pump and a tin shed, did a battery-recharging service.

One enterprising boy, who grew up to own a transport fleet, started up in business collecting accumulators for recharging in a massive old twin pram, wheeling it over to the garage and bringing the charged batteries back.

Progress, creeping at a snail's pace, reached the village, first with piped water and gas, then electricity came striding across the fields on pylon stilts and creosoted poles.

We had a new radio set and discovered that 'London Speaking' people did not suffer from permanent catarrh, nor did real music sound as if it had been trapped in an old treacle tin before it dispersed itself across the ether.

The gamekeeper happened to be in our kitchen soon after we got our new set and he told us an unbelievable tale.

'His Lordship' had just come back from London, where he had witnessed a remarkable demonstration from the B.B.C. He had seen a radio set with a glass screen in front and not only had he listened to the broadcasters, but watched them moving on the screen, and them at least three streets away. Videograph or television, it was called.

Mum and Dad both said that a wireless set that could make moving pictures was something they would believe when they saw one for themselves.

I wish they had.

Unwillingly to School

There have been more changes in the pattern of country life in the last quarter of a century than in any time in our traceable history.

Agricultural methods have advanced so rapidly that many landworkers now operating in the highly mechanised farming industry once cultivated the land with implements that had remained virtually unaltered since the middle ages.

This quiet revolution has affected every aspect of rural community life, and nowhere is this more noticeable than in the changed conditions for country school-children.

I sometimes see a group of animated infants eagerly awaiting the arrival of a mini-bus to transport them to school. At mid-afternoon they disembark, chattering like magpies, clutching poster-painted masterpieces and happily relating the day's happenings at school. For young children attending the pre-war village school it was a different story.

There was no school transport and in mid-winter children from outlying farms and cottages left their homes before day-break to walk the goblin-haunted muddy miles to school, not daring to be late. It would be dusk before they returned.

I was lucky, for although I lived almost two miles from the school by road, there was a short cut across the fields and I had two pairs of winter boots and a waterproof warm coat.

For other schoolmates who had to make do with one pair of boots, the muddy farm tracks meant perpetual cold and wet feet while chilblains were a seasonal plague.

The standard farm-hand's wage at that time was 32s. 6d. a week. This might be augmented if the wife did field work cut-ting winter cabbage or picking brussels sprouts.

Any offspring too advanced to stay strapped in a pram at the end of the cabbage rows was 'put on the roll' at school. These toddlers trekked to school with their bigger brothers and sisters.

The school-master was a Mr. Steelman, and never was an individual more aptly named. He was small of stature, with a cadaverous face and iron-grey hair. The cold grey eyes that glared through his steel-rimmed pince-nez spectacles invoked the same hypnotic effect on a timid four- or five-year-old as a stoat outstaring a cowering baby rabbit.

He was assisted by his wife, a dessicated woman with bony hard-hitting hands, who habitually wore a mouldy green hand-woven skirt and two thick black drooping cardigans all through the year.

She needed them in winter, too. The entire school was housed in one long high-pitched draughty room. Near a wooden partition, jammed into permanent disuse, a free-standing circular combustion stove sulked fumes or glowed red-hot, depending on the direction of the wind.

In addition there was an open fire at the 'babies' end of the room. And babies the first year pupils were. Walking long distances to school, often coming from families with incomes that could barely provide the basic nutritional necessities, it was no wonder that they frequently keeled over off their seats asleep.

The old feudal social system still lingered on in our community and this percolated down to the 'babies' class in the school. The higher one's parents rated in the status scale, the nearer to the fireplace one sat.

Pride of place went to a girl named Jessica, the daughter of 'His Lordship's' steward. She came to school wrapped in a travelling rug in a wicker-work basket carrier on the back of an estate hand's bike and I detested everything about her, from the sausage curls in her auburn hair, to the mud-free soles of her brown kid buttoned boots.

Next came the son of a prosperous farmer, the postmaster's daughter, the blacksmith's tubby son, an overweight girl from the local inn, and then myself. Six to a form we sat, and I can only think that I made the front rank on sufferance, because Dad happened to be a stalwart of the parish council.

The other five children were all plump and I invariably cliff-hung to the edge of the form by half a cheek.

Lessons were written on slates and erased with the aid of spit and sleeve, or the hanky that we had to wear pinned to the front of our frocks and jerseys. At all other times we sat with folded arms or with our hands placed on the top of our heads.

Singing lessons were not conducive to a love of music. Each May we practised for Empire Day. The local dignitaries always attended the school celebration and Jessica of the auburn curls always sang the solo part.

One year when she came out in spots, three of us lesser fry were detailed to sing her parts. The hymn was 'All Things Bright And Beautiful' and I was supposed to sing solo in the verse that runs 'The rich man in his castle, The poor man at his gate, God made them high and lowly, And ordered their estate'. This I did not believe, and not even our sycophant headmaster could make the words come from my mouth. I sang loud 'La-La-Las' instead and suffered later on.

Although I curtsied to our honoured visitors with all the rest, Dad was warned that his youngest daughter was showing some very radical tendencies that would need to be severely curbed.

We did get cheap school milk, but school dinners were a future dream as far as our school was concerned. Looking back, the contents of our dinner bags demonstrated the poverty of our times.

Again I was fortunate. My mother used to fill a pint enamel milk can with either soup or rabbit stew, to supplement bread, cheese and fruit. Many had to make shift with dripping sandwiches, or bread and mixed-fruit jam.

Many a school dinner came to grief by falling off the prongs of an improvised toasting fork pushed through the bars of the guard round the 'babies' room fire.

By grace and favour, my can of rabbit stew was heated on the top of the combustion stove and various other 'dinner children' were afforded a quick dip of their stale crusts in my stew. It soaked up the runny part and I was left with the solid bits in which I would often gain remnants of someone else's fish paste spread.

Under the guise of being taught 'housecraft', the older girls were sent across to the schoolmaster's house. There they were taught bed-making, laundry and rudimentary cooking by his wife. Cookery consisted of making onion soup and baked egg custard, a basic in our teacher's diet.

When I reached the dizzy academic heights of being in 'Standard Six', I too was instructed in these culinary arts, and was happy to discover that, unknown to other pupils, the big girls working in the school house kitchen had been waging a secret war of retaliation and revenge.

Solemnly, each one added her contribution to the custard, and I spat with the rest.

The schoolmaster's moods became more and more eccentric and then quite suddenly he was gone. His replacement was a gentle, spell-binding man who showed us that our narrow world was a storehouse of country lore and historically interesting things.

He taught us that words were wondrous weapons and talked about our heritage of the unchanging land.

A branch of the county library is open in the old schoolrooms two afternoons each week. Its musty atmosphere still smells of chalk and steaming leather boots, conjuring memories of children of another age who are still young enough to be active in the new.

Cooking Them Dratted Germs

To Mum, illness was like a bad smell on the landing: something to be dealt with ruthlessly, effectively and without wasting precious time.

She took anything short of actual surgery in her stride and her simple remedies brought about some speedy cures, possibly because being 'made well' was such an uncomfortable business.

It was sheer lunacy to cough in the first few weeks of the year. In addition to the usual sugar soaked in Friars Balsam and eucalyptus that took the plating off the spoon and left the victims convinced they were the unwilling stooge in a fire-eating act, there was an 'after Christmas' bonus.

Having regained your breath and wiped your streaming

eyes, your mouth was filled with a great dollop of goose grease.

Willingly, or by the sheer necessity of having to breathe despite a firmly gripped nose, you swallowed it and then submitted to having goose grease plastered on your chest.

A distinct smell of sage and onion wafted from under your liberty bodice well into spring.

It only needed Mum's hand to feel a hot forehead and we were off again! Two dozen onions and a few chillies were boiled up in an iron pot while sand-filled stone jars that had been heated in the oven warmed the patient's bed.

In a flannel nightshirt topped by a woollen cardigan and cocooned in the bed clothes, even the most rebellious knew better than to refuse the basin of pepped-up onions.

Mum called it, 'cooking them dratted germs'. While perspiration oozed from every pore, bed and steaming patient were covered by Dad's best horse rug. Dad disliked the idea but the horses never seemed to object.

Strains, sprains and circulatory troubles were easily dealt with. Horses and humans simply shared the same bottle of embrocation, Mum's contention being that if the cure hurt more than the complaint, it would all feel better soon.

Chilblains called for a slightly different method of approach. The first line of attack was oil of wintergreen and salt, massaged in with all the delicacy of a rotary sanding machine.

Stage two involved first catching a sheep and pulling out a handful of its fleece. Having wrapped one's swollen toes in the odorous greasy wool, how you got your shoes on afterwards was a problem that you worked out for yourself.

Inner cleanliness was a fetish with our Mum and every Saturday evening saw the family downing massive doses of liquorice. Not for us the luxury of a long lie-in on Sunday mornings!

Spots, pimples, and being in love were all symptoms of the same complaint, all requiring a mixture for cooling down the blood. This was obtained by mixing the yellow powder of 'flowers of sulphur' wih treacle ladled from a barrel in the corn shed.

The same stuff was administered to horses with a poor or 'staring' coat. I never saw a horse with pimples and it did nothing for our hair, so I don't imagine that it can have worked in reverse.

Sometimes Mum discovered interesting knowledge by accident, and, while she was delighted when it proved to be of practical use, her patients were sometimes grudging in their thanks.

She knew why misery masked the pretty face of a querulous young wife who called each week to purchase eggs and a recent observation led Mum to think she could possibly help the girl.

There was a whispered confidential chat and the customer departed with two bottles under the dozen eggs in her rush basket.

Mum disclosed that when she had strained and bottled the Morella cherry wine, the behaviour of our normally placid farmyard fowls, after they pecked at the fermented cherries, led her to believe that the juice might be particularly potent.

Mum's therapy obviously worked, for everyone was delighted with the news of an impending arrival. But happiness is a fleeting thing.

When the couple had four children in as many years they placed the blame on Mum and developed a kind of hate fixation for our innocent cherry trees.

Mum immediately imposed sanctions on that year's crop of cherry wine and gave it to an honoured few, only those in a state of wedlock qualifying. Definitely excluded was Aunt Bet's husband, who needed no encouragement and had a roving eye for a pretty barmaid.

When the juice from the fleshy leaves of the plant that flourished on our lavatory roof failed to cure a sudden crop of warts that covered my hands and arms, Mum called in a specialist.

She had seen his handiwork before and had great respect for an old man who most people regarded as being little more than a worthless tramp.

We called him 'Cockle Billy', for he eked out an existence gathering shellfish from the foreshore and transporting them to nearby towns in a squeaking, buckle-wheeled old pram.

He bought my warts for a shilling piece and buried them under the flowering currant bush. My warts vanished and for years I trod gingerly near that bush, afraid that I might find a crop of warts growing like mushrooms from the ground.

Mum had an uncanny instinct for sensing when any of her scattered family was sick and we attributed this to the fact that she had a Romany grandmother.

I often wonder if that could also account for the most remarkable bit of home nursing that I have ever seen.

The old threshing machines that travelled from farm to farm before the advent of combine harvesters all had 'Threshing Johnnies' who slept rough, lived rough and were as hard as nails.

Their job was to cut the bonds from the sheaves with vicious sharp hooked knives and feed the corn into the revolving drums on top of the machine.

One of these men once cut his hand where thumb and forefinger meet, slicing it almost to the bone. He lost balance and caught his injured hand in the machine.

The thresher stopped and he was assisted to the bench beside the farmhouse door. In his filthy state tetanus was a real danger and he was losing too much blood, but terror of 'the 'orspital' far outweighed his fear of bleeding to death.

Mum came bustling on the scene and without a word tore the strings off her apron, tied one round his wrist and the other round his upper arm. I was detailed to find an old but freshly laundered sheet while Mum sorted out the mangled flesh with a gentle, infinite care.

She went into the corn store and came out carrying the biggest cobwebs she could find. Before an open-mouthed, goggle-eyed girl and a group of men who were sure that now they had seen everything, she slapped the cobwebs over the wounds. She bound the patient's hand and fixed a sling to rest his arm, then went about her daily tasks as if she did that sort of thing every day.

She would never discuss the incident except for one occasion when she told me that instinctively she had remembered hearing an old lady talking of the same sort of situation and remedy.

Within a week or two that hand was completely healed.

Don't ask me how – I only wish I knew.

We smiled at my old Mum and her cures, but they were based on common sense, confidence and the most unpleasant brew she could concoct.

Now we queue in overcrowded waiting rooms, breathing in each other's germs and spreading those we have ourselves, to get a bottle of strawberry flavoured linctus that we take religiously for the first three doses then leave with the row of other medicines on the shelf.

A gallon of Friar's Balsam, a gallon of eucalyptus, half a hundredweight of sugar lumps, someone with the personality of my old Mum to dish it out, and present day sugery queues would vanish like mist before the sun.

Please, no goose grease for me though, because I don't wear a liberty bodice any more.

Whitsun Fete

Whit Monday was always something of a relief. The ordeal of having to keep the new Whit Sunday dress clean and intact, the suspense of wondering if by some mischance I had been included in the list of Sunday school prize-winners, was over.

On the only occasion that I was selected to scramble over children's outstretched legs into the aisle and tread the never-ending strip of grey coconut-matting, the vicar consulted both his list and the flyleaf of my prize to verify my name, declaring that it justified his belief in miracles.

But that was yesterday and now it was Whit Monday, traditionally the day for the vicarage fete and children's treat.

All morning long Vicarage Lane was busy with wagons

transporting chairs and crockery from the village hall to the vicarage paddock. Men with mallets sorted out tangled ropes and struggled to erect the large marquee, while harrassed ladies scuttled round, putting old and faded curtains over trestles and setting out their stalls.

Order always emerged out of chaos soon enough for the flags of empire to flutter from the tops of tents and between the avenue of trees in the vicarage drive before the grand opening.

After dinner I was released from the rag curlers which corrugated my scalp but did nothing for my hair. Scrubbed, polished and magnificent in yesterday's new dress, I went to the fete, complete with mug and spoon.

All along Vicarage Lane the strains of a band, giving forth with *Blaze Away*, heightened the excitement. My two older sisters, somewhat hampered by their first pairs of silk stockings, struggled to keep my pace.

'Her Ladyship' always declared the fete open, economically wearing the same 'cabbage rose' hat and using the same speech every year.

It meant that everyone automatically clapped or laughed at the right time, but could concentrate on which stall was likely to offer the best value for the spending money that burned in the pocket or was clutched, sticky, in the hand.

The sultry sun shone down upon the sweating City Silver Band, roasting in their splendid martial uniforms as they played *Colonel Bogey*, *The Merry Widow*, and selections from *Show Boat*, with all the fervour their panting lungs permitted.

There was little time to visit all the stalls, so I by-passed the ones that would not sell out quickly and concentrated on buying a halfpenny glass of shocking-pink raspberry sherbert, a toffee apple and some sticks of peppermint twist, all sticky and gooey in the heat.

The postmistress presided over the sweet stall. The ogey-pogey-eyes, the liquorice chews and giant humbugs, along with all the other old stock that had hung fire on her shelves all winter, were dusted off and sold at a cut rate.

The band sopped playing to let the schoolmaster attempt to blow his whistle through a megaphone. Feeling very important, those of us who were 'in it' ran across the erstwhile sacred turf of the vicarage lawn and went into the house.

In a kitchen that smelled of beeswax and stale cabbage we put on crepe-paper dresses, the wings and the crowns of silver paper stars, so laboriously made at school.

The leading lady howled with nerves, forgetting every line she ever learned, and I was glad. I knew my part quite well because in fact it consisted of one word, and then I got it wrong!

While we were dressing, a heavy shower, thundery but of short duration, sent people running to the shelter of the tents, but the sun came out as we were led out through the vegetable garden and through the wicket gate to the shrubbery that was the backcloth to the tennis court, our open air theatre.

A deputation of anxious Mums sent the vicar as spokesman to tell the schoolmaster that their precious daughters must not perform barefooted as he had intended.

Dancing around on damp grass would do quite hideous things to growing girls' insides and the least we could expect was galloping consumption.

The schoolmaster suggested that it was the perfect solution to his overcrowded classroom, but glanced at the hovering gaggle of mohers, fearsome in their cherry-laden hats, and gave ground.

I looked down at the brown buttoned boots that encased my ankles and was delighted to realise that Titania would be forced to trip on to the stage in knee-high, black lace-up boots.

Oberon and Snug outraged our fairy dignity by suggesting that they could see our navy bloomers underneath. A battle royal ensued and I was hauled out of a heap of rotting, rain-sodden lawn clippings, my paper dress soggy and torn, dripping dye on to what ever it touched.

Only my protruding ears prevented the crown of stars from completely covering my face.

The schoolmaster's long-suffering wife, prompt-book in hand, crouched in a wet laurel bush. The scholmaster announced that his pupils would perform Act 3 of A Midsummer Night's Dream and the old horn gramophone, wobbling on a rickety cane table, started up the music of Mendelsohn's Overture.

Like early Christian martyrs we were pushed into the arena and I tripped across the lawn in my drooping paper dress and brown button boots.

The maypole dancers followed us, weaving their coloured lattice patterns. Being left-handed, with a tendency to turn in the opposite direction to everyone else, I had once succeeded in getting the ribbons in a hopeless knot and was forbidden to attempt the feat again.

The Brownies' action songs were not for me either. Brown Owl once fell over one of our straying cows asleep on her front porch.

She landed in the evidence of its visit and that started a feud.

The children's acts were planned to let the stallholders and band have an early tea but, soon after the Brownies let 'Little Redwing' rest in peace, the band struck up with the *Grand March* from *Aida*.

Every child in the village, be they Church, Chapel, Catholic or Hottentot, lined up in a procession to the children's tea.

While the younger children munched their way through piles of sandwiches, cakes, and jelly, melting and tasting waxy in a cardboard dish, the older folk slipped off to have their tea.

The echelons of society were clearly defined. The elite were invited to drawing room tea in the vicarage and it cost them two shillings and sixpence. Farmers and tradesfolk sat on the verandah and were charged two shillings. Tea on the lawn cost one shilling and sixpence, while lesser folk stood drinking penny cups of tea from the urn and bought buns from a stall.

After tea, the coconut shies, the hoopla, skittles and other games of chance came into their own. 'Bowling for the pig' was a great attraction and many a cottage sty was cleared on the offchance of winning it.

The pig, a runt from our blue sow's last litter, had been squealing all afternoon and created a diversion by getting free and charging at full gallop into the open french window of the house.

The Sunday school teacher went round with a cake that she had baked herself, inducing people to guess the weight at two pence a time. She asked Jack, the bachelor shepherd, if he would like to try and in clear large print for everyone to see, he wrote just one word, 'Heavy!'

When, by some odd fluke, she won the bowl-off for the pig, however, Jack volunteered to look after it for her and gave the gossips enough ammunition to last them through to Michael-mas.

The greasy pole was fun. Three poles firmly fixed like a football goal were plastered with cart grease and in the 'All-comers, knock-out contest' each contestant, armed with a sack of straw, had to climb to the other side using the sack to dislodge his opponent en route.

In the tug-of-war, where the vicar's and the farmer's teams fought their yearly battle, everyone felt the vicar's side to be the underdogs and at some disadvantage.

The farmer's team knew there was a stone jug behind the cedar tree and that it contained something that would give them strength, while the vicar's team pulled faces over their sour lemonade.

While the farmer urged his team along in language they

could understand, the vicar's supplications were of the 'Pull chaps, pull' calibre.

The evening wore on and as dusk fell the trees around the lawn were magically transformed with coloured lights.

From the verandah, the old gramophone blared tinnily for the couples dancing on the lawn. The bandsmen were free to mingle with girls who had made sheep's eyes at them all the afternoon.

Among the deserted tents, Dad and my brother loaded crockery and chairs into the wagon and, tucked up on a pile of old curtains, my Witsun dress all stained and anything but white, I rode down the vicarage drive.

The music of the *Distiny Waltz* still drifted through the trees and pervading it all was the scent of lilac and bruised grass.

Post Hole Willy

Post-Hole-Willy used to live in a stone-built cottage at the far end of Glebe Lane.

Most people in the village called him daft to leave his old home and buy a flimsy new bungalow that was 'nobbut a rabbit hutch on a pocket-hanky plot of land'.

But boyhood memories of his Granny's log fires on the chimney corner hearth wouldn't warm Willy's rheumatics now that he had grown old.

Although he had long since hidden the smoky old fireplace behind an aggressively ugly tiled surround and plaster boarded the solid stone inner walls, rising damp still turned his best boots mildew green, while slugs and snails left slime trails on the mat inside the door.

Daft or not, Post-Hole-Willy sold Stone Cottage, bought his bungalow and still made money on the deal.

There have always been two schools of thought as to whether he is 'a Ha'penny short of a shilling' in the head.

I know that behind the stolid, slow witted face he shows the world, there's a crafty old schemer with a goblin sense of fun that first earned him his name.

Years ago he came back from the Army, toothless, unmarried and boasting a small pension, a sitting bird for our widowed distant cousin, May.

They married and thereafter Cousin May wept public copious tears, bewailing the loss of her much-lamented first.

Having bought a wife, Willy bought some second-hand teeth, strictly a social asset, too precious to eat with and removed in times of stress.

Strangers being introduced sometimes shook a hand that clutched a still-warm upper denture.

Family pressure forced Dad to find Willy employment on the farm. Hedging, ditching and fencing were safe winter jobs where no-one could go wrong. Willy did his best.

Enthusiastically burning clippings from a hedge that he had just trimmed, he set fire to the hedge.

He fell face first into a deep mud-filled ditch and the fence posts he erected blew down in a breeze. He tried again but the posts still leaned like drunken sailors on a rolling deck.

The milk of Dad's forbearance became skimmed.

"Will," he said. "You didn't get the post holes right."

"Post holes?" asked Willy. "What be they?"

Temptation leered and Dad, no saint, replied, "If you don't know, take the wheelbarrow over to the hurdle maker and ask him for a barrow-load of post-holes."

Smiling cheerfully through his china teeth, Willy wheeled the wooden barrow five miles up and down the lanes.

The perplexed hurdle-maker scratched, thought, then asked which sort of holes Dad wanted, round or square?

This floored Willy's powers of reasoning. He knew there was something about square pegs in round holes but, to be on the safe side, trundled his barrow back to ask Dad.

"Round ones Willy, you're using round posts!" Willy set off back on his third five-mile trip.

The hurdle maker, solemn faced, said,

"Round ones, eh? Did Harry say what length?"

"Blogger me," said Willy, flagging now. "I ain't going back and from again. Give us a load of whatever size you've got."

Half-past nine, pitch crow's-wing dark and Cousin May a-hammering on the door.

"You mean to say you've sent poor little Willy for a barrow-load of holes?"

"Round ones," said Dad, as if that helped. Ruffled, she squawked and clucked like a broody hen. She'd had one husband slip the net and if Willy wasn't much, he kept her warm at night.

The gate hinge creaked and Willy, a trifle short on wind, came limping to the door.

"Here, boss, those post-holes be blamed airy-fairy things."

Not a glimmer of a smile showed on Willy's face.

"They'd have been terrible awkward to stack on the barrow, so I caught the afternoon bus at the woodyard and went to the agricultural merchants in the town. They said they'd charge it to your account."

Already hovering in the red in the balance at the bank, Dad asked Willy what on earth he'd bought.

"Well, first, the wheel of the barrow has run so far and so fast it was nigh on bursting into flames, so I bought half a gallon of cart grease and a half-hundred-weight of binder twine."

"Binder twine?" Dad was stuck for words.

"That's right. I took it back and tied the start of one ball to the hurdle maker's gate, knotted the end of each ball to the start of the next, and threaded the twine through all they old holes. You'll find any that dropped off the barrow when you collects up all that string."

A wasted day, four hours overtime, cart grease and a half-hundred-weight of cats-cradled useless twine, all for a barrow load of holes. We never did decide just who fooled whom.

Soon after, Post-Hole-Willy as he now became, set himself up as a handyman, and had the Trades Descriptions Act then been in force Willy would have been on shaky legal ground, for everything that he put up fell down.

Sweet Smell of Revenge

The feud between my father and The Admiral's Niece began one Speech Day at our village school.

The wooden partition dividing the two class-rooms had been propped back and the 'top class' desks, pushed together in three rows, were covered with a strip of thin coco-matting to make an improvised platform at one end of the school-room.

On this a group of familiar figures, crammed close together on chairs brought over from the schoolmaster's house, strove to appear dignified as they avoided putting their heels in still-full inkwells or lost their balance as a chair leg slipped into the gaps between the rickety old desks.

The schoolmaster, centre-stage, had exchanged his egg and

gravy bespattered woolly waistcoat for a mildewed cap and gown, but his assistant teacher wife still sported two drab 'cardies' and kipper-box, polish-starved boots.

Beside her sat the vicar, beaming beatifically, baby-pink and shiny-faced, as if his most recent occupation had been an attempt to boil himself in a bath.

His Lordship's steward was there, deputising for 'His Nibs', and not obviously overjoyed at the prospect of an afternoon in a hot, ill-ventilated schoolroom, facing a group of grubby children who were probably laying odds on how soon he would nod off to sleep.

A prosperous fruit-grower, ram-rod straight, sat glaring down. With the apple scrumping season just ahead he seemed to be imprinting a picture of our individual faces in his mind.

In an aura of parma violet scent, and the feather from her hat probing the schoolmaster's left ear, sat The Admiral's Niece.

'Uncle, the Admiral' was a shadowy figure, long deceased, but his niece still set the standards of social niceties as far as local society was concerned.

And right on the end of the platform, with his bowler hat on his knee, sat my Dad, smart in his Harris tweed suit and his shining Sunday boots. All Mum's efforts to get the studs into his starched shirt front and his tie tucked under his stiff collar had been worth it.

Like King George V he looked, only smarter.

I prayed that his pink-painted bedroom chair wouldn't slip off the edge of the stage, and that he would remember the words for his vote of thanks.

On a card table, covered by a Union Jack, was a bunch of flowers in a painted pickle jar, a pile of essays and some books. These I had an interest in, for one could soon belong to me.

The Admiral's Niece, who was to present the prizes, gave an essay award each year and, possibly because I was the only one to write on two sides of a piece of school paper, my effort on 'Why I Want To Join The Navy' had gained the highest mark.

A bumble bee, trapped in the shut windows above the stage, disturbed the dancing dust motes and filled a vacuum of boredom as the speeches droned on.

Unmindful of a deep contralto voice offering advice to 'Those about the leave', I watched the bee until I noticed Dad's right foot tapping in irritation, a storm signal usually reserved for the fools who forgot to shut field gates, or my older sisters when they came home late.

Then the gist of the speaker's remarks filtered through the cobwebs of my mind.

"Low-born country children that you are, do not be dismayed."

The Admiral's Niece's impassioned tones washed over us in waves. "No one among you need go unemployed. There is always domestic service for the girls, and the most simple idiot among the boys could work on the land."

The fruit-grower turned an apoplectic shade of mauve and as Dad stood up to give his vote of thanks, I knew from his tapping foot that practising his set speech had been a sheer waste of time.

"Madam," he began, "the countryside does not necessarily breed fools, nor does noble birth preclude bigotry and patronising condescension."

We may not have understood the long words, but we knew that the Admiral's Niece was not amused. When she reminded Dad that he was not addressing a dairy maid, her face turned crab-apple sour as he replied:

"I realise this, Madam, for I do not believe that you could milk a cow."

The schoolmaster studied the coco-matting between his feet and the vicar, tilting backward in his chair, looked as if he might be praying for the imprisoned bee.

Nevertheless, Speech Day continued and a small procession of prize-winners, undecided whether to bow or curtsey, bobbed across the stage.

The Admiral's Niece held my essay, 'Why I Want To Join The Navy', in her hand, offered some constructive criticism on it and said,

"Now who is entrant number nine?"

I knew, so did the schoolmaster, but as she consulted his list, The Admiral's Niece gave me one long withering look, extended a glacial gaze in Dad's direction and announced that she had been reading the number upside down. The winner was, in fact, entrant number six.

A surprised lad, who never dreamed that three lines and a page of blots could rate a literary award, ploughed through sardine-packed children to collect his prize. I did not covet his volume of 'Selected Sermons On Sectarianism' any more than I had really wanted to embark on a sea-going career.

The sea was the stuff that Sunday-school treats were made of.

There was always the farmyard pond and a fleet of sheep-troughs to sail from tadpole time until the leaves of the poplars carpeted the surface of the pond.

Prize-giving and the school day over, it was to the solitude of the pond that I escaped. A sheep-trough punt, clothesline prop propelled, is, strictly speaking, a one-man craft, but I was always prepared to carry passengers for trips around the pond. Customers were few, however, because their mothers seemed to be averse to their offspring going home with slimy, water-stained clothing or pond weed in their hair.

As far as Dad was concerned, the incidents at Speech Day were finished with and, if I had been unfairly treated, the injustices of life were facts that I would have to learn to face. Meanwhile there was a clover crop to cut and carry while the weather held.

Day followed sun-baked day. The pond grew steadily more

shallow until it would have been possible to paddle from side to side, had not the bottom been knee deep in evil-smelling mud. The hot weather affected Mum's laying hens, but if egg production had fallen off, the customers to buy them had rapidly diminished since the Speech Day episode.

Spitefulness over a paltry prize was one thing; depriving Mum of her egg money was another. This time Dad would do more than tap his foot.

If we hoped for rain it was not only to save the parched crops, but because The Admiral's Niece was holding a garden party for her social equals. None of the local ladies was invited, a fact that made one disgruntled lady renew her order for butter and eggs from Mum, despite the displeasure that The Admiral's Niece would show.

The pond had never been so low, an ideal time, Dad said, to clean it out. It stank to high heaven and even Jack, whose personal hygiene left more than a little to be desired, since he never reckoned to wash, complained that "Her didn't 'alf 'um," as he shovelled semi-solid sludge into a dilapidated tip-cart.

The task was finished by mid-afternoon, Dad hitched Phyl, the old half-blind mare, to the shafts and led her slowly out of the farm gate.

"Near side wheel looks a bit dodgy, Harry," Jack called as Dad set out along the lane.

"It will get there if I take it easy," Dad replied.

Half an hour later and he was back, leading Phyl but without a cart.

"I can't understand it. I must have clipped the verge just outside The Amiral's Niece's garden wall, and the rim of the wheel fell off. Old Humph reckons that it will be tomorrow afternoon before he can get it repaired. The hot weather shrank the wood.

"As you say Jack, that pond mud don't half hum and there is that poor lady with all her guests just over the wall."

Dad grinned a little, then, straight-faced, said no-one could move a cart with a broken wheel.

Ballet Equestrienne

Daisy Hackett said that if I held my ear close to the telephone post I would hear messages passing overhead, but no matter how I tried the only sound I heard was the wind in the wires.

Not for me the chance to eavesdrop on the parson pleading for his unrequited love. Daisy Hackett professed to hear it all.

"He says he loves her worse'un toothache!"

"Who?" we asked, intrigued.

"Listen and find out," was all that Daisy would divulge.

"Oo-err!" The other children, crossing their hearts and hoping to die, swore that they could hear the conversation too. Unenlightened, I came to the conclusion that I had been born with the wrong-shaped ears.

It bothered me and I was not sorry when Alfie Hart, riding his father's bike, called out that the self-binder had almost finished cutting winter wheat up on Foxley Bank. The other children ran up there to watch the sport.

Much as I liked rabbit or hare pie, I hated those last few circuits of cutting a cornfield. As the standing corn grew less any animals or injured game instinctively sought sanctuary towards the centre of the field and when that shelter disappeared they broke cover or crouched, petrified with fear. 'Guns' stood on one side and anyone nimble enough to chase the terrified rabbits waited on the other.

With the others running ahead, I pondered on the problem of my ears, convinced that they were in some way deformed.

I knew that they were perpetually forced forward by the scalp-tight braided plaits in which my mother endeavoured to contain my slippery 'mouse-coat' hair, but an intensive study of my shadow gave no clue as to where the fault might lie.

It perplexed me until I realised that the slim telephone post in School Lane carried only two insulating cups and four thin wires. Ears as misshapen as mine would probably need a larger post to listen-in. The thick one on the corner of Plough Lane should be just right.

It smelled of sun-soaked pine forests and creosote. A resinous gum exuded from its cracks, but I still heard nothing but a vibrating low-pitched hum. With both arms encircling the post, my fingers explored the outline of a notice on the side. That, I reasoned, could easily prevent any telephone conversation from coming down the post.

The poster made enthralling reading. 'Grand Circus and Menagerie. See Titania and her Ballet Equestrienne; Alfredo the Fearless; Wild Beasts of the Jungle. Admission from sixpence up.' The illustration showed Titania as a dainty ethereal creature far removed from our clod-hopping country ways.

Cloistered and enclosed in the stuffy school-room on the

following day, we heard rumbling wheels and a traction engine travelling through the village at the top end of School Lane. Alfie Hart, tallest in the class, could just see out of the bottom panes of the school-room window had he dared to look, but he was sitting cowering under the schoolmaster's glacial stare.

"Reckon it was threshing tackle or the steam plough," Alfie said at playtime.

"Wasn't then," I argued, smug and feeling smart as paint. "It was the circus moving into town."

They asked me how I knew.

"I found out while I was listening to the telephone post," I said.

"Now let Daisy Hackett pretend she heard the parson talking sloppy to Miss Ash!"

It would be hard to imagine anyone less likely to inflame male passion than Miss Ash. She was a shrewish little woman with halitosis, a permanent digestion problem and an aversion to soap and water. As the village organist and teacher of pianoforte, she suffered from the added disadvantage of being disastrously tone-deaf.

She coached my 'brainy' sister through 'Ezra Read's Easy Tutor' for one hour every week. Mum, full of maternal pride, would stand enraptured as my sister plodded painfully through *The Maiden's Prayer, The Robin's Return* and the *Blue Danube Waltz*, punctuated by off-key promptings and attacks of wind.

There was no music lesson for anyone on the afternoon that we heard the circus lorries pass through.

When I got home from school Miss Ash, looking dustier and more dishevelled than ever, was having hysterics in the kitchen, pausing only to draw breath and swallow down great gulps of Elderberry Wine, Mum's standard medicine for bringing back colour to one's cheeks.

"To be confronted by a lewd looking little man in a loin cloth in the lane was bad enough," she sobbed, "but when I saw that he was actually encouraging a great brute elephant to steal apples from the trees, I poked the pair of them with my gamp, but the wretched beast picked up a trunkful of dust from the side of the road and blew it in my face!"

Another glass of medicine disappeared, she stopped for a quick scream and was off again.

"One does not expect to meet a wagon load of monkeys displaying their disgusting habits and believe me or believe me not, they all had blue behinds! It is just not safe for a decent, respectable person to venture forth alone!"

Appalled at the prospect of hours of Miss Ash, I volunteered to walk her home across the fields.

Swaying slightly and slurred of speech, she imagined that lustful men lurked behind every hedge and was so relieved to reach her house intact that she gave me a shilling and promised to show me how to play Chopsticks on the piano when next it was safe to call.

Anything as exotic as a circus was an extremely rare occurence. I had never been to one before, but nothing was allowed to interfere with harvesting and if I went I would have to go there by myself.

Dad gave me sixpence, three weeks' pocket money in one go. This, with the shilling I had saved, gave me one and six.

Doing a mathematical calculation on the dust of the barn floor, I figured that two fourpenny bus fares, plus the sixpence admission, would leave me with four pennies to spare. It felt wonderful to be rich.

The circus looked much less glamorous than I had imagined it would be. The Big Top had more patches in its canvas than our stack cover tarpaulins at home. Nevertheless, there was a long queue waiting for entry and a long wait before I could say, "A sixpenny ticket, please."

"You're in the wrong queue young'un, menagerie tickets is around the back."

I argued but there it was in black and white.

'Menagerie sixpence, Circus seats from one and six'.

So the menagerie it had to be. Disillusion was complete.

A moth-eaten old lion, a group of dejected monkeys – Miss Ash was right, they did have blue behinds – an elephant with eye trouble and both fore and hind legs hobbled with chains, and two skinny skewbald horses, standing on less straw than my brother would have put in his rabbit hutch.

A man with leopard skin trousers came into the tent, followed by a frowsty woman dressed in trailing tulle and tarnished tinsel.

"Right then Alf, let's get them harnessed," she said, then led the horses out.

"And now, the great Titania!"

The ringmaster's voice carried through the canvas walls of the Big Top. I left the menagerie tent and walked the five miles home.

If that fat woman could be 'Titania, the ballet dancer on a horse', then so could I. I would use the old net curtains that kept the birds from the blackcurrant bushes for a dress and ride Jim, the horse that was the same age as myself. He had an even temper and a broad back.

Privacy was essential for the first few practice rides and since Sunday was the only day that he was turned out to graze, I skipped Sunday school and led him down to the far corner of his meadow by the elms. Draped in blackcurrant stained net, with Jim wearing ploughing reins on his halter, I got up on his back.

Riding Jim was nothing unusual, but he took objection to the hobnails in my Sunday shoes on his bare back and made straight for the low branches of the elms. That is where I stayed.

As Dad said as he extricated me from yards of hampering net hooked up in the tree, few are blessed with beauty, artistry and poise.

The rest of us must work.

Sunday School Treat

Chapel children, night clothes clad, stare enviously from upstairs windows in the village street, crying or jeering at us because they cannot come.

We, the children from the church, stand shivering from excitement and the chilling damp of an average summer morning.

Clustered around the open shutters of the gloomy forge we watch the blacksmith bellowing his smouldering hearth into roaring, spark-erupting flames, a foretaste of the fires of hell that the parson warns us of each Sunday in the year.

This year we are safe, for we have been to Sunday school and service frequently enough to gain reprieve. The fact that we are congregating by the forge is proof that we who stand

and wait have all been good. No back-sliders are allowed to come!

We hear the chugging engine of the Flying Dutchman's bus, (Daily services to outlying districts. Outings and tours a specialty). The bulbous, brown, solid-tyred charabanc comes rattling up the village street.

Rough boys and older girls jostle and push, rushing to claim the back seat first and get a longer ride. The vicar counts our heads; "Three to a seat, and all sit down!" He tells the Flying Dutchman to proceed, for "All are safely gathered in." At last we are on our way.

My gentle sister, first one from our parts to win a scholarship for more than a decade, has taught the slower children how to say their prayers, so qualifying to sit beside the Sunday school teacher up in front. It makes me proud to think she rates a seat all to herself.

I have found a perch halfway down the bus, wedged between plump Emmy and her flesh-encumbered Mum. Emmy gets 'poorly' if she can't sit by the window, while her Mum's fat overflows the edge of the seat, and I sit sandwiched in between.

"Emmy, here's the dripping toast you didn't eat before we left."

Emmy munches her late breakfast, visibly and audibly enjoying every bite while we rush by the fields of standing corn at a breakneck twenty knots, down one hill, gathering speed to take the hump-backed, tummy-dropping bridge, and charge on up the other side, changing down through the gearbox, gradually losing speed, shuddering, juddering. Clutch is engaged and 'Clunk!' the Flying Dutchman finds his bottom gear. The heavy-laden bus crawls slowly on and up.

Meanwhile Emmy's face has gone an interesting green; it happens every year!

"You'll have to stop, my Emmy isn't well."

The Flying Dutchman knows that if he does, he'll never start again and, posing deaf, drives on.

My string-handled, paper carier bag that advertises Mr. Brown's wet and dry fish is hauled up from the danger zone and my new seaside bucket is sacrificed to the cause.

At the top of the hill, the other children cheer because the sea is in sight. My vision is restricted to the ham-like arms of Emmy's Mum, mopping up her bucket-clutching child.

Down the hill and through the little seaside town, until we stop and unpack, like sardines walking from their tin.

A cold and drizzling wind is blowing off the sea. Emmy's Mum says "Thanks" and ceremoniously hands me back my half-full bucket, advising me to rinse it in the sea. The tide is out and half a mile away, but I trudge out across the shingle beach until I reach the waves and, all alone, imagine that there is nothing in the world but sea, the lowering clouds and me.

Salt splashing in my best brown button boots, I run like mad to find my sister and my friends; there's nothing more scarifying than the thought of being lost in a strange town.

Emmy, fully recovered, is on the swing boats, eating chips from a paper bag.

It is far too cold to linger on the front and, safe with my sister, we cross the esplanade and go across into Penny Arcade. We use up all our pennies, save the two that Mum says we must always keep 'in case', then watch the tall boys, laughing, holding up their shorter friends, trying to cram four eyes into the visor meant for two, to find out for themselves just what it was that the butler saw.

Across the sea, a line of blue marks a break in the clouds. It is going to clear up. The sun comes out and like lemmings we are drawn toward the sea.

Removing boots and socks, we younger girls tuck petticoats and dresses in our knicks, screaming as the cold waves creep between our toes, while braver ones walk out in the water, right up to their knees!

One or two, who go to the seaside more than one day in the

year, have gone to the extreme of wearing swimming suits; with chattering teeth and blue-faced with cold, they say it's lovely when you're in!

My sister, neither child enough to tuck her skirts up in her pants, nor old enough to join the vicar and his wife drinking coffee in the Grand Cafe, envies us our paddle.

The intelligence that gained her a higher education overcomes the problem and works out the way for her to have a dip. I must stay on the beach, while she goes off towards the council bathing station. Some good few sea-wasting minutes and she is back, tripping like Aphrodite to the sea, clad in a yellow stockinette swimming costume, two sizes too large and boldly printed right across the rear, 'Property of the Urban District Council'.

The sun has sulked again, so in a large glass-fronted shelter we eat jam sandwiches for lunch. Conscious of a debt of gratitude, Emmy's Mum shares a pint of winkles with us, taking the 'gob-stopper' hatpin from her head to show me how to get them out. This time the bucket comes in handy for the shells.

It settles in for rain and doubting disbelief runs riot in my soul. Surely the Lord could let the sun shine on this one day in the year. Was it for this we went to Sunday school in ice and snow? For this we stamped our chilblained feet in a draughty, cold church hall, consoling ourselves that it was all worth while to be allowed to go to the summer seaside treat?

Death, heaven and hell are a million years away, the seaside is here and now! It seems the obvious time for Deity to signify He knows that we have tried. And then He lets it rain!

My sister calms down my rebellious spirit and lets me try to catch six ping-pong balls in a shrimping net. A boy beside me catches five from the fountain jet of water; the man in charge takes his hand off the button, the water subsides and the balls disappear. We protest, volubly and at length, that it is a swindle and my sister, education bent, takes me off to see the town museum. 'Closed for lunch, open at 2.30 p.m.'

Back past The Gem Cinema, its placards boasting 'Come inside and see what France is really like!' My sister can speak French, which astounds us who find it hard to write and spell our native tongue. She would like to know more about France so, screwing up her long hair in a bun and looking worried, in the hope it makes her look sixteen, she buys 'One nine-penny and a half.'

The dim light of a tiny torch pilots us through the Stygian darkness to sit in the front row. At least it is warm and dry in here.

France seems to be a dreadful sort of place, where the nicest thing that happens to a sweetly pretty girl is that she is dipped in wax and ends up as a statue. Her friend is carried screaming to a boat that's bound for South America. It says so underneath!

I can't see why she is making such a fuss, the gentlemen around her seem so friendly, but my sister says it is far worse than being dipped in boiling grease.

The Blue Grotto Cafe is the venue for our Sunday school tea, curled-up, dry cucumber sandwiches and lovely creamy sticky cakes.

Emmy, full to the teeth, regards the last cake on the plate and with ladylike delicacy, wraps it in her paper serviette and puts it up her knicker leg, to eat on the way home.

There is an hour to kill before we can depart and in the bay a cargo ship is heading for the harbour. The vicar suggests that we might like to go and see it dock.

My sister is reluctant to go. The film this afternoon showed what could happen to a girl who wanders near sea-going ships. Mum would be cross if we did that, then woke up bound for Buenos Aires.

The welcome, familiar bus is just across the road and 'everyone will please remember where they sat before'. I hope that someone forgets but fate decrees that, once again, I act as buffer state between fat Emmy and her Mum.

Knowing too well that once we reach the hump-backed bridge and start to climb the hill on the other side, Emmy will start to bawl and be sick again, I take Dad's stick of rock and Mum's giant peppermint humbug from my bucket and pass it on to Emmy, now engrassed in her squashed, sat-upon cake.

It is quite a job to lift my leaden-weighted lids. Perhaps I'll go to sleep till we get home. Tomorrow I must start another year, laying up treasure in heaven and making sure I qualify to go on next year's Sunday school outing to the sea.

Harvest Bunfight

Lockley Harvest Gala is one of the few remaining threads from a pattern of living as remote now as the rural world of Jethro Tull.

In a working year not overblessed with festive occasions Lockley Harvest Sports and Supper, otherwise known as 'His Lordship's Bunfight', brought a bonus work-free Saturday to each autumn.

It was a long walk from our village, but no-one willingly missed 'the Bunfight', since it gave us the opportunity to glimpse life as it was lived behind the high walls surrounding Lockley Park, His Lordship's country seat.

The main entrance was on the other side of the estate but at 10.20 precisely on 'Bun-fight' morning an under gamekeeper unlocked the huge iron gates at the bottom of Lockley Hill. We trooped in and along the tree-lined, mile-long drive.

Children from Lockley School and ours, segregated from their parents, washed and inspected behind the ears, waited in subdued lines as their school teachers briefed them yet again.

It was forbidden to damage the turf, pick any flowers or fruit or be 'excused' behind a tree. There must be no staring at the statues. These, it was explained, were Art, portraying heathen gods and therefore of no interest to us.

Aphrodite, Adonis, Circe, Ceres, Juno and Saturn were consequently studied in great depth, providing the first instruction in basic anatomy to every goggle-eyed child. Two-headed Janus, damaged by a misplaced shot at a low-flying pheasant, had lost a chunk of his marble. The uneducated tenantry knew him as 'Old Minus', whether they could read the writing on his plinth or not.

No child must behave boisterously and should 'Young Master Frederick', known to his contempories as 'Right Horrible Fred', compete in any race, he must not be jostled or pushed. As His Lordship's heir he would naturally win.

Otherwise, the youngsters were free to enjoy themselves before their own races began by watching a twenty-over cricket match between His Lordship's XI and the Farmers' team.

Since all the inhabitants of Lockley village and a good percentage of our own were tenants of the estate, His Lordship's side comprised the best cricketers from both communities, plus any house guests – 'London folk' to us.

The Farmers' scratch team seldom won when the bowlers dutifully avoided His Lordship's stumps and the fielders felt obliged to drop each catch.

While the cricket match was in progress, the womenfolk and smaller children gathered near the yew arches that screened the back terrace lawns.

Her Ladyship, her female guests and the Lockley district nurse came out through the conservatory doors and down the terrace steps. Infants were hauled from their prams and toddlers had their faces 'quick-licked' clean. The nurse jostled the mothers into groups, according to their offspring's age.

Her Ladyship progressed along the ranks, pinching cheeks, admiring clothing. Showing the correct amount of indecision, she chose the best and bonniest baby in each group. It was immaterial that the chosen child was so bloated that it suffered from croup for nine months of the year.

Weight was the deciding factor, just as prize winning porkers or spring lambs were adjudged to be those that gained the most poundage in the shortest time. Her Ladyship's criterion of a healthy baby was much the same.

A snack lunch was served between the two innings of the cricket match, but by then the school children who had sat still for so long were wriggling and remembering that they were forbidden to 'go behind a bush'. Not that they would voluntarily have done so, for using the gardening staff's 'offices' was a highlight of the day.

When most of our homes lacked piped water and had wooden privies 'out the back', the tiled walls, polished mahogany seats and gleaming white porcelain bowls were a source of admiration.

To tug a chain and unleash 'The Niagara (Patent Pending)', was both exhilarating and terrifying as the rushing water flushed and gurgled in the cistern overhead. It was an experience to savour as often as one dared.

With the cricket charade over for another year, the children's races could begin. Three-legged, sacked, egged, spooned and hampered by their Sunday clothes, each tried to outrace the others, ever mindful that if 'Right Horrible Fred' took part, then he must set the pace.

Each competitor was rewarded with a toffee-apple, usually a windfall Worcester shrivelling in a rock-hard burnt sugar shroud.

The men's events provided much more fun, with local rivalries emerging and each participant determined to take home any livestock that was going free. Climbing the greasy pole faster than anyone else meant a weaner pig from the home farm to fatten for Christmas in one's garden sty. Tossing the tree trunk, heaving the hammer, tilting the bucket – each contestant stood the chance of winning a young cockerel or laying hen. Then the obstacle races, scrambling under stack covers, over pig nets, through swinging barrels and a sluggish flowing stream.

The athletic activities culminated in the tug-of-war, Lockley team against our own. This was the most partisan contest of them all, since a guinea and a cask of cider were at stake.

Eight men from each village, taking the strain on a four-inch rope, dug the heels of their Sunday boots into the resilient turf, undid their collar studs and, eye-balls protruding, heaved.

By now the electric lights in the glass covered coach-house yard beckoned our attention. It was time for the annual Harvest tea. Sheaves of corn and mop-headed chrysanths decorated the wrought iron uprights supporting the glass roof, flags of the empire decorated the walls, and bodies crammed together to get seated round the trestle tables on which the feast was set.

'Right Horrible Fred' presided at the children's table, liberally spattering his guests with remnants of the pink blancmange rabbit that crouched on green jelly grass.

The grown-ups tackled a much more substantial meal, which everyone was expected to help in clearing away. This gave the more inquisitive a chance to see the cavernous back kitchens of the 'big house'.

'Order for His Lordship'. Mouse quiet, we listened to his usual annual speech, gave three cheers for the king, the estate, and a good harvest and then began to sing.

His Lordship always started with *The Farmer's Boy*, and we

dutifully sang the choruses. For several years a singer, announced as being Lady Cordite, warbled *Cherry Ripe* or *Lo Hear The Gentle Lark*. Having acknowledged the applause, this individual would reveal himself as the estate secretary in 'drag'.

Children who had never seen a wig were impressed, their elders muttered that 'Yonder chap were summat odd'.

When a genuine contralto gave a recital of German lieder, our response was cool indeed as we sat waiting for her to remove her hair and gown.

We came out on to the familiar lane at the bottom of Lockley Hill and went our separate ways home.

Distinctly feudal, definitely homespun, His Lordship's Bunfight produced enjoyment and spontaneous laughter. It generated a humorous vitality that, despite the 'star attractions' displays and sophisticated side-shows, the efficiently run present-day Gala lacks.

Rabbit Stew

That season had been a never-ending series of disasters and, not to put too fine a point on it, we were broke. Late frosts had halved our fruit crop, the season's hay had gone up in a stack fire and, as a finale to the summer, an outbreak of swine fever plunged the bank balance down below the thin red line.

True, the yield from the hard-won harvest was still an unknown quantity. That would stay in the barn until we were solvent enough to get it threshed, but Dad would borrow from no one. What he could not pay for we would not have.

We were rich, he said, in everything but money and if there was no cash in the kitty there was no need for us to starve.

Economy would be our password and we would build up our

resources in any legal manner we could. These then were the circumstances that led to what for me will always be the days of rabbit stew.

Not that butcher's meat had ever been a frequent feature on our menus. In more affluent times there had always been a fattened pig to provide meat for the winter, but now the sties were empty and burying swine fever victims in quicklime had killed our taste for pork. Previously we often had a Sunday chicken dinner, but now every egg layer counted and if one found its way into the pot it was some egg-bound old boiler, 'killed to stop it dying', as my mother used to say.

In those pre-myxomatosis days it fell to the ubiquitous bunny to provide the mainstay of our meals and should anyone ever feel inspired to compile and publish a 'Hundred and One Things to do with your Rabbit', I could contribute to every page.

We ate them stewed, we ate them roasted, boiled with dumplings, frittered, fried and battered, 'rabbit in the hole' or rabbit pasties and a thick pastry lid covered many a 'mystery' pie.

That was not always one hundred per cent rabbit, but who were we to argue if some suicidal pheasant chose to end it all by putting its neck in the noose of a snare.

We had a gentleman's agreement not to poach the squire's pheasants, but if the squire was a gentleman I knew his son was not. That, to my way of thinking, made the whole thing null and void. One of the estate gamekeepers who often used to drop in at mealtimes knew how we were situated and would compliment Mum or me on our 'feathered rabbit' pie.

Earlier in the year I had found an injured tame rabbit by the roadside. I took it home and within a fortnight there were eight. Each had a name, they grew fat and flourished, then all but one were sold to swell our funds. Mum said that there would be no wild rabbit for that year's Boxing Day dinner, we would eat the remaining tame rabbit instead. It was just like being asked to sit down and enjoy a meal made from one of the friendly farmhouse cats.

Even when it was nothing but stock and stewed bones, its pelt, scraped, salted and treated with alum hung in reproachful accusation, curing and nailed up on a board.

Later Mum would use it to line mittens, ideal for cold winter working on the farm.

As the cook book says, first catch your rabbit and if ever there were double standards on a subject this was it. The dear little flopsy, cotton-tail, story-book bunny close-cropped pasture, decimated young corn crops and chewed his way through the shoots of growing trees. It was the countryside's most ravenous nuisance, yet to catch a rabbit was not regarded as pest destruction but poaching, on any land one neither hired or owned.

Some of our farms were badly affected for, although it was our crops that they cleared, the actual rabbit warrens were mostly just inside the squire's woods on the other side of the hedge. There were often dozens of rabbits grazing and with the asking rate at a shilling a rabbit from the butcher, this seemed a source of income worthy of being explored.

The saddler sold rabbit snares unofficially and Slippy Springer the poacher watched with interest as I bought mine. "Setting up in opposition then, girl?" he enquired then, walking home beside me, gave a discourse on his art. A good poacher, according to Slippy, was one who ran quicker and thought faster than his opponents.

He offered to set my snares out for me and soon there were hingles, as he called them, set out in every rabbit track in Stony Field.

"You won't catch much tonight but you should do better the night after," he warned me. "You want to walk round them about half an hour after the rise of the sun."

I couldn't sleep for thinking of dead rabbits and was up and over in Stony Field before it was really light. By the time I was half-way round I had found thirty rabbits, far too many to carry in my bag.

I saw some movement in the hedge in the field's far corner, and there was Slippy carrying an empty sack. He looked surprised to see me, then grinned and helped me carry my rabbit catch home.

"You know something?" he said as he puffed along beside me, "I reckon that besides running and thinking faster, I'd better add getting up earlier to my list."

On a fifty-fifty basis, Slippy volunteered to use his ferrets to clear the burrows on our land. Sometimes the ferrets would 'lay-up' with a dead rabbit and, full-tummied, would go to sleep underground. There was nothing for it then but to sit and wait if the project was legal, otherwise one cut one's losses and ran.

While I had been a part-time rabbit catcher, Mum had been engaged on her profit-making scheme. In addition to fur-lined mittens she collected every bright piece of cloth she could lay hands on, cut it into strips and hooked it into enormous kitchen rugs. Our clothes line often bore some extremely weird and gaudy garments that Mum had unearthed in some second-hand clothes shop, borne home in triumph and washed. With corn sacks for backing, Mum's bright patterned rugs were virtually indestructible and were snapped up by the hardware store in town.

Scrap iron was sold to gipsies and everything we could produce that had a marketable value was sold. Each pound that we acquired was laboriously entered in an old account book until Dad was able to start using black ink instead of red.

One day, while Mum was serving up the inevitable rabbit stew, she told us that a man had called that morning. He had been out driving and lost his way.

"Such a nice man," Mum had thought him because he had noticed what she was making and had actually purchased a pair of her fur-lined gloves.

When she asked him to step into the kitchen while she wrapped them he offered to give her ten shillings for a pair of ornaments on the kitchen shelf.

"I told him that you would be in within minutes Dad, but he was in a hurry to be off, although he promised to be back."

We looked at Great-aunt Polly's china shepherd and shepherdess with new respect. Tricksters were an alien element in our lives but if the stranger was interested in figurines Dad thought it a worthwhile idea to check up on their value.

Mum and I took them to a reputable antique shop in the town and sold them for more than we dared hope. Now there would be money to pay for threshing the harvest and the price of corn was high.

"We ought to celebrate," said Mum. "Let's buy a pound of steak."

Flanagan's Summer

Strangers to the village looked askance to see Flanagan sunning himself in the Post Office window.

But regular customers knew that he kept to the 'official' corner, ignoring the temptations beyond the cards of pot-menders, flypapers and sweating cheese that defined the limits of the grocery section.

His unusual black and tan markings saved him from being drowned at birth, thus forfeiting the first of his nine lives.

Life No. 2 and four inches of his tail were lost acquiring the knowledge that a mowing machine moves faster than a half-grown kitten stalking rabbits in a hayfield. The remaining stump of tail sprouted like a fluffy, multicoloured shaving brush in contrast to the rest of his smooth coat.

His tattered ears and scarred eyelids, a legacy from fighting other toms, gave him a wild piratical expression. In fact Flanagan was an extremely ugly cat, but every litter in the vicinity seemed to produce black and tan kittens and the village people recognised him for the character he was.

Tom the cowman, whose rough hands could send static electricity tingling through the fur along his spine, was Flanagan's friend, as was the fishmonger who fed him titbits from his reeking, flyblown van. The vicar, who twice yearly pinned a notice on the Post Office door in an effort to find 'good Christian homes for unusual charming kittens', harboured extremely uncharitable thoughts about Flanagan and Flanagan knew it, but realised that the vicar was too gentle to transform words into deeds by way of a well-aimed brick.

The only human who caused Flanagan to arch his back in sheer dislike was a loud-voiced, flat heeled female, who now stood complaining to his mistress that the unhygienic, misbegotten tom-cat should be banned from wandering in the shop. The object of her venom extended and retracted his claws, glanced at her through half-closed eyelids, then darted past her size eight brogues, hurrying towards the fish van that had pulled up in the square.

The same hectoring voice demanded fresh fish for 'the Rose of Sharon, my pedigree Persian Queen', while Flanagan sniffed at the melted packing ice that dripped a slimy trail along the road.

He had no idea what a 'Persian Queen' might be, but he knew there would be good pickings from the unfilleted plaice she was going to eat.

Flanagan followed the hefty brogues until they entered the glass conservatory that served as the side entrance to Rose Villa, and through the glass saw a gorgeous female cat with a silky coat that shone like rain-washed slate. He put back his head and yowled like any farmyard tom, before a size eight brogue dispatched him from the premises with unexpected accuracy.

Nothing daunted, he took cover in the privet hedge and waited for the lovely creature to come out, keeping vigil all day and night without success. But next day, when the flat-heeled shoes pounded past his hiding place, he called to the cat beyond the glass again. She was obviously impressed but stayed inside her prison.

Flanagan knew the 'hard to get routine' and slipped away, returning with a young leveret which he placed beside the door.

The cat inside sniffed and scratched ineffectively, but Flanagan leapt at the latch, throwing the weight of his body against the door until it creaked open and the prisoner was free.

Sharon, born to a world where pedigree breeding was a financial undertaking, raised on a diet of cooked fish and yeast tablets, groomed daily with scented flea powder, was the most unnatural female that Flanagan had ever encountered.

She picked daintily at the strange tasting young hare, then meekly followed Flanagan through the fields of young wheat and into the undergrowth of a wooded valley. There, in the base of a hollow ash tree, Flanagan and Sharon found a place for shelter and warmth.

In a few days Sharon lost her pampered show-cat look, growing sleek and supple.

Flanagan brought food to her and cleaned her coat with his rough tongue until the hunting instincts that generations of careful breeding had submerged stirred again and Sharon hunted beside him. All summer long they ran wild in the woods, stalking food or playing like kittens, chasing dancing leaves.

The £10 reward for the safe return of the valuable 'Rose of Sharon' caused a nine-day wonder that sent every village child prying into ditches and old barns, but no-one worried about Flanagan. He had gone off courting before.

One avid anti-vivisectionist gave her opinion that cat

snatchers were abroad but as the village poacher said, his dog ferret had escaped but he didn't accuse anyone of stealing it for laboratory experiments.

The yellowing reward notice faded in the August sun and was forgotten.

Clattering combine harvesters echoed to the valley woods and Flanagan set off to catch the easy prey that huddles limp and lame on the edge of stubbled fields. He hunted alone, for the shimmering heat made Sharon's distended body an intolerable burden and the birth of her kittens was imminent.

The sun had swung across the sky but Sharon had only managed to produce one offspring, while her brain and body concerted together in a cacophony of pain that held her screeching and screaming for relief.

Another creature disturbed the peace of the summer evening and petrified rabbits crouched in their burrows, until the danger passed beyond the range of their senses.

This creamy coloured animal stood on its hind legs to sniff the blood in the air, establishing the direction of its target and insinuated its fluid, undulating body towards Sharon.

The poacher's ferret was out hunting too.

In her agony Sharon was unaware of the danger until the ferret's teeth closed on the helpless kitten and, despite her frantic struggle, the ferret had torn a second kitten from her before merciful blackness engulfed the stricken cat.

Flanagan, dragging a full-grown partridge in his mouth, sensed danger as he struggled through the wood. A jay screamed out a warning and Sharon's last agonised call triggered off the primeval wild cat instinct in her mate.

A spitting, snarling, scratching fury sprang at the satiated ferret, and they writhed in an undefinable mass of flying creamy brown and black and tan fur.

Flanagan felt needle sharp teeth grinding on the bones of his haunches, and as a retaliatory measure, darted talon claws to seek and scratch at the retina of the ferret's unblinking

eyes. At last the ferret lay lifeless and in the trees a magpie signalled that the woods were safe again.

Licking his wounds, Flanagan discovered that his hindquarters were lead heavy and not inclined to move. He
crawled to Sharon and cleaned her blood-flecked coat, mew-
ing quietly to her until she stirred and tried to rise.

Slowly, deliberately, Flanagan took the supine cat by the
scruff of her neck and dragged her, kitten-like, down through
the woodland and across the stubbled fields, each corn stalk
probing and prodding his torn body and useless hindquarters.

It took a night of struggling, resting and struggling on again
before Flanagan reached the village. The sun was up before he
reached Rose Villa to caterwaul and scratch against the door,
with Sharon still cradled gently against him.

The loud-voiced woman, drinking early morning tea, heard
the unfamiliar sound and hurried to the door.

"Sharon!" she bellowed, and Tom the cowman, hurrying
past on his way to work, was in time to see her slipper-clad
foot take a goalkeeper's kick at Flanagan, dispatching him
across the sun scorched lawn, to land under the privet hedge.

Tom realised that Sharon needed veterinary help, for years
of inbreeding had turned the normal process of birth into a
hazardous business and, on the whitened doorstep, delivered
her of an abnormally large black and tan kitten.

The woman, stunned to silence by Tom's caustic tongue,
found voice again.

"Ruined! It's no good for either showing or breeding now.
Get rid of that mongrel kitten, too!"

Tom gathered the cat and kitten in his arms.

"I wasn't reckoning on leaving them here. You'mm too
handy with your feet.

"I know where they will be welcomed, but you're too daft to
see that old Flanagan had the sense to bring her where she
could get help. I heard a commotion in the wood last night
and found a darned great ferret lying dead, with enough cat
fur around to fill a cushion.

"That old tom cat must have fought like a tiger to save his mate. I wonder where the old rascal is?"

Tom found him lying still and glassy-eyed for, under the dark green dusty hedge where it had begun, Flanagan's summer had ended.

Sheep-Dip and Home-Made Wine

Whenever campions bloom, my mind's eye re-creates the sun-soaked summer evening that found our village policeman lying with his helmet over his face and ladies bedstraw twining in his hair, oblivious of his steaming uniform, ruined and reeking of sheep-dip, or of his bicycle lying bent and battered in the stagnant ditch. Wheat-wine bewitched, he simply did not care.

The day had been warm, ideal weather for dipping the recently-sheared sheep.

Sheep-dipping to rid them of parasites and prevent them being maggot-blown by flies was obligatory by law and the police had to be informed when this operation was taking place. This ensured that our guardian of the law would put in an appearance, verify that we were complying with the law, sign the appropriate forms from the Min-of-Ag-and-Fish and then depart.

Since we were a comparatively law-abiding lot – give or take an overlooked dog licence or two and a bit of poaching – our constable was glad to spend the sleepy stillness of a summer afternoon watching lesser men struggle with strong-willed, stubborn sheep that were reluctant to be dipped.

Before insecticides became available we used a dip that was arsenic based, so that when the sheep emerged they looked as if they had been caught in a shower of custard.

The dipping tank was an oblong wooden trough, rather like an oversized bath tub, with a ramp and platform at each end.

The theory was that the sheep would walk up the ramp. There, one of two men would turn it on its back and, with both men holding a leg at each corner and a third man covering its nostrils and mouth, the sheep would be lowered gently into the dip.

But our sheep were distinctly unco-operative and objected to the indignities heaped upon them. Shaking their shorn fleece in disapproval as they stood draining on the second platform, they walked down the ramp, ludicrous comedians mincing along in wet long johns.

Not being hefty enough to handle wet and struggling sheep, I was designated 'sheep's chiropodist', trimming back overgrown hooves with pruning shears and treating any foot ailments with a liberal coat of stockholm tar.

Every village had its reservoir of casual labour, men prepared to help out when extra labour was required. Being a 'one man, one girl' set-up, we often relied on this kind of help.

Although a neighbouring farmer lent a reciprocal hand, our third man at sheep-dipping time was always Jack. Some regarded Jack as a grubby old man who was so mean that he relied on the sheep shearers for his annual haircut, but to him it was simply a matter of priorities.

The other men of the village could do as they chose, but it seemed sheer waste to pay out sixpence to have the squire's groom cut his hair with horse clippers in the 'pent-us' of the blacksmith's shop on Saturday afternoon.

Besides, by having his hair cut once a year at shearing time, it grew long enough to keep the draughts away from his neck in bed all winter long.

Washing, too, folk made too much fuss about.

"Takes all the natural oils out of 'un," Jack maintained, and reckoned that we had much to learn from sheep.

"Look at they. Only bath once a year, and then it's because some Jack-in-an-office says they must. It's certain that they don't get dipped for choice."

Arguing that sheep get washed with rain made no impression.

"Aint's I out in all weathers, too?" was Jack's stock reply, and there was no gainsaying that. Nevertheless, when we went sheep-dipping, we always tried to keep upwind from Jack.

Our constable was always trying to reform Jack to more hygienic ways, so that when they came in contact with each other at our dipping tank, the atmosphere was acrimonious as well as strong. The smell of sheep-dip-saturated clothing that had been on Jack's back for weeks on end was almost unendurable for everyone and it was not by accident that Jack joined the sheep in the tub.

He was convinced that in some way the constable was responsible for his immersion and although Dad offered to stop operations while he got a bucket of warm water and some clean old clothes so that Jack could change, Jack refused and carried on.

The tension eased with the arrival of Mum, carrying a jug of cider and a dusty bottle of home-made, ice-cold wine.

We thought Jack uncommonly sporting to refuse anything but a mug of cider, leaving the policeman to tackle the cool wine.

"Very mild and most refreshing," was his verdict, coming back for another swig.

"I'll go down to the house with your missus Harry, to sign the cattle papers and perhaps she could find another glass of the cold drink."

He was back within a few minutes, looking slightly red above the dog-collar of his tunic.

And at that moment Jack was preparing to drive Billy, our old ram, up the ramp and on to the platform. With an evading jump, Billy darted out of Jack's grasp, turned smartly on one hoof and charged at the policeman's rear, just as he was approaching the dipping tank.

When he surfaced, brushing sheep's wool and filthy yellow sheep dip from his eyes, he felt around for his helmet and mustering what dignity he could, strode down the yard to the pump, and there with her usual gentle tact, Mum soothed his ruffled pride, sluiced off his tunic and offered him another glass of wine.

Since it was just a cooling, home-made summer drink, he saw no reason to refuse. He came back to the dipping pen to collect his bike surprisingly cheerful considering that his uniform was turning a peculiar shade of green.

Sheep-dipping was finished and everyone but Jack was cleaned up ready for our evening meal when an anxious police-sergeant came to the door.

Our constable should have rendezvoused with him two hours before, and now he was nowhere to be found.

Where the first bend curves down at the top of Lockley Hill the summer flowers fill the banks waist high and there I found him, sleeping in the sun. No-one mentioned Mum's wheat wine, and Jack explained to the sergeant that a sheep-dip bath can have a mighty peculiar effect on folks that wash their 'natural oils' away.

Doris

We had a telephone answering service long before the arrival of automatic exchanges and STD. It was run by Doris, daughter of the postmisress. She alone understood the intricacies of the exchange switchboard in the storeroom of the village Post Office Stores.

Doris knew if the person we were ringing had gone out and where they had gone, where the district nurse was likely to be and why and the wholesale price of brussels sprouts as quoted to Charlie Carter by a city market salesman the previous day.

Few felt the need to have a phone installed when the blue enamelled sign above the store-room door invited everyone to 'Telephone From Here'.

Telephoning was an awesome business. Even Doris

addressed the mouthpiece firmly, as if there was an uncontrollable hound tied to the other end of the line. Asking Doris to phone for us dispensed with the need actually to use an instrument that most of us regarded with distrust.

Doris took messages for non-subscribers. The information, 'Cousin Albert going to hospital with his leg', scribbled on blue sugar-bag paper and delivered by children going home from school, was just the bare bones. Doris would relate the meat of the message as soon as one called at the Post Office Stores.

When Doris was off duty her mother acted as stand-in. It was never 'Number, please' or 'Trying to connect you' when Doris's Mum was in charge of the exchange. Instead a voice broad with accent would enquire:

"Who did 'ee want to chat to then?" and knowing, advise the caller to "Just hang on while I puts this-yere plug in that there hole and finds out who we've got."

The crowning achievement for our village exchange was a call from Mrs. Wall's sailor son. He rang from Australia at two o'clock one morning to tell his mother that it was his wedding day and to introduce her to his bride.

The bridegroom's mother, with steel curlers in her hair and wearing a coat over her nightie, stood in the clutered storeroom among the bags of haricot beans and packets of porridge oats, awestruck that Doris was capable of using the wonders of a scientific age to connect her to her son.

Old Dubber Wall, the bridegroom's grandfather, refused to be impressed and voiced doubts in the shop the following day. If Australia was the unnatural sort of place where folks could get married and telephone around the world at the time of night when decent people were in their beds and fast asleep, he was not sure that the tenuous link between Doris's switchboard and the antipodes was entirely a good idea.

Explaining international date lines and time lags was useless. No-one was going to tell Dubber that if he died eating his breakfast in Britain he could still be alive at teatime in Australia.

Dubber resigned himself to the fact that the silly young shaver had got mixed up with a topsy-turvy parcel of odd folk who didn't know that day is light and night is dark.

"Originals, they call them," said Dubber, quite convinced that his new grand-daughter would turn out to be some nocturnal being to whom the laws of gravity did not apply.

Doris, queen of the headphones, probably bent every rule in the telephone operator's handbook but she sorted out our problems, saved our twopences and was sometimes instrumental in saving our lives. When a runaway tractor crushed a farmer's son Doris's telephonic tracking service located a doctor on his rounds and got him to the accident within a matter of minutes.

Then Doris dropped a very large stone in the placid pond of our rural existence by divulging that the switchboard in the storeroom would soon be obsolete. The small brick building in the course of erection in the corner of the orchard by the shop was not, as rumour had it, a public convenience. It was the new telephone exchange.

"I am being automated," Doris explained regretfully. Ethel Tappit, spokeswoman, expressed the customers' concern and shock.

"Automated? How disgusting! You don't want to give up so easy, girl. You're not so long in the tooth that some chap won't come along and wed you, decent like. There is always Perce the post. Automated indeed! What will they think of next?"

Indispensable and seemingly as indestructible as a leather coat that gathers a few wrinkles but never seems to age, Perce the village postman was a much a part of the local scene as the mounting steps by the churchyard gate. Having shunned the spinster-spun webs of marriage, his small market garden and his postal round had been his life.

His fruit and vegetables always seemed to flourish and mature weeks ahead of neighbouring gardeners' and Perce reckoned that he knew the reason why.

"I talks to 'em when I'm weeding and hoeing, see! Now if that were a wife she would answer back. Besides, you can't sell your old woman like you can a bunch of carrots."

His Post Office bicycle was his pride and joy, brought out to be dusted, oiled and have the tyres pumped up each Saturday afternoon, then put back in the shed.

Perce did his postal rounds on a tricycle built like an ordinary cycle with a box car on the side. It was extremely difficult to ride and few children who grew up around here escaped scarred knees from injuries inflicted while attempting to ride and stay on Perce's trike.

The tricycle box carried mail, parcels, greengrocery, odds and ends of shopping orders and anyone with strong nerves requiring a lift.

Perce always started his rounds early so no one really objected if it was sometimes gone eight o'clock before the mail arrived. We knew that Perce would have lit a fire and got in a day's supply of fuel for the arthritic old lady along School Row, looked in to see that Amos had not had another funny turn and probably delivered a medical prescription to an outlying farm.

If Perce was actually delivering mail he wore his postman's hat. If it was a business or social call he took it off.

Should the two coincide he would first deliver the letter wearing his hat, then remove it while he served the greengrocery order.

There is a gentle incline down Plough Lane. Perce always took advantage of this to sort out his letters as he free-wheeled down the middle of the road. When the tricycle was superseded by a small van Perce was too set in his ways to let mechanisation alter his routine.

Local drivers realised that they were liable to be confronted by Perce checking the mail as he drove along Plough Lane. The verge, though wide, bore many tyre ruts from those who had chickened out.

I once had a passenger who abandoned ship as Perce approached. Stopping a good headlight's width away, Perce called out, "Two lettuce or three?"

My somewhat shattered visitor asked if it was a country custom to choose the amount of mail one wanted and commented that it must be highly irregular to carry greengrocery around in an official mail van.

"Ah," said Perce, picking up a bunch of shallots. "Things is different here to what they be in town. I carry such as these, so that if I get hi-jacked I can stuff these onions up the bandit's nose. Powerful things, onions. Better than tear gas, onions are."

By comparison to the Post Office services our village has known, urban communications seem very tame indeed.

The Saga of Florrie Ford

To the true countryman, the land is a living thing to be respected and farmed as if one expected to live for ever. This was the doctrine Harry preached and one that I understood before I was taught to read or write.

School was just for 'book-learning'. Real education came from tending the living land.

Since the basis of good cultivation stems from the ability to use a plough, Harry deemed it necessary to train me in that art. I sat on an upturned bushel basket in the draughty cart-shed, using bath-brick to remove the rust from the brist-board of a plough.

"Keep on polishing, boy, and keep 'un greased and shone."

That this 'boy' was in fact a spindle-shanked, skinny-ribbed

girl with plaits made not the slightest difference, I was there
to watch an expert 'set' a plough.

Wielding a huge spanner to adjust the coulter that cuts
through the soil vertically and the share that slices horizon-
tally beneath the surface of the soil, I tried to get them
properly spaced and lined up with the beam or frame of the
plough.

If I had got it right, the furrow would be neither too shallow
nor too wide. The brist or mould-board I had polished was
fixed to the wide end of the plough share and curved out along
the length of the beam, thus forcing the soil to turn over as
the share cut through it.

It took a few grazed knuckles before I got it right.

When the days of chill depression came and Harry, sick in
health and bank-balance, was struggling to keep faith with
his beloved land it was time to put that training to the test.

Marking out a field had appeared to be easy until I tried.
'Set the furricker a good rod wide' – a furricker or headland
being the space left for the horses to turn at either end of the
field. I remembered that one rod, pole, or perch, equalled
five of Harry's strides; seven of mine still left the horses with
their noses through the hedge. My mark-line looked as if we
had traced an outline of the inlets on some craggy island
coast.

The test of a good ploughman 'opening up' a field is in
getting the first furrow arrow-straight. The time-honoured
way to do this is by tying paper to a thatching rod and standing it high in the hedge at the opposite end of the field. This
acts as a guide, sightlined between the ears of the nearside
horse all the way down the field.

If the plough is set correctly, with the horses pulling together and in step, if one can keep the reins taut and still
grasp the handles to steer the plough over stony ground, the
furrow will be straight. I knew all that but wished that I could

explain the procedure to each uninterested horse. My permanently waved ploughed field became a local talking point all winter long.

I ploughed three fields that winter and the old men who congregated to put the world to rights in the blacksmith's forge agreed that if the first two had furrows as crooked as the hind leg of a knock-kneed mare, the third field was a 'fair old job'.

They advocated a continuous diet of 'beef pudden' to add the weight and stamina I lacked. At least the ploughing was finished before the back end of the year.

There is a country belief that to have the plough in the barn and the brist-board in the house on Christmas morning guarantees good crops at the following harvest. This is superstition based on fact. Frost makes ploughed earth friable and easier to work and the worst of the wintry weather comes in the New Year.

Harry mistrusted handling more horse power than he could stop with a sharp tug on the reins but reluctantly decided at last that he would have to go 'mechanised'.

The second-hand tractor salesman gave a demonstration drive round the stackyard, gave a brief discourse on the art of tractor driving, collected his money and left. The vibrating monster blew monoxide smoke rings from the upright exhaust as Harry climbed aboard.

With the full weight of his boot on the clutch, he ground the lever around the groaning gearbox until it obviously engaged, opened up the hand-throttle, lifted his boot and gazed steadfastly ahead. The tractor gathered speed – backward.

"Whoa there, whoa," he bellowed, tugging at the steering wheel as though reining in a headstrong horse. The tractor at full throttle reversed toward, then through, the splintering weatherboarded side of the barn. The revving engine spluttered, coughed and died.

The stalled silence was coloured by a repertoire of oaths as

Harry invoked great balls of fire to descend upon his head if he should ever listen to a smooth-talking salesman or a horse-shy girl again.

He stumped off to the stable to regain his dignity and re-move the spliters from his seat. He never attempted to drive again.

I couldn't leave the tractor snuggled up to the dribbling corn sacks, it looked all wrong.

The engine started reluctantly, and I found one of the three forward gears. I drove slowly through the barn doorway and, gathering speed and courage, did a lap of honour round the stack-yard, by which time I had been selected to be tractor driver to 'Florrie Ford'.

Life with Florrie Ford was never dull. She detested cold mornings and many a chivalrous male retired hurt, convinced that Florrie's starting handle had ruined his manhood and fractured his wrist for good measure. The answer to her sulk-ing was to surprise her with some bicep-building swings, sprint round the mudguards of her iron-cleated wheels and waggle every control that moved.

With a following wind and a downhill run Florrie could notch up a good 10 m.p.h. in top gear.

With a 28lb. weight lashed under the seat to prevent me being tossed around like a bean in a bucket, ploughing, har-rowing and cutting corn became easier thanks to Florrie Ford. We tackled land reclamation, tearing up twenty acres of sour pasture, the subsidy for which was four times the money Flor-rie had cost.

Any hesitation or misfiring responded to a thump on her fuel tank and I kept her going with cart-grease, wire and bin-der twine. This earned me the reputation of being mechanically minded.

Florrie chugged along for several years but one day she started to make internal rumblings going down a steep in-cline. The rumblings became a grinding clunk, Florrie stopped suddenly but the heavy load of feeding stuff hitched on behind did not.

I took a worm's eye view of a nettle bed and emerged to see Florrie on her side and definitely dead.

"Scrap iron. To think I wasted ten good pounds buying that old thing." Harry stared at the wrecked tractor in disgust and marched off to hitch his beloved horses to the plough.

Jim

A skein of plovers flying west were strung out like a black necklace across the sunset sky. From the saltings a curlew cried like a lost soul.

Out in the estuary a ship's siren wailed in melancholy unison and as the cold east wind rustled the rushes along the dykes, the familiar marsh became a desolate, God-forsaken, frightening place.

Following the rutted tyre marks of the lorry I hurried back toward the farm and slammed the marsh gate shut behind me.

Dad was walking dejectedly across the yard and as I caught up with him the floodgates of misery that had held fast all that dreadful afternoon suddenly gave way. Jim had been part of my life, all my life; now Jim was dead.

Both our mothers had been surprised to have us. Mum had given the iron rocking cot to the gipsies the year before I arrived, and on the day she brought me home from the hospital Dad found the old half-blind mare in the process of giving birth to Jim, a beautiful chestnut foal. So there we were, two unexpected offspring of ageing mothers.

Being an afterthought, I was often left to my own devices and long before either of us could see over, instead of through, the paddock gate Jim was my pet and playmate.

Even when he was old enough to work the fine young chestnut horse still had the ridiculous habit of sagging his forelegs, drooping his head over my shoulder and rubbing his neck along the side of my head.

He greeted the quietest of my three brothers in this way too but to strangers Jim would react like a devil horse, ears flat, tail swishing and back hooves flying.

Soon after I started school I was dared to call Jim from the playground and he jumped three hedges and the school fence to reach me, but the moment of glory was short-lived.

The bell that sent the children scuttling into lines brought the schoolmaster into the playground. I tried to pretend that the slobbering horse, his head resting on my shoulder, was a figment of the teacher's imagination.

The marks that his steel ruler made on my legs were proof that I failed. It was a very subdued child who led Jim back to the pasture by the forelock of his mane.

Dad realised that in Jim he had a possible prize winner for the local horse show. Harry Applethorn the wagoner decided that a horse pill would improve Jim's chances.

Administering a horse pill is a simple operation until you try to do it! Theoretically nothing could be easier than inserting a bullet-shaped pill into a hollow tube, placing one end of the tube at the back of the horse's throat, then blowing down the tube so that the pill shoots down the horse's neck.

Harry, a short man with legs so bandy he couldn't stop a pig in a passage, stood on a corn bin to administer the pill while Dad led the submissive horse into position to receive it.

Harry blew and Jim coughed simultaneously. There was a look of startled dismay on Harry's face; he gulped and after a burp that would keep a baby wind-free for months, Harry said that he had swallowed the pill.

He always reckoned afterwards that it cured his rheumatics.

It takes more preparation to get a horse ready for showing than it does to get a bride dressed up for her wedding. Jim was groomed for hours, his mane and tail braided with red, white and blue ribbons.

As he paraded around the show ring, high stepping his polished, dancing hooves, the chestnut horse was the most beautiful thing in my world.

When the judges held their final scrutiny Jim was among the final entries. Unable to contain my excitement, I ducked under the ropes at the edge of the ring and Jim was so pleased to see me that he sagged his head on to my shoulder.

I was hauled back by the seat of my cotton knickers, something snapped and I had to sit still after that! As if to demonstrate that he was fed up with being a fiery steed, Jim stood with his head down between his front hooves, looking more like a broken down clothes horse than a cup winner, which resulted in his gaining a 'highly commended' rosette instead of the coveted cup.

My brother used some binder twine to mend my drooping drawers and neither Jim nor myself were anybody's favourites on the way home.

On the day that Harry Applethorn passed out with pleurisy while driving to market, Jim had somehow known that he must turn the cart and bring him home.

We heard him coming up the slope at full trot until he stopped abruptly beside the garden fence, stamping and rattling his breastgirth impatiently.

No one called Jim 'that fool horse' after that.

When war came, Jim and I, now in our twenties, were still together. During that summer, when our quiet country skies became a battlefield, we gathered in the harvest as the gallant few fought overhead.

One morning, when the vapour trails scrawled death across the clear blue canvas of the sky, Jim decided he was going back to the barn although we had scarcely started to load the wagon.

Nothing would calm him and we went back to the stock-yard with half a load.

An airbattle broke overhead and, as we watched, a bomber broke formation and hurtled, screaming, earthwards. As it reached the ground it disintegrated and the harvest field was littered with burning debris and exploding ammunition.

Young soldiers with old men's faces and eyes that mirrored the hell of Dunkirk helped us in the harvest season and, in our unchanging country ways, found healing respite before they faced the futility of war again.

Apart from that we relied on casual workers from the labour exchange and it was one of these who ended Jim's working days.

When men are afraid they arm themselves with weapons. This half-wit was scared of the playful, teasing horse and cut himself a long hazel switch.

Jim, who had never known cruelty, went berserk as the moronic fool lashed out at him with the hazel whip. Both horse and cart rolled over a steep bank. Jim never galloped again.

His weakened back made him walk like a tired old man and he spent the rest of his days grazing in the pasture on the edge of the marsh, coming in to his warm stall at night.

The unchanging pattern of seedtime and harvest went on despite the army lorries beneath the camouflage nets under the elm trees, the soldiers who were billeted in outhouses and an army workshop in the barn.

Frightfully efficient officers would gaze across the marsh, mutter about defence and security and more barbed wire and iron spikes would appear along the sea wall between the saltings and the marsh.

We often had to round up straying sheep and cattle because the soldiers had no time to worry about closing the marsh gates.

Complaining seemed futile – until one October afternoon.

A cold easterly gale made the elm trees creak and sigh so I went out to call Jim back to the warmth of the stable. The pasture was empty and the marsh gate swinging in the wind.

Impatient at the extra work and chilled by the biting wind, I hurried across the marsh but there was no sign of the old horse.

"Jim," I called, my voice doing battle with the whining, wailing wind. Knowing that he would come if he heard me, I ran along the dyke calling, calling. I found him in the sedge of the reed-filled ditch.

Black, stinking mud plastered his chestnut coat as he writhed in a devil's skein of barbed wire. Several coils of the dreadful stuff were scattered around.

Two small clips held each concertina-wound, tight-sprung, snaking coil and Jim must have sprung one with his hooves.

I took one look at the terrified struggling horse and ran, devil driven, to get help. With every breath tearing at the lining of my lungs I started the tractor, while Dad got ropes and pliers.

As we passed the soldiers we asked their help with wire cutters and sped on, every nut and bolt of the old tractor rattling in protest as it was driven full throttle over the bumpy marsh.

The next half-hour was an unending nightmare as we struggled with the wire and pulled Jim from the morass and all the time his eyes followed me, imploring help.

We stood covered with filthy slime, hands and clothes torn, our own blood mingling with Jim's, and a sergeant who had left Europe by way of Dunkirk went into the reeds and was violently sick.

Dad went off to do the only thing we could to help the old horse now while I knelt beside the panting animal, stroking his torn neck and talking to him until gradually he quietened.

He tried to lift his head and instinctively I knew what he wanted me to do. It seemed an eternity before I heard the slaughterer's lorry coming across the marsh but, cramped, cold and stunned, I still managed to hold Jim's head on my shoulder.

As the lorry came close Jim moved his head and tried to rub his neck against me as he had always done, but suddenly it became too heavy to hold.

I let his head slip gently to the ground.

The horse slaughterer didn't need to use the humane killer he was carrying.

The soldiers cleared up the wire and the lorry went off with its pathetic cargo.

"It's just a casualty of war," said the sergeant. I felt a desperate need to be alone and volunteered to walk back and close the gates.

A skein of plovers were strung out like a black necklace across the sunset sky. From the saltings a curlew cried like a lost, tormented soul and from the estuary a ship's siren called in dismal unison. The once-loved marsh became an eerie, hateful place.

Following the rutted tyre marks of the lorry I ran towards the farm and slammed the marsh gate shut behind me.

The Hut

The village Cultural and Recreational Memorial Hall sounds somewhat impressive considering that it was an ex-Army workshop, bought cheap on site at the end of World War 1.

We called it The Hut and, despite constant patching and shoring-up, it was reaching the limit of durability.

The moment of truth came during the Harvest Home Supper, when a section of the plaster-board ceiling parted company with the rafters.

Having graciously received the traditional bouquet, our distinguished guest of honour collected ceiling-white and dust in her freshly set blue rinse as the remnants of a starling's nest made splash-down in her soup.

Tom Grommet slipped home to collect a hammer and nails while we all moved along a place, just like the Mad Hatter's tea party.

Everyone tried to laugh off the episode as jolly rollicking fun, but it was plain that the evening had lost its magic for our guest. She discarded the notes of her after-dinner speech, tersely suggsted that we start a rebuilding fund and left before Will could begin his annual rendition of '*Buttercup Joe*'.

There is a mountain of money between recognising the need for a new village hall and being able to build one. Like seed sown on stony ground, the crop of cash or fund-raising schemes was pretty sparse.

Earlier generations had managed to transform an Army hut into a village hall and, seeking inspiration from their example, we looked back through The Hut committee books.

The grand inaugural happening was a church social and the minutes of the very first meeting record the vicar's disapproval of the purchase of French chalk for making dancing possible on the unpolished surface of the floor.

Still stored in the ladies' cloakroom, behind a box marked Coronation Bunting 1937, is a framed notice forbidding any gentleman to swing or lift his dancing partner off the floor, or dance in so close proximity as to be unseemly.

For a 'Cultural' hall, edifying activities appear to have been spread thinly down the years. A neighbouring curate and his wife gave occasional piano and cello recitals, labouring valiantly with an out of tune piano and a cello that was never quite on key.

It takes a powerful imagination to envisage farm-hands flocking from the fields to sing along in 'An Evening Of Toccatas And Fugues'. Give or take a few, the duo seems to have had a faithful following of eight.

Their performance of *Air On A G String* had more response but I am given to understand that, thanks to the New American movies, the audience was mostly adolescent youth under some delusion as to what a G string really meant.

Fan's Failings: A Morality Play must have been a mind-bending cultural experience. One uncensorable scene called for the villain to catch Fan in the kitchen, compromised by the absence of her blouse. Rather than risk inflaming the male populace the modest Fan demanded that she be allowed to wear her camisole above instead of underneath her petticoat and vest.

This was pretty racy stuff according to local standards but Fan displayed her naked forearms in the cause of culture and it is not on record that any of the audience went berserk.

Against the vicar's dissenting vote, The Hut became a gambling hell of cribbage drives and whist on every second and fourth Wednesday of the month.

The hand-printed posters advertising any village festivity always carried the proviso, 'If wet, in The Hut' and the records show that despite the belief that the sun shines on the righteous the vicarage fete seemed singularly unfortunate in its choice of weather through the years.

I am left-handed, with a tendency to take off in the opposite direction when asked to turn to the left or right, a failing later responsible for getting a driving test examiner disorientated and lost on his own testing route.

At the fete in question I was detailed for the school maypole dancing team. Dressed all in white, with paper flowers in my hair and clutching my coloured streamer as if it were the bearing rein of a wayward horse, I clumped through *Gathering Peascods*, remembering my strict instructions to 'follow the girl in front'. Halfway through *Ruffti-Tuffti*, chaos! I lost track of my pathfinder and found that I was travelling in the opposite direction to all the rest.

Pressing on regardless, my maypole ribbon became a trip-wire, leaving the other dancers lying around in heaps with the ribbons just a multi-coloured knot.

It took a king-sized pair of scissors to sort out the muddle and believe me, one has never plumbed the depths of humiliation until one has had one's paypole streamer publicly pruned.

There were village concerts every year, but none was more ambitious than the 'Welcome Home' effort at the end of the last war. The entire village seemed to be involved. No opportunity for rehearsal was lost.

The blacksmith's wife became the Spirit of Freedom and Light and her part in the grand finale should have been sheer show-stopping spectacle.

She stood on a cider barrel centre stage, supporting her banner of freedom and brandishing her flame of light. Actual flames being somewhat risky in a wooden building with a pitched felt roof, the torch effect was achieved by disguising a battery-lit cycle lamp in silver paper hung around with the anti-radar metal foil strips that wartime aircraft used to drop.

Unfortunately the initial impact of this scene was lost.

Where curtain up should have revealed a darkened stage lit only by the Flame of Light illuminating the Banner of Freedom, a glow-worm of light from a flat battery shone on to the face of the blacksmith's wife as she appealed to any cycle-riding, public spirited member of the audience to let her borrow a front lamp.

Mis-cued, unheralded and unlit, the flag-bearing cast representing 'Our Gallant Allies' stumbled across the stage.

There were minor skirmishes and chaos reigned supreme. It was a howling success and there has been nothing to match it ever since.

Nowadays fund-raising village concerts are just not on.

Television-satiated as we are, no one turns out on a wet wintry night to hear *On The Road To Mandalay* sung in a voice that developed a flat tyre just north of Chittagong.

Our Tramps Supper seemed a social success and looked to be a financial winner until, comparing notes while washing up, we realised that the gentleman so scruffily disguised was no one's invited guest but the genuine article, contributing only his 'livestock' in exchange for a slap-up meal and the secretary's purse.

Simple, memorable occasions have made The Hut part of the fabric of our lives. Wedding receptions, harvest suppers, parties, all have been entered in the old ledger that opens with the account of the acquisition of one ex-Army hut and a plot of adjoining waste land.

The market value of this waste land has now made it possible to plan the new village hall, a real and much needed asset to the community. No one bothered about acoustics or amenities in The Hut, yet past laughter and happiness must have soaked into every wood-worm-riddled board. To watch it being dismantled will be like tearing up a favourite comfortable coat.

Sam Lamb

Regularly during the winter a flock of mallard flew across the valley to their distant feeding grounds out on the mud-flats of the estuary.

On the dreary days when mist has clung clammy and damp as a wet sheep's fleece we still heard a stirring of wings and conversational quacking as the mallard passed overhead at daybreak and each afternoon.

One day their routine was altered. As they passed, the leading drake broke formation, wheeled and glided down to settle on Church Field pond. He spread his wings, duck-dancing across the surface to display the irridescence of his plumage. His companions, confused and calling, circled in disorder, separated, then flew on.

One drab female turned back, losing height, then flew down beside him, fluttering her wings in courtship as she joined her new-found partner in a cacophonous duck duet.

Moorhens foraging in the rough grass of Church Field went scurrying back towards the pond, ludicrous comedians in green and yellow tights and flippered feet, their heads all jerking forward with each exaggerated comic step.

There was a lot of disyllabic croaking and quarrelling before the waterfowl conceded that the mallard had established squatters' rights on Church Field pond and they must exist together in a state of cautious neutrality.

It happens every year.

Even the gregarious rooks sensed that there was an indefinable difference in the day. Since early morning the colony had been noisily arguing in the elm boughs or disengaging from aerial combat to fly down and strut menacingly towards another rival, ignored completely by the placid grazing sheep.

A few amiable birds were already inspecting last year's nests, refurbishing with neighbours' twigs, indignantly protesting if another pair attempted to raid their own.

Dutch elm disease had reduced the trees in the rookery and the siting of new nests would give some indication as to the weather ahead, according to the old country lore, 'Rooks build high: calm, fair and dry; rooks build low: cold, wet and blow.'

There was a new warmth on the wind, the sun was out and the land stirred from cold winter's sleep. Birds sought their mates and from this day shepherds knew that they must watch their ewes, no matter when lambing was due to start.

My prosaic Mum had a name for this one day. She called it 'Bedspread Washday', symbolising her salute to spring.

This was no ordinary laundering Monday, formidable as they were with the basic preparation for washday being to first cut up a tree, light the copper fire and pump water from the well.

There was a copper on each side of the open fireplace in the farmhouse scullery.

In earlier times the larger copper had been used for beer brewing and scalding fresh-killed pork. The smaller had the mundane purpose of providing bath water and coping with the weekly wash. On Mum's Bedspread Washday both coppers were stoked and filled.

Bedspread Washday was a devil's sabbath with every currant bush sprouting cushion covers and fringed plush tablecloths. Between the line-posts honeycombed counterpanes and patchwork quilts billowed in the breeze and on impromptu clothes lines between two plum trees mattress tickings and unwieldy chair covers flapped water on the unwary walking up the garden path.

Indoors, the witches' cauldron coppers produced a soap and soda fog, from which emerged my Bedspread Washday Mum. Not her usual easy-going self, but a Mum all shiny faced with the bun of her hair askew and each wisp lank with dewdroplets of steam.

A 'chop-more-firewood', 'turn-the-mangle', 'pump-more-water' Mum, quick to anger, hard to please.

Bedspread Washday dinner, 'bubble and squeak', impregnated with the taste of primrose soap. No pud. No tablecloth. A meal served on the still damp whitewood kitchen table, copper-water scrubbed. One learned to eat up and go.

Dad was always sure to need a hand with thatching the hurdle gates to make lambing-pens, or one could volunteer to go around the sheep and check that no in-lamb ewes had rolled over on to their backs, something that happens to pregnant ewes. Their struggling to regain their feet can exhaust them and cause death.

It was on such a Bedspread Washday that I found Sam.

A sheep will usually clean its new-born lamb until it bleats and struggles to its feet and if the lamb does not respond the mother's distress is very real. When I found Sam his mother was grazing disinterestedly some way away.

At first I thought that I had found a premature still-born lamb but as I picked up the minute cold body I felt a butterfly fluttering heartbeat. Holding him in one hand and pressing his ribcage with the other started respiration.

Sam gave a feeble bleat.

Cade, or hand-reared lambs, were nothing new, as there were one or two weaklings or orphans every year, but Sam was the smallest lamb I had ever seen. I popped him into my woollen mitten, tucked him down inside my coat and hurried home.

The kitchen fireplace was barricaded by two huge old-fashioned clothes-horses draped with airing bedcovers.

Wrapped in an old flannel nightie in a shoe box on the hooked rag hearthrug, Sam might well have been in a purpose-built incubator.

By evening he had acquired a taste for milk laced with brandy but the problem now was how to keep him warm all night. There can't be many lambs that are carried upstairs wrapped in a flannel nightie, wearing a tea-towel nappy and improvised sponge-bag waterproof pants. I kept him warm that night. By morning Sam was trying to balance himself on weak and wobbly legs.

From that point life revolved around Sam's frequent feeding times. He followed me everywhere and tried to converse in grunts and bleats. Being adopted by a lamb small enough to wriggle through a sheep-proof fence means waiting at the village bus stop, all dressed up to go to town with the blacksmith's son and seeing Sam trit-trotting down the lane, pitifully bleating 'Maa'.

The bus conductor was perplexed. Fare scales for dogs he understood, but passenger lambs were not catered for on the company schedule. Consulting the driver, he decided that Sam would travel free. If the bus inspector came aboard I might try to disguise Sam as a pair of sheep-skin gloves.

The bus crews had changed shift for the return journey and the new conductor had a disagreeable face. Sam travelled home in a twopenny carrier bag from the fish and chip shop, while a friendly fellow passenger sat with 'Two of cod and six of chips' newspaper-wrapped on her lap.

Sam never grew large enough to contemplae his being sent to market and we would never let him run the risk of being eaten with mint sauce, but he had his uses. Turned out among a flock of sheep, he would come running when I called.

The others would always follow him and, like the eastern shepherds, we could lead our sheep instead of driving them along, thanks to Sam Lamb.

At the Sign of The Star

Mid-December brought a howling north-east gale that roared across the valley, flinging the full force of its fury against the farm.

For days it raged, then swung round to become a whining easterly wind that penetrated every crevice of the house and sent one two-coat-clad to work about the farm.

At night the new moon rose blood red and tilted on its back, a sure sign that we should shovel snow before it waned.

By now the cattle had been brought down off the hills to shelter in the warmth of the enclosed yard. The Hereford bullocks, like a group of disapproving aunts glaring at a precocious child, disdainfully twitched steaming nostrils as the half-grown collie pup chased imaginery rats from the straw

I scattered in the yard. Soon they were hock deep and the pup floundered in litter that was deep enough to last two days.

Tomorrow would be Christmas Day, yet in the isolation of the farm, with no sound but the cattle chewing the cud and a flight of starlings chattering their way to roost in the high holly hedge, it seemed like any other working day. I thought of town-bred girls and momentarily envied them their brightly-decorated, bustling shops, their office parties and the centrally heated warmth. They never went to work wrapped like lumbering Eskimos, yet I would never really want to leave the farm and have my parents struggle on alone.

A sound to conjure up high summer cut across my thoughts above the starlings' din and the flapping of the galvanised sheet that had come adrift from the wind-wrecked hen house.

I heard the sound again. The pup heard it too and raced along the farm track to the lane but soon returned, his tail between his legs. Snapping at his heels was a narrow-gutted whippet, thin enough to show each rib beneath his sandy skin.

A combination of ungreased axles, roughshod hooves, clanking buckets and drag chains makes a gipsy caravan sound unmistakeable in some undefinable way. A sound that goes with warm haymaking days and harvest time, for in my world gipsies appeared in early summer and vanished when harvest ended.

To see one in the lane on Christmas Eve was very odd indeed.

It turned into our gate, a dilapidated canvas-hooded cart pulled by a shaggy, thickset cob. A tall young gipsy wearing a week's growth of beard and a baggy old army greatcoat tied round with binder twine led the tired horse. I went to meet him.

"The guv'nor about?" he asked. Dad, seeing our visitor, had hurried back from the kale field.

"You can't stop here!" he said, before the gipsy even asked.

The young man wanted to pull his wagon to the leeward side of the holly hedge, promising that he would move on at dawn, but Dad was adamant.

"I don't doubt that you will be gone, along with all the fowls!"

The Gipsy flushed. "I'm no Dideki, moosh! Joe Kemp gives you his word! I saw old Uncle Manny's sign beside your gate and thought you would let me unhitch here tonight. Old Manny once sold you a horse."

Dad remembered the patriarchal old Romany, whose family group had worked the fields some seven years before and asked if he were still alive. The gipsy smiled.

"Oh, Dordi. I'm heading for his winter camp before the weather breaks. He's got a warm new wagon waiting for me there. Go on 'chavi', let me stay tonight, the old girl's back is hurting her something cruel and the nag is walking on its knees."

Mum came into the yard and Joe explained that he had been picking sprouts to earn enough money to buy the new wagon, but his woman wasn't well so he had headed back east to rejoin his tribe.

Joe's 'old girl' had remained inside the cart but now the flap was pulled aside and we saw the anxious face of a girl no older than myself. Mum looked at her then whispered to Dad who shrugged his shoulders in resignation. Tiny Mum was taking charge! She spoke gently to the girl, climbed the three-rung ladder into the cart, then emerged again.

"The poor thing's miserably cold and in considerable pain."

Addressing Joe from the height of his third rib she added, "Young man, you will have to travel fast to get to winter camp before the baby arrives!"

Because the frozen canvas cover was as draughtproof as a moth-eaten sack, Dad allowed Joe to pull the van into the open-fronted cart shed, its tin stovepipe chimney protruding at the back. We went back to finishing our tasks, keeping a watchful eye on the 'Gippos' as we worked.

The smell of the soup Mum carried across the yard in a big blue jug made me feel glad to get in for my tea in the cosy kitchen and our visitors in the cart shed receded from our thoughts as Christmas Eve preparations progressed.

We were reminded of their presence by a hammering on the door.

Mum and Dad rushed out thinking that the car shed was going up in smoke, but an agitated Joe said,

"My old girl is taken bad. You've got a kind face lady. For God's sake come and help."

The girl crouched beside a biscuit-tin sized stove, her eyes having the same terrified expression as a wild animal in a trap. Mum got her to the bunk-like bed, its linen remarkably clean and white.

We had no phone, the district nurse was miles away and it was obvious that the baby was impatient to be born. Mum suggested taking the girl into the house, but both husband and wife were determined that their true-bred Romany son was not to be born under a 'gorgio's' roof. However they agreed that no newborn babe could survive in ten degrees of frost and compromised by accepting the use of the lambing shed, an outhouse with an open fireplace that had saved the lives of countless new-born orphan lambs, and Joe went off to light the fire.

The baby settled the question by arriving with an almightly yell which brought Joe running back across the yard.

"Dordi, moosh! I've got a son. I'll call him Manny, since old Manny's sign guided me here."

Midnight saw us cutting up Mum's flannel petticoats to clothe the newborn child and mother and babe were settled for the night. We saw a shooting star as we crossed the yard to go indoors; a sign, Mum said, of a newborn babe.

Joe bought the ruined hen house and our Christmas Day was punctuated by the sound of hammering in the cart shed. By Boxing Night the cart had taken on a most peculiar shape, for Joe had completely covered the canvas hood with tin, making it weatherproof and relatively free from draughts.

The ice was melting in the cattle troughs next day and high banked snowclouds were building in the sky when Joe hitched up the horse and backed the cart up to the lambing shed door.

With his wife wrapped up in one of Mum's goose feather quilts and the baby snug in his orange box crib, Joe was ready to move off.

"We're 'Kushti' now, Guv, thank you kindly." He took Dad's right hand and clapped it to his own, a Romany gesture of good faith. Turning his head he called, "You right there, Mary girl?" and the reply was lost in the noise of the rattling cart.

Dad and I followed them along the farm track to the gate.

"I wonder what old Emmanuel Kemp will think of his namesake," Dad reflected, but something strange had clicked in my mind.

"Dad, Joe called his wife Mary, the baby's name is Emmanuel and he was born among the cattle at Christmas."

Dad saw my line of thought. "Look love, it's coincidence. Joseph Kemp is a Romany, his wife an ordinary girl and they only stopped here because of a gipsy mark somewhere beside our gate."

The thoughts of this kind of bush telegraph intrigued me and as the wagon rolled down the lane and out of sight I searched round for the sign.

Some minutes later, on the smooth bark of the beech tree by the gate, I found the symbol Old Manny cut some seven years before. It was carved in the shape of a Star of Bethlehem.

The Luck of the Bees

Busy as a scuttling field mouse, Madge was gathering dandelions along the old wood road.

"Late they are this year," she said, her scrabbling fingers furiously decapitating flower heads.

"Dandelions should be fit to pick for making wine on St. George's Day."

Eyes that do not really notice what they see could dismiss as weeds the plants that Madge turns into wines, lotions and healing balms. She seems to know the name and location of every wild flower growing along the isolated paths she wandered as a child. Madge's father had been a drover.

These men would, single handed, undertake to drive flocks of sheep or herds of cattle over long distances between the upland pastures or farms and the cattle fairs, stock sales, and markets that were held throughout the year.

Motherless, Madge had accompanied her father along most of the old droving tracks that criss-cross the southern part of the country, walking all the way.

In a childhood not over-blessed with soft living, Madge's first memories are of being buffeted by scampering sheep the same height as herself and sleeping under a tarpaulin shelter, snuggled up against a tick-scratching collie dog in an effort to keep warm.

With the onset of winter Madge would be boarded out while her father lodged at a men's hostel near the city market, undertaking short journey work.

Sometimes pity would stir a kind-hearted country woman to offer shelter to the waif Madge must have been, but all too frequently it was a strictly commercial transaction.

Ask Madge her age and all that she can verify is that she is as old as her tongue and a little older than her teeth. She thinks that she must have been about nine during the winter that she ran away.

"Dad and I had walked a flock of sheep to Stow Fair in Gloucestershire that autumn," Madge recalls.

But their stay in the town was only short, for her father had the prospect of taking an enormous flock seventy miles across country and wanted to get started before some other drover undercut his price.

"It began to rain in torrents as we left the village of Stow and somehow I just knew that the coming winter would be bad." It was.

The journey over the Cotswolds, bleak with gale-driven rain, was a nightmare. Sheep, lame with footrot, held up their progress and the father, frantic to reach their destination, knew he would never get there hampered by an exhausted child.

Had circumstances been better, Madge is convinced that he would never have left her with the 'minder' as he did.

As soon as the money for her keep and winter clothes had changed hands and her father had gone on his way there was no pretence that she would be treated as one of the family, 'the family' being a hard-faced woman and two loutish sons.

Their treatment of her was so bad that Madge knew that to survive she must try to find her father.

These then were the circumstances that half a century ago sent Madge, sick, sore and starving, past the cottage on the edge of Penny-pot Wood.

A rat trap seems a singularly unlikely instrument of destiny, but the occupants of Penny-pot Cottage, troubled by rats in the hen house, had set one beneath some brushwood by the hedge.

Madge, passing, saw the hard cheese bait and in trying to spring the trap caught her foot in the steel teeth.

Gentle hands released her and carried her into Penny-pot Cottage, a new life and a new home.

Madge still recalls the heaven of lying on a worn leather sofa with both feet wrapped in warm poulticed linen, drinking warm milk and eating crusty bread thick with butter and honey.

By the next morning when she woke it was settled that she should stay with Aunty Beech, as she was told to call her new-found guardian, until her father came for her.

But first they would have to tell the bees.

Young as she was, Madge had encountered madness on her travels. Was this bee nonsense the worm in the apple of her new paradise? Aunty Beech led her around to the back of the house and addressed the roof.

"This is Madge. With your approval she has come to stay."

Madge was shown the room where she would stay, providing that she kept herself scrupulously clean and did nothing to offend the bees. It had a sloping ceiling, marred near the dormer window by a moist golden brown stain which oozed a sticky substance that occasionally dripped down into a large white jug.

There had been a swarm of bees in the cottage roof for time out of mind and in all probability the penny pots of honey sold at the cottage door gave name to the house, the woodland and the lane.

They certainly provided Aunty Beech with the basis of her livelihood and like a magnet drew generations of children to spend their precious halfpennies and farthings at the cottage in Penny-pot Lane.

By the time I was old enough to realise that Penny-pot ginger-beer and home-made sweets were an economical proposition Madge was grown up and Miss Beech an old lady who spent most of her days watching the bees at work.

In May and June she kept a bunch of keys handy in case the bees should swarm.

Claiming the ancient law of right of way to pursue her swarming bees, she once entered the Manor House.

She marched straight through the front entrance and out of the back door, clashing the keys on the frying pan as she ran. When they settled she collected them and took them home in her straw hat.

It was worth the long walk to Penny-pot Cottage to buy nutty toffee and ginger beer made in stone bottles with corks that came out with a champagne pop, half-penny a foaming glass. My mind's tongue tastes it now.

Miss Beech maintained that bees could foretell bad weather and bad news. They were in a state of turmoil on the day she died but, remembering instructions, Madge told them of her passing and begged them to stay under her protection and not take their luck away.

Health regulations forbid the continuation of the sweet-shop in Penny-pot Cottage parlour but Madge still sells honey and uses her knowledge of herbs and the places where they grow.

You might see her driving her old car to the herbalist store in the town, or out along some lonely country drove.

Hillside tracks where no bracken grows, overgrown lanes, pilgrims paths, Roman roads, routes marked only by dotted lines on maps: the old drover's routes still exist, the places where a drover's half-starved daughter and a tick-infested collie once walked.

A Dog Called Moses

Yard dogs were frequently unhappy, neglected creatures. More than a few outlying farms had a wretched collie tethered to a draughty barrel for a kennel, dragging out its existence on a length of rusting chain.

Kept to deter prowling foxes or warn off unwelcome strangers, they deteriorated into whimpering apathetic curs or became ferocious hysterical manhaters. If one broke free it invariably ran berserk, attacking cattle, sheep and fowls and had to be destroyed.

Working dogs fared somewhat better. Only a minority of shepherds believed that a hungry dog, trained to fear its master, would round up sheep more efficiently than a well-fed pet. Most shepherds took pride in the breeding, physical condition and prowess of their dogs, yet one of the greatest canine characters I ever encountered would have been laughed out of the arena at any sheepdog trials.

His name was Moses. Hugh found him in the rushes by the road up on High Common, a windswept wilderness of wheeling lapwings, stunted gorse and Hugh's summer-grazing sheep. A small-built man of interminable energy, Hugh tried to make a living from hill farming the upland pastures of High Common and his twenty-acre hired holding down below the hill.

His wife, having to make every copper count, begrudged the cost of feeding a pup too amiable in disposition for a yard-dog and certainly not bred to work with sheep.

There was much speculation about the background of a pup which had inherited the characteristic drooping ears and large paws of a spaniel, the bone formation and facial expression of a labrador, a rag-bag mixture of grey, black and brown curled coat and no tail to wag at all.

But Moses stayed, growing rapidly and developing an almost telepathic understanding of his master. Soon after he arrived Mrs. Hugh caught Moses trying out his bark for size, then watching the reactions of her flustered hens.

She made a ruff of quill feathers, a country cure for chicken chasers, threatening to tie it around his neck and leave it there until it dropped off.

Moses took the hint and ignored the chickens. Within months Moses needed no more instructions than a conversational "Let's get those darn fool ewes over here then" to send him off to round up the flock. He had become a lolloping knock-about clown of a dog, liable to catch his long flapping ears under his front paws and turn somersaults when the ground was rough.

Hugh drove a battered hard-topped jeep purchased, so rumour had it, in a pub at closing time in 1945. The States-bound American sergeant swore that it was definitely war surplus stock since he would not be needing it again but Hugh wasted no time in covering its camouflaged bodywork in the same red oxide that he was using to paint a galvanised tin roof.

Crouched low over the steering wheel with Moses at his side Hugh in his old jeep became part of the local scene and more than one person had reason to remember his tendency to cut the engine and coast down hills.

November mist shrouded the hillside as a quaking salesman staggered into the village pub, convinced that he had encountered the occult. He had stopped to clean his windscreen up on High Common and swore that a ghostly army truck driven by a leering dog-faced devil with huge hairy hands had materialised out of the mist, glided noiselessly past and disappeared.

No-one mentioned Hugh's left hand drive jeep or Moses's habit of sitting with his front paws on the dash. The salesman paid for several rounds before his courage returned and he drove away.

Soon after, Hugh and Moses were involved in a much earthier incident. Hugh was not averse to acquiring any sort of fertiliser to improve the productivity of his smallholding and he knew where there was some pig-manure that could almost be termed a liquid asset. Loading an empty 100 gallon tank into the jeep, he drove over to the other side of the common as soon as it was dark.

While Hugh was busy with bucket and shovel a police patrol, pursuing a notorious law-breaker reported to have been sighted in the vicinity, set up a checkpoint on the bridge at the bottom of the hill.

They heard a vehicle cut its engine and come coasting down the lane.

With torches flashing they signalled it to stop. Hugh slammed on the brakes but the lurching sudden halt set up a backwash of pig manure, engulfing Hugh and Moses and settling inches deep over the floor. The policeman on the offside was flattened by a flying muck-covered dog but Hugh, submerged in misery, sat trying to explain. One could smell as well as see Hugh's jeep approaching after that.

In the dusk of an early spring evening Hugh, with Moses at his heels, took a last look around the lambing ewes on the hill. The flock were settling peacefully but Moses, restless, stood trembling and sniffing at the wind, his hackles raised and thunder rumbling in his throat.

Hugh had never seen him so disturbed and wondered what was wrong; then in the dusk he discerned a shape more wolf than dog sidling down towards the flock like some loping beast of prey.

The first disturbed ewe stood nervously stamping and calling to her lamb. The marauding yelping dog broke cover, throwing the lamb high in the air and ripping through the fleece of its mother.

Hugh was not carrying his gun and knew that Moses was no match for the killer dog. He ordered him to stay. For the first time in years Moses disobeyed.

Hugh ran toward the carnage of torn sheep and the furious flailing mass of flying bloodflecked fur that was the fighting dogs.

He eventually drove off the killer, still trailing its broken chain. Moses lay quite still.

With daylight there would be more dead ewes and stillborn lambs. Tomorrow Hugh would find out whose yard-dog was missing and alert his neighbours to hunt for the killer.

Meanwhile it was getting dark and he had a hole to dig.

It's Just Not Cricket

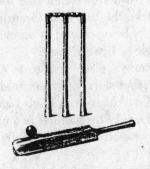

Those misguided enough to have been born over at Lockley Green would have you believe that one could come to our village as a babe in arms, remain here all one's life and still be an old foreigner when one was planted six foot deep. It's what is called living in a close-knit community.

Time was when any local girl caught glancing sideways at a lad from Lockley way ran the risk of feeling the flat side of her father's hand. The rivalry between the two communities has mellowed somewhat since the days when duckpond dunking was an inter-village sport and now we meet for a 'friendly' match at the start of every cricket season.

But make no mistake, there is no idealistic nonsense that it is the game that matters and not the result when our village team plays Lockley Green. It is the score that counts and gamesmanship is such a practised art that one could believe the Ashes were at stake.

As pitches go, Lockley club have every right to feel superior. Their pitch, encircled by majestic horse-chestnut trees, is in the home farm paddock of 'The Park'. Our pitch was quaint rather than picturesque when it was on the village green.

Hardly spacious, cramped perhaps, a straight drive from the snowplough end invariably meant that some unfortunate fielder sent to retrieve the ball from Granny Gammon's garden ran the gauntlet of being chased by an evil tempered old gander and his gaggle of hissing geese.

Now that 'granny's place' has gone and bungalows with huge picture windows skirt the green, tiddly-winks would be a safer game to play. Hugh from High Common Farm volunteered the use of one of his pastures as a pitch and if our team has a secret weapon, psychologically speaking, Banky Meadow is it.

It tends to demoralise visiting teams to find that our cricket pitch is sited halfway up a hill. It has been known for new fixtures, disorientated from driving around the lanes endeavouring to find the field, to draw up at the gate, stare at our sloping pitch in disbelief, then depart before Albert our club hon. sec. can get down to welcome them and undo the wire that ties up the gate.

That wire is a necessity, for the club shares Banky Meadow's fifteen acres with three redundant rams and thirteen inquisitive Hereford heifers. At practices and home matches a group of small boys are bribed to keep them at the far end of the field, but they seem to take an intense interest in the game and frequently outnumber spectators two to one.

Their presence tends to unnerve the fielding opposition, not used to having to watch out where they put their feet.

It makes no difference if the pitch is 'holding moisture' or not. If we win the toss our team bats first, the theory being that the opposition will be so exhausted with all the running up and down hill that their protesting calf muscles will inhibit their ability to score.

There is another advantage in batting early on. By tea-time the sun is behind the bowler's arm from the cattle-shed end and many a Lockley wicket has been lost on this account.

Don't imagine that we have no facilities. We have. Our pavilion is rain-proof if nothing else. It may not be so architecturally pleasing as Lockley's. That was built to commemorate the twenty-first birthday of an Edwardian squire's son, known to earlier generations as 'The Right Horrible Fred'.

Ours was donated by a local supporter who went over from open range chicken farming and wanted his largest henhouse shifted to make space for his battery sheds. It may not have a clock tower as Lockley pavilion does, but you would be surprised what useful lockers nest boxes can make.

Albert Parsley has worked wonders converting the place.

When farm wagons were still being made down at old Humph's yard, Albert was the chap who painted them and did the distinctive decoration with squiggly fine lines. Now he potters, painting everything and anything he can.

Albert was never very popular over Lockley Way, having got a girl from Lockley Bottoms to the altar steps before his commonsense and local pride made him marry a village girl instead. It was a local victory when 'young Albert', as he was then, was commissioned by the squire to repaint the face of Lockley pavilion clock.

Very smart it looked too, but for several undetected years it marked the passage of time with five dividing lines between each roman numeral. No-one noticed.

Albert kept his practical joke against Lockley to himself until, goaded by successive defeats at bowls, cricket and the annual tug-of-war, he taunted the jeering Lockley-ites as being the only village where they worked for seventy-two minutes to the hour by the clock and never knew they were doing so.

Now Albert amuses himself by painting the cricket club score-board in Old English script. He has made a special set of number plates to hang on it when we play Lockley Green. Try reading a cricket score in Roman numerals. Psychological warfare at its worst.

As batsmen, the Chappel family from the dairy have always provided the backbone of our team. With organisation, the problem of their having to nip home at milking time is overcome. Substitutes cover the fielding side and if perchance they stay in while their comrades' wickets all fall, the stalwart supporter ladies who spend hours spreading marge and slicing cucumber for sandwiches turn off the oil stove under the tea urn.

Having done so they then apologise for the delay in serving tea and listen for Hugh's old jeep returning, holding up proceedings long enough to give the band of volunteers a chance to help the Chappels with their chores between batting and fielding.

No-one will admit it, but to my mind this year's brand of gamesmanship has reached the ultimate where our local derby is concerned.

The first match with Lockley is an away game. Perce the postman, giving a daily report on the state of their pitch, said that he had never seen it looking better.

An inbred hang-up from the forelock clutching days when village kids knew better than to beat 'The Right Horrible Fred' at the races that were held on Lockley cricket pitch makes us tread carefully on its turf, as if the wicket were hallowed ground.

But it was something less than perfect for this year's match and looked as if it had broken out in a brown soil rash.

"Dear me," said a member of our team who shall be nameless.

"I thought that Banky Meadow was the only place round here to be plagued with moles. Set mole traps up there this year and you can catch 'em two at a time. Do a lot of damage overnight, moles can!"

Whatever else it is, it's hardly cricket.

An Arch of Iron Flowers

Walk along any village street and you will notice that most old cottages still have a horse-shoe nailed, points uppermost, to the lintel of the door. If one house appears to defy superstition by having a reversed horse-shoe above the threshold the chances are that this is where the blacksmith lived.

Until recently, customs and beliefs dating from pre-Christian times still prevailed among those whose livelihood depended on the land. Being at the mercy of nature and the soil was a very chancy business.

By placating whatever powers ruled the seasons they hoped to escape ill-fortune on the land and in the home.

Iron was believed to ward off evil influences. An iron poker placed upright against the bars of a sulking fire would drive the devil from the hearth.

A horse-shoe placed above the entrance to a dwelling was double insurance. It would deter malevolent spirits from entering and, providing that the points were kept uppermost, the good fortune already in the house would not escape.

The blacksmith, by the very nature of his trade, was immune from evil influences and witchcraft; an upturned horse-shoe was the symbol of his trade.

A master-farrier had the right to mount three reversed horse-shoes in pyramid formation above the entrance to his smithy and his home. The smithy was the news centre for farming and local gossip.

The smith was a key craftsman, respected and relied on by a community which depended on his skill in using iron for their plough-shares, coulters and harrows and for keeping their horses shod.

The technique of horse-shoeing has remained unaltered for centuries, as has the apprenticeship and training for the blacksmith's and farrier's trades.

Bert, our village blacksmith, came from a long line of craftsmen, but it was not customary for a smith to train his own son. Beng small in stature when he left school, Bert spent three years as beer-boy, pumping the huge pear-shaped bellows of the forge fire for most part of the time. He was seventeen when his articled apprenticeship began.

The unpunctuated indenture papers read like some medieval document whereby he signed that he would 'faithfully guard his master's secrets, neither waste, lend or sell his master's goods'. He would not 'absent himself from his master's service by day or night, but in all things act as a faithful apprentice toward his said master and all of his'.

In return his master promised to teach and instruct, 'finding sufficient meat, drink, lodgings and all other necessities'.

By his twentieth birthday Bert was earning ten shillings a week and ending the first part of his apprenticeship.

The second part would not start until he had passed a traditional test of strength.

He would still be regarded as 'the boy' until he could put his forearms under the anvil and lift it clear of the smithy floor. It made sense; a blacksmith needs strength as well as skill. A sway-backed shire horse, weighing over a ton and reluctant to be shod, has an uncomfortable tendency to lean on the farrier when its hoof is lifted off the ground.

Lifting the anvil was a ritual watched by interested spectators. Once this was achieved the apprentice was grabbed and held down while the master farrier cut a fringe in the lower edge of his pupil's muleskin shoeing apron.

This signified that he was now considered worthy to work at the anvil without supervision and the fringe of his apron could be used to flick the hot iron scalings away. Still held firm, the apprentice submitted to having a nail hammered into the heel of his boot until he cried out 'Beer', acknowledging that he would pay for a pint for every witness of the ceremony.

For the next four years Bert's status was that of journeyman or improver, not yet qualified to call himself a master smith.

By the time that the seven years of his training were complete Britain was at war and, believing that 'Kitchener Needed Him', Bert volunteered as a farrier in the Royal Army Service Corps.

The gentle countryman who had seldom seen the sea found himself in a sinking troopship, cutting panicky mules loose and swimming with them to some Mesopotamian beach.

Having shod untameable mules and survived the carnage of the Dardanelles, Bert came home with medals on his chest and a pair of spurs cut from the heels of Johnny Turk.

He moved into the house beside the forge and, as a master farrier, proudly nailed three reversed horse-shoes on the lintel of the door. His skill was soon recognised. The old-time horsemen, who guarded the secrets of their horse medicines so jealously, favoured Bert by passing to him their various cures and remedies.

If he had a kicking mean-tempered horse to shoe Bert put a few drops of some aromatic mixture on his hand, stroked the beast from the nostril, up along the arch of its neck, down across the withers to the hoof he wanted to shoe. He would sometimes calm a horse by breathing in its nostrils and could gentle a horse as opposed to breaking it in. In all his years he never needed to hobble a horse or throw it to get it shod.

Regularly each morning at 6.30 the smithy shutters opened and, like some tocsin bell, Bert's hammer striking the anvil as he turned iron bar into horse-shoes warned the surrounding countryside that the new day had begun.

He worked in close conjunction with the wheelwright and shoeing the wheels was a spectacular procedure, involving the services of two men and a boy. Behind the 'Pant'us' – the partitioned part of the smithy where the horses were actually shod – was a circular steel plate with a centre spindle on which the wooden wheel was clamped.

The iron rim, cut a fraction smaller than the perimeter of the wheel, was put through an iron-bending machine rather like an old-fashioned mangle with three rollers, then shut and placed in a nearby circular pit piled high with faggots of kindling wood.

The fire burned fiercely until the iron rim was cherry red with heat. It was lifted from the fire with long-handled tongs. If the heat was exactly right the iron would expand to fit the wheel. Sometimes it required a touch of the hammer before it bedded in.

Immediately the rim was in position, and before the hot iron set the wood alight, it was cooled off with wet sacking and buckets of water. As the iron contracted it fitted tight upon the wheel.

Bert and old Humph the wheelwright would listen to a farm cart trundling along the village street and without seeing it know if it was one of theirs.

Prize-winning Clydesdales, racehorses, gipsy ponies, donkeys, Bert shod them all. Pompous landowners knew better than to treat the craftsman who shod their hunters as anything less than equal.

Tongue-tied farmhands smouldering under injustice confided in Bert as he replated their hoes and in his quiet way he set things right with their employers.

Repairing a leaky kettle was as much a matter of pride to Bert as was the wrought iron arch he fashioned when electricity was connected to the church. Almost secretively, the light above the churchyard gate was suspended from Bert's handiwork.

The age of farm horses passed and the shoeing side of the business dwindled to become almost non-existent.

Nevertheless, mechanically minded farmers realised that Bert could repair, renew or remake broken equipment cheaply with no waiting and no fuss.

If this happened to be fiction Bert would have lived to reap the reward of contentment and a ripe old age. He didn't. Coal dust, which demands the sacrifice of miners' lungs when first it is hewn, made Bert pay the price of working in the pollution of a smoke-filled forge.

The smithy was demolished and few things remain to show that Bert existed at all.

Above the churchyard gate there is an arch with climbing vines of flowers and fruit that look so real that each veined leaf appears to have been in some strange way bewitched and turned to iron and there are three reversed horseshoes, pyramid-fashion, above a cottage door.

Nelson

Nelson is a very old one-eyed donkey. He has long droopy ears and a coat that appears to have suffered innumerable attacks by maternity-minded moths.

His doleful, docile appearance is deceptive. That which Nelson misses with his flying heels, he catches with a sharp nip from his yellow teeth.

For years he belonged to Ikey, an itinerant who used to accompany the corn-threshing outfits from farm to farm. These 'threshing johnnies' slept rough in barns and sheds wherever the machine was working and where Ikey bedded down, his donkey slept too.

If objecting workmates demanded that Nelson should be turned out for the night, his continuous sleep-destroying braying made them change their minds. He would obey no-one but Ikey and sensible people kept well clear of both Nelson's front end and his rear.

When the threshing season finished, Ikey and the donkey would sometimes occupy a shepherd's decrepit hut, tucked away behind the dry-stone wall that divides the upland meadows from the open moorland of High Common.

Ikey looked like a character from the Old Testament.

He was a powerfully built man with a black beard, bushy eye-brows and dark penetrating eyes. Unlike most of the threshing johnnies, he was clean and tidily clothed.

He was uncommunicative, had a strange accent and whistled haunting, foreign-sounding tunes.

The fact that he was a 'furriner' explained the strangeness of his ways.

And he had strange ways. Having quietened a rampaging stallion and cured a horse which the vet had advised to be destroyed, he had the reputation of being a 'horse charmer'. There was nothing magical about this, there were old horse-men who knew how these things were done, but that is another tale.

To the village children Ikey was the local bogey man and many a recalcitrant offspring was threatened with being 'given to Ikey for his donkey's dinner'.

At threshing time it was a somewhat chastening thought to know that Ikey and the donkey were sleeping in the chaff-house by the barn.

The cumbersome procession of the threshing outfit travelled very slowly on the narrow country roads. A chuntering traction engine with massive wheels hissed steam and smelled of coal smoke and hot oil. This pulled the high, wide, box-shaped threshing machine, invariably painted red and tarpaulin-sheeted against the wet.

Attached to the back of the thresher by a massive iron tow-bar was the engine driver's mobile home, a wooden caravan like an old-time seaside hut, trundling along on wooden, iron-banded wheels.

Lashed behind this came the baling machine, piled high with straw to keep its canvas feed sheets dry. The road vibrated as they passed. Bringing up the rear were the threshing johnnies wheeling ancient bicycles or trudging along in broken hobnail boots. Last of all came Ikey, leading Nelson harnessed to a low-sprung cart.

A traction engine had an insatiable thirst. If the water trough or tap was more than a hosepipe length away it was a treadmill task to keep the monser from running dry.

The engine driver was in charge of the operation. He saw that the countless pulley wheels and drive belts were working properly, supervised the grading of the grain and kept the gauges of his highly polished engine at their correct levels, but never went on top of the threshing machine.

Only two people were allowed up there, the bond cutter and the feeder. A farmhand pitched the sheaves from the corn stack across to Ikey, who was the bond cutter. He wielded a murderous curved knife to cut the binder twine that held the sheaf together, then tossed the loosened sheaf across to the feeder, who fed it into the revolving drums of the machine.

Through a process of flailing and sieving the grain passed down through chutes into two hundredweight sacks hooked on to the front of the machine.

The straw that came out of the back and passed on through the machine did not emerge as the 'square egg' straw bale that one sees today. This was tied into long straight-stalked baled straw that would thatch a roof.

The chaff or outer casing of the corn husk and the rough straw 'cavings' were disgorged underneath the machine and a relay of workers with long wooden rakes dragged it out on to sacking carrying cloths.

This was a dusty unpleasant task for if oats were being threshed the chaff was so light that it would blow all round the yard and the long 'bearded' spikes on barley chaff irritated and stuck into one's skin.

The threshing machine made a deep melodious humming sound and with every sheaf that was consumed, it alternated key. This built up a rhythm, setting a pace by which the whole outfit worked.

During the threshing season Nelson grew fat on fodder from the farms and surreptitious feeds of oats but in early summer Ikey and his donkey would disappear for weeks on end.

It was during one of Ikey's absences that Miss Mattie, a retired lady, acquired a broken-winded horse. She had encountered a travelling tinker ill-treating it along the lane and in her brisk, efficient way had put the fear of the law in the poor man but ended £10 poorer and the owner of a sick and lousy horse.

That evening Ikey appeared outside the gate.

"I'll look to that 'roarer' you have bought missus," he said. Miss Mattie showed him to the outhouse where the sick horse lay.

"My life!" Ikey exclaimed, then went inside and closed the outhouse door. Next morning Ikey was nowhere to be seen but the horse was up and feeding, breathing normally and free from lice.

Thereafter, bundles of fodder and straw would be tossed over the hedge of the small meadow by the house.

This went on for years, long after the threshing machines had given way to combine harvesting. No words passed between Miss Mattie and Ikey, yet one morning Miss Mattie found a grubby envelope on her front door mat.

Inside were banknotes, and the cryptic message,

"Going to my home. I told Nelson he is yours."

She found Nelson grazing with her own old horse and his harness in the low sprung cart inside the gate.

Ikey never returned and, although Nelson would allow no one to harness him to the cart, he let Miss Mattie put his halter on.

She alone can coax him from his stubborn moods. He seems to settle down for months on end, but at times develops a nomadic urge and breaks out to wander far away.

Invariably Miss Mattie has to retrieve him from someone's stackyard. He stands immobile, refusing to be coaxed until she appears and takes him home.

Last week, when mist clung to the valley all day long, Nelson went missing again. Hugh the hill farmer heard him braying pitifully up on High Common and found him standing in the doorway of the old shepherd's hut.

When Hugh eventually got inside the hut to mend the broken door he realised that some vagrant had been using it, for the old iron stove was warm.

For once Nelson neither bit nor kicked, but allowed Hugh to stroke his neck and lead him home by the forelock of his mane. To use Hugh's words, it fair gave him the creeps.

He reckons that the poor silly hold donkey thought he would find someone he knew up there, but an animal as unintelligent as a donkey would never go out searching for a long-departed friend.

Or would he? I don't know.

Stay There Till I Get Back

Oone would never imagine that Will, placidly pedalling to the post office for his pension, could create a minor panic.

Yet nothing has caused so much excitement since the forestry tractor driver tipped a trailer-load of firewood over Tom Grommett's backyard fence and drove away, leaving Tom's missus trapped in the outside privy with a ton of tops and butts piled against the door.

Will rides pretty high in the saddle, his bike being a Home Guard relic issued at the time when his anti-invasion orders were that he should cycle up the hill and defend Britain and the water-tower against the advancing Nazis with a sharpened bill-hook.

Nowhere does Will ride more slowly than when he passes Plough Cottage, an ancient wattle and daub house with a thatched roof which has changed owners several times since it was sold for seventy-five pounds when the village saddler died.

The latest owner has pulled down, built up and altered the old place with more enthusiasm than skill.

It took him some time before he learned that country crafts-men won't be rushed. One does not try to convert a thatcher to a time and motion routine on a frosty morning when the dressed straw is difficult to yelm. Nor does one mention dirty words like plastic straw.

When he confided to the landlord of the Hare and Hounds that he intended to extend the latest extension to make a log-gia and a patio, Will was able to report that these fancy-sounding additions were nothing more than a lot of poles and an unevenly paved back yard.

Will reckons that it is all this foreign travel that gives some people such ideas.

As Will slowed down for his weekly look over Plough Cot-tage garden wall last Thursday, he heard a curious echoing sound that he described as being 'something like that radio chap that busts his charts'.

Will held on to the top of the wall to keep his balance and turned his good ear towards the sound. There was no one in the garden and nothing looked amiss although the paving slabs of the patio looked more uneven and had a hole in the middle. Perhaps that blamed-fool-new-chap was building a fountain or a pool.

The second time Will heard the sound he realised that it was coming from the hole.

As soon as he walked on the wobbling paving stones to in-vestigate Will knew that the owner of Plough Cottage had discovered that it had a well.

Leaning precariously over the void, Will could see him standing on a sloping wooden sleeper a dozen feet below. Beneath him was some murky looking water.

"Well I never. What are you doing down there?" Will couldn't think of anything else to say.

"Get me out," the answer echoed up.

"You just bide quiet and I'll see what I can do." Will is getting too old for this sort of caper, but slowly and methodically he placed a ladder across the hole and found a tow rope in the boot of the owner's car.

It barely reached the upstretched hands and as Will explained, if he tried to pull unaided he would fall in too and there wasn't room for the pair of them. He hauled the rope back up and, in a moment of inspiration, grabbed a pole left over from the loggia building and an old horse collar which hung on the garage wall, a relic of the days when the building had been the saddler's shop.

With the pole on one end of the rope and the collar on the other, Will crawled back along the ladder and painstakingly placed the pole across the rungs then lowered the horse collar down the well.

"Now you just haul yourself up a bit and put your legs through the collar. You can dangle there, safe and comfy as a babby on a swing till I get back with someone as is heftier than I."

As soon as he could get enough breath to pedal his bike Will rode to raise the alarm to everyone he passed before he reached the Hare and Hounds.

Some of us dialed 999. The poor man was soon hoisted out of the well and a small crowd stood watching the several fire brigade appliances and police cars that dashed to the scene.

They discovered that there was at most a foot of water in the well. One neighbour reckons that the wailing sirens and general disturbance have made her free-range poultry egg-bound all this week.

The chap from Plough Cottage bought his rescuers a drink in the Hare and Hounds.

Even old Harry Applethorn, who tends to do his oldest inhabitant bit with strangers, was treated to a pint.

The shallowness of the water in the well was becoming something of a joke until Harry Applethorn upset everything by remarking that if younder chap had fallen down a hole not more than twenty feet in depth, it was the rainwater tank he had found and not the well.

"That be nigh on a hundred foot from bottom to top. So deep that when I was an unbreeched boy they used a horse to turn the capstan and drawed the water up through pipes made of wood. Bored out of elm they was, and neither water nor frost affected them. Many a time I was put on the old horse's back as it plodded round and round."

The man from Plough Cottage hadn't bargained on having one well, much less two.

With all the alterations no-one could remember the exact location of the well. There had been loads of rubble and top-soil dumped on the garden and, being a town-bred chap, he could see no way of discovering where it was.

When he was told to get Walter working with his twigs his disbelief showed on his face. Water divining? He had always thought it to be folk-lore, archaic mumbo-jumbo. Nevertheless he would be grateful for anyone who might help educate him in country ways.

At first Walter's forked hazel rod found the course of the water main, then lay unresponsive in his hands until he clambered over a pile of rubble.

The twig dipped and jerked and Walter stuck a marking peg in the ground.

Digging to find an old well is no job for one man or even two. At such times everyone lends a hand. They worked in a circle some way out from the peg and dug down until they found a ring of flagstones where the horses used to walk round and soon after struck the worm-ridden wood of the lid of the well.

Everyone's rubbish is being tipped down Plough Cottage well.

The spring interior mattress and old fridge that a passing motorist deposited in the vicarage hedge, old sinks, demolished pig-pounds. At this rate we could be in with a fighting chance in the tidiest village stakes.

There is one sobering thought. Piped water was a rare amenity in the country until about forty or fifty years ago.

Most rural houses and groups of cottages depended on a well.

The majority of wells were haphazardly sealed, covered over with soil and promptly forgotten.

Should you have acquired the cottage of your dreams, do establish that you have nothing more lethal than fairies at the bottom of your garden, and not a slug-infested well.

Granny Morgan's Pride

'Sale This Day.' A notice-board tied to the gate-post directs buyers to the auction and Barn Field gateway is becoming a tyre-churned pool of mud.

In the last few weeks of his leasehold old Mr. Morgan cleared out the farm buildings and now the accumulated tools of a lifetime are set out in lots across Barn Field.

Dairy utensils, Granny Morgan's pride, stand rain-soaked and mud bespattered, ready to be sold. Sheltered in the empty cart-shed, her heavy farmhouse furniture, polished with love and beeswax down the years, collects grime and fingermarks from the woodworm-seeking hands.

The massive old kitchen table serves as a rostrum for the auctioneer, scrubbed whitewood desecrated by mud-clogged boots.

The auctioneer raps on the old milk churn with his gavel and the sale begins. So does the rain.

The first few sundry lots are a jumble of old pitchforks, scrap metal and feeding troughs. The auctioneer's monotonous chant, gibberish to the uninitiated, pushes the bidding along.

"Lot 12. One cheese butt with lid." A sale porter holds up a round wooden tub drilled with small holes. No one bids.

"Come, I won't waste time on unimportant items. Who will say 20p?" Still no one accepts the auctioneer's offer and Granny, glaring beneath an umbrella, seems ready to prod him for giving offence.

Her cheese butt unimportant? Such ignorance could only come from a town-bred man.

Granny Morgan, perpetual motion in a floral wrap-around pinny and arch-supported shoes! Ageless, seemingly no older than the day she scorned my up-bringing because at twelve years old no one had taught me to make cheese.

"My dear soul, you shall learn this very week," she said. I knew better than to argue.

Outside the sun was shining, but the small amount of sunlight that filtered through the thick glass of Granny Morgan's dairy was diffracted by ivy branches trailing across the panes.

It gave me the goose-pimply sensation of being inside a chilly green bottle. I watched her lift the cheese butt on to a trestle and line it with a muslin cloth.

The bowls of milk and rennet that she had set to 'curd' were tipped into the butt and I was instructed to set a pan underneath to catch the drips and to 'poke a skewer at they old holes so that the whey do run off quick'.

The lid was placed in the top of the butt and a seven pound weight put on that. Each day Granny twisted the muslin cheesecloth tighter and at the end of the week she tested it to see if it was ready by pressing her finger on the top.

"When 'tis neither mish-mushy nor too hard, you takes the cheese from the cloth and roughs it all around with a knife to give it a firm crust. You puts 'un to ripen on an open-slatted shelf or wraps it in clean muslin and hangs it from a beam out of nibbling reach of they old meece."

I begrudged the lost hours of playing time, not realising the compliment I had been paid.

Grany's cheese equalled Stilton at its best and cheese-making is an art that is often only divulged by one generation to the next.

"For the last time, 20p for the cheese butt." I brushed a raindrop from my forehead with my sale catalogue and the auctioneer's gavel rapped on the milk churn. "All done and sold at 20p." I still don't know if I intended to bid or not.

The next lot. "One barrel butter churn with stand", was an instrument of destiny where one of the local lassies was concerned.

Ethel, a village girl, used to help Granny Morgan with the dairy work. They made butter on two days of the week but when the Saturday churning was finished Ethel was free to go home.

Ethel had a boy-friend, a broad-shouldered lad with brilliant black hair and a tendency to smelly feet. As she churned the butter Ethel dreamed of the day when she would have the right to wash his socks.

Their romance was a pretty torrid affair by local standards, insofar as she rode home from work each night on the crossbar of his bike and they went to the pictures together every Saturday afternoon.

They saved enough money to put down the deposit on a ring and planned to visit the jewellers on their next trip into town.

The next Saturday was cold and frosty and try as Ethel might the cream would not turn to butter in the churn. She was still turning the handle as the bus went into town.

Her Romeo met another girl in the pictures and from then on, Ethel walked home from work alone.

For weeks Ethel salted the butter with her tears, her love-life thwarted by a butter churn. Now she is the wife of a prosperous American and flies home every year to see her Mum.

She sure would have raised a bid in gratitude to see the old barrel churn had she not been Stateside today.

Now the tractor and heavier implements are being sold and are bid for by the lifting of an eyebrow, the nod of a head or a gentleman pretending to take out a hanky to blow his nose.

Old Mr. Morgan confides that the potato digger has sold for almost double the price that he first paid, so he thinks it has earned its keep.

If there is a more god-forsaken job than planting potatoes, it must be picking them up but when an old neighbour has a crop that is spoiling to be harvested, everyone lends a hand.

As Granny Morgan says, 'tatty-upping' is a hungry-making job and her 'helper's dinner' almost compensated for acquiring a hairpin bend for a back. She served up cheese and potato pie; baked apples, cored and filled with spiced brown sugar; vanilla junket with grated nutmeg and enormous quantities of scalding hot, sweet tea. All of which is both easy on the purse and time and marvellous to eat.

It seems unbelievable that no one will eat a 'tatty-upping' dinner at Granny Morgan's kitchen table after today. The last lot is 'all done and sold'. The buyers are departing and lorries and loaded trailers ooze their way out through the gate.

Granny and old Mr. Morgan look across the fields of the little farm that will now become part of a vast farming complex, then walk across to lock the door of the empty farmhouse.

The relentless rain beats a tattoo on the old kitchen table, mud-covered and abandoned in Barn Field.

So Long at the Fair

D an's wife said that he could please himself, she would gladly accept a lift home from the town. Her feet were near worn out with 'trapesing' around the fair, and the afternoon bus had 'been and gone and not come past'.

Dan hesitated, then got in the car, muttering that he couldn't abide women drivers and could have quite easily walked.

Overcoming apprehension, he settled in his seat.

"I grant that fair-going is a tiring old job," he admitted, "but the Horse Fair is nothing like it was.

"There were few high days and holidays in the poverty-stricken times folk call 'the good old days', nor was there much cause for jollification. Horse Fair week was something different though.

"We dubbined our boots, strip washed down and changed our shirts though t'were only midweek, then, spruced up like bantam cocks, we went off into town.

"Them as was fit walked, the young 'uns were pushed and the farmers lent their wagons and teams to take such old folk as wanted to go to the fair.

"The town fairly 'eaved with folks. Gipsy wagons were pulled on to the cobbles one side of the market cross and the fairground caravans on t'other. There were some rare old fights between the two.

"Horses by the dozen waited to be auctioned off in Market Street and the pens in the cattle market were full of stock.

"There were swingboats, stalls and sideshows, freaks and fortune tellers and a chap as would pull your teeth for sixpence. Of course it was a hiring and firing fair in those days, as well I know."

Dan fell silent, drawing hard on a foul smelling short-stemmed pipe and reflecting on the Horse Fair as it was just before he was fourteen.

That year Dan went blithely to the fair wearing new boots and his father's cut down coat. He took scant notice of the conversation his father was holding with a gentleman farmer.

His mother told him to mind his manners and say his prayers and then Dan realised that he was a fully fledged stable-hand, engaged for the sum of £10 a year with free bed and board plus one pair of boots, a pair of breeches and a new shirt every year.

His straw bed was in the stable loft which he shared with the wagoner and a groom. Meals were eaten in the back kitchen of the farmhouse.

Sunday meant mutton for dinner. For the rest of the week 'pot-wallopers' were the staple diet. These were a mixture of flour, rough suet and water made into a solid dough, wrapped in a cloth and boiled for hours.

There was much competition and rivalry as to which farm had the smartest turn-out at the fair and by the time the next Horse Fair came round Dan was very much 'one of the lads'.

He rode beside the wagoner in a newly painted farm cart, their team of shire horses high-stepping their polished hooves and jingling the burnished brasses of their harness.

Dan had helped to braid their manes and tails with red, white and blue ribbon, 'wearing the worsted' as the old horsemen said.

He had to hand most of his first year's wages to his mother, but with a whole florin in his pocket Dan felt as affluent as a lord as he strolled round the side shows.

He thought he might risk one penny on the moving picture machines and chose one labelled 'Frolics by the Sea'.

Dan had never seen the sea and, while he was mildly interested in some ladies with naked forearms spasmodically splashing in the water up to the bottom of their knee-length bloomers, he was so fascinated by the jerking waves of the sea that he invested in another pennyworth.

He never got full value for his money, for a resounding thump on his back almost sent his eyeballs through the eyepiece, then he was hauled upright to face his 'maister's' wife, a righteous lady who railed at him for being licentious and lustful.

She ordered him to go and mind her pony which was tied up to a hitching ring on the back wall of the chapel, well away from the temptations of the fair.

A very gloomy Dan leaning against the chapel wall watched the 'maister's' wife and the wagoner approaching, the wagoner carrying a set of harness.

"Fancy," said the 'Missus', "I've just bought a second set of harness for the pony and it's almost identical to the one he's wearing now."

"What harness?" asked Dan. The pony had been standing with just a halter on when he had arrived. He got one hiding for the harness being stolen and another because the 'Missus' had bought it back.

Three hidings on one Horse Fair day Dan could stand, but to be made to put the remainder of his florin in the chapel poor-box was too much. Daniel joined the ranks of the un-employed.

There were two kinds of horse-trading at the fair. While the auctioneers were selling horses which were being paraded up and down Market Street, in Three Bells Lane the gipsies and dealers conducted a horse sale of their own.

Horses sold cheaper there, but it took a knowledgeable man to find a real bargain. All the greasy-legged, lousy, workshy nags were there with the horse-fakers.

Old horses with grey muzzles walnut-leaf-stained brown, and with filed down teeth stood looking fit for nothing but the knacker's yard until a likely customer approached.

As the dealer engaged the client in conversation the horse would suddenly become very lively and muster a fast trot down the lane.

"Good for years of work," was one phrase.

"Horse-jollying" was another. It was simply and sadistically achieved.

For days before, the wretched horse would have its head close tied between two stakes and be driven frantic by the dealer's assistant hammering on a bucket with a stick or rat-tling a tin full of stones inside a sack, just under its nose.

As the sale the demented creature had only to see the same man standing with the terrifying bucket or sack in his hand to become lively and agitated. Nothing would look more in-nocent to the mug out to buy a cheap horse.

Any 'gorgio' buying a horse was fair game, but horse-trading between gipsies was different. Almost ritualistic haggling with raised voices, posturing, much shaking of heads and walking away.

Just as suddenly a price would be agreed and the bargain sealed with a slapping of the transactors' hands.

The seller always returned a silver coin for 'luck money'.

This the buyer spat on, rubbed and placed in his pocket to ensure good fortune on the deal.

Dan recalled that the farm-hands often bought clothes from the stalls at the fair. His wife said that she had bought a bargain that very day.

There was rustling of paper in the back seat of the car and the conversation went something like this:

"Whatever is them then, mother. Let us have a look."

There was a disgusted grunt.

"They are tights Daniel, three pairs for twelve pence."

"Tights!" Dan exploded. "You have as many brains as a pig has got pockets. Silly old gal. Two pair has one leg shorter than t'other and the third was made to fit the shape of a little old toad.

"Ain't you been going to the fair long enough not to buy old 'rubbidge'?"

"At least I haven't bought any Wonder pills." Dan's wife deflated him with a glance and went on to recall the year that some chap calling himself Doctor Watson sold special tablets, the formula of which contained some mysterious ingredients derived from the glands of apes.

They were guaranteed to put new life in men.

It attracted a lot of custom to the 'doctor's' stall at the fair.

The following morning several village men stood self-consciously waiting to attend the weekly surgery held in the back room at the post office. Each one carried a container, ranging from jam-jars to flower vases, all containing bright green liquid.

"Yes," said Dan's wife, "and there wasn't a wife among us that didn't go in fear and dread of having a green baby all that year."

"Women!" snorted Dan. "They do say that at one time a man could auction off his wife! No, the fair ain't what it was!"

The Fragile Fortress

We fed the calves by lantern light that morning and by daybreak I had the cart loaded, Jim harnessed and stood waiting, impatient to be off.

Mum hurried across the cobbled yard, tucking stray wisps of hair up under her best velour hat, stabbing the purple cabbage-rose trimming with a lethal looking hat-pin as she went.

"Check that nothing is forgotten," she called. I checked.

Several complaining cockerels chuntered in their crates. There were eggs, butter, bushels of Blenheim apples, seven snared rabbits and mistletoe that I had cut from the apple tree in the yard. I had even remembered a horse rug and the enormous umbrella in case it rained.

Mum was the wrong shape to clamber into a two-wheeled

tip-cart and no sooner was she heaved in than she wanted to get out. "Wait," she said, "I have left the shopping bags on the table." I went back and collected them, all six.

Then we were off, with Jim's hooves ringing on the road-way, gravel crunching beneath the iron-shod wheels and Mum, myself, and the horse each making individual minia-ture fog-banks as we breathed in the morning air.

Mum was anxious to reach the Christmas produce market early and get low lot numbers so that our items for sale would be auctioned first.

Then we could get her Christmas shopping done in time for us to get back home by dark.

Our produce went under the hammer and Mum totted up how much shopping money she had made. My seven snared rabbits and the bunches of mistletoe had earned me twelve shillings and I did mental mathematical gymnastics to divide that to buy presents for my brothers, sisters, nephews and nieces who seemed to increase in numbers every year.

Dad was no fool to opt out of driving Mum to the Christmas market and I knew enough to let her tackle her Christmas shopping by herself. She started off with a variety of straw and string bags hung on one arm, pursuing bargains as if she was preparing for a siege.

Hawk-eyed, she watched the grocer's scales go down and if it didn't the cowering counterhand would be denounced as 'nothing but a nip-cheese' to other customers in the market-day busy shop.

As each shopping bag got too heavy to carry she would blithely deposit it on the couner of the nearest shop, inform-ing the unsuspecting shopkeeper that she would soon be back.

Then I would retrace the route of her shopping spree, col-lecting the bulging bags. Sometimes she would forget which shop had been honoured with her left luggage. That morning I drove round looking for 'a place where they sold socks'.

Through the doorway of a frightfully select Gents Outfitters and Tailoring establishment I saw Mum's overfull straw shopper on the glass-topped counter.

Right on top was a butcher's sixpenny bargain sheep's head, grinning out of a bloodstained newspaper wrapping as if it was as pleased to see Mum as she was to find it. As she explained to a youthful assistant in a celluloid collar, one 'hurdle bumper' equals two basins of brawn and three of broth, and if you have never heard of mutton brawn you didn't know my waste-not-want-not Mum.

While Mum had been shopping I had spent most of my twelve shillings and solved my Christmas present problem bidding for, and buying, a miscellaneous lot in the market.

Lumped together in a dull metal log-box with a broken lid were several china vases, a shaving mug and a pile of books.

Mum loved reading, the shaving mug would do for Dad and there appeared to be enough vases to give my sisters a present each.

'One copper log-box with sundry items' had cost eight shillings of my twelve and, in a whirl of teenage self-indulgence, I lashed out on a one and elevenpenny pair of artificial silk stockings and a pint sixed bottle of Ashes of Carnation scent at one and six.

Two hot pies and a mug of tea for Mum and me cost sixpence.

Still solvent to the extent of one penny, I hauled Mum back up into the cart and drove home along the lanes.

With Mum safely indoors I could move the log-box from under the chicken crates where I had hidden it and in the corn store examine what I had bought. The books, mostly romantic novels, would delight Mum, who loved a long weepy read.

The shaving mug when washed and polished would please Dad.

At the bottom of the lucky-dip log-box was a cardboard container and inside this were gramophone records ranging from Mozart to *The Merry Widow* and Marie Lloyd. These I felt would give Mum a Christmas bonus and I took them indoors.

There were several oven-ready chickens which had been ordered and, having spent the day shopping, we plucked and trussed them by lamplight in the kitchen after tea.

As we worked and sat there talking the conversation turned to the subject of Mum's youth.

At the age of thirteen as a scullery maid, she had shivered night after night in an unheated, unceilinged attic. From that window she could look down into the ballroom of a grand hotel.

Listening to the music and watching the dancing had brightened her unendurably drab existence and the strains of that music had echoed down her years.

"Such glittering ball-downs, such beautiful waltzes as you would never believe," she said.

As she sat in her old cover-all hessian apron plucking chickens, with the feathers falling into an old tin bath, I put one of the 'bonus records' on and the lamp-lit kitchen was filled with the music of Lehar's *Merry Widow* waltz.

It was soon filled with feathers too, for Mum dropped the chicken and whirled me round and round the kitchen table, teaching me how to dance.

On the next day Christmas preparations began in earnest.

The kitchen range gobbled fuel like a starving monster and no sooner was the oven emptied of a batch of baking than it was filled with clean dry bricks. Heated, these would be put in old stockings and used to air and warm the extra beds.

There were bedroom fires to lay and logs to carry, but none of the extra work mattered. Mum's children who had grown and gone away were coming home for Christmas and the family would once again be safe within the fortress of her love.

Each year I rustled up enough of the festive spirit to welcome Uncle Fred but my quota of goodwill stopped somewhat short of Cousin Daisy his daughter and Aunt Bertha, his domineering wife. They were by our standards wealthy and often condescended to spend a 'good old country Christmas' at my hard-pressed parents' expense.

There were always pre-visit 'don't put mice in your aunt's slippers' lectures and I was forbidden to tell Daisy tales of headless horsemen and vampire bats. But on principle I had collected four dead spiders and deposited them in Daisy's single bed.

The house was alive with fire-lit welcome then, in a Christmas Eve mistletoe-kissing uproar, the family circle was complete. In our under-the-eaves little bedroom, Daisy displayed her crepe-de-chine French knickers and asked if I had noticed how like Ginger Rogers she had grown. To me she was just a chubby-built girl with acne and steel curlers in her hair.

She said that she had brought me a pesent. I conceded that she had a surprise waiting, knowing that she had yet to find the spiders in her bed.

"Yours is a pair of real silk stockings," she told me and pride demanded that I found something to give her in return.

All that I had to sacrifice was my pint sized bottle of Ashes of Carnation scent and I begrudged every farthing of the one and six that it had cost.

The blacksmith's son had volunteered to mend the copper log-box for me and on Christmas morning he brought it back, polished and burnished for me, an additional present for my Mum.

Daisy, reeking of Ashes of Carnation, stood simpering under the mistletoe, waiting to be kissed.

"Phew, have they been making you carry mildewed hay?" the blacksmith's son enquired then kissed me, needing no mistletoe at all.

Christmas passed in a plum pudding haze of laughter until it was, by family tradition, time for Mum to sing *The End Of A Perfect Day*. Then, candle-lit, we went to bed.

The fires in the bedroom grates would turn to cold ash by morning and like that ash Mum's world would soon be scattered to the winds. The fragile fortress, defended by her unselfish love, had withstood the onslaughts of another year and her family circle was complete.

Paradise

Paradise is a large white jug patterned with roses and for-get-me-nots.

It is full of strong, sweet tea and is carried by my mother.

A yellow straw shopping bag nearly as deep as I am high drags on the dusty path as I struggle along the lane, fascinated by the sun hat perched precariously on my mother's head, defying the huge hatpins and bobbing up and down as she hurries on in front of me.

We walk between the poplar trees, their leaves rustling in the breeze like the sea on a shingle beach.

By the half-built haystack she spreads out the faded blue cloth. The wagon wheels beat out a rhythm as the haymakers come, eager for their meal.

Cottage loaves broken into quarters, hunks of cheese and onions that set my mouth on fire and me too happy to refuse because I am near my Dad, sharing his tea.

The warmth of the sun, the laughter of the men who tell my mother that she makes her cottage loaves to match her shape.

The hayfield scent, mingling sweet briar and honeysuckle. That is a sort of paradise.

Paradise is a March night, with the sky so filled with stars that a little star shoots across the sky to find a less crowded space to shine. In Twelve Acre meadow among the thatched hurdles the flock of sleeping ewes stir and rise as they see the lantern at the gate.

They walk towards me and we pass the time of night.

Here and there the proud mums nudge their lambs and tell them to lay still.

Outside the circle of the light, a plaintive call. One old ewe has rolled over on her back and cannot rise.

There, beside the quiet hedgerow where primroses shine white against the moss, we wait. She has no fear of me and I do not fear the night.

When at last she stands, her lamb beside her, the gate is quietly closed and thick cocoa, drunk beside a kitchen fire, drives out the March chill so that I go to bed with easy mind.

Paradise is a copper beech tree standing like a bride with auburn hair. The blossom-covered cherry orchard is her wedding dress and the hawthorn banks her train.

Paradise is a field of April wheat having its hair combed.

Bess, the half-blind mare, pulls the light harrow but suddenly stops.

No amount of 'Come-on' or 'Giddup' will make her budge.

In front of her great shire hooves is a skylark's nest and no amount of straightening up will hide the fact that in the middle of the field's lined tapestry there is a corrugated curve.

Paradise is sheep-dipping time when the newly shorn sheep, looking like city gents caught office-bound in underpants and vest, are dipped in custard-coloured wash to drive away the monster-looking tick.

The local constable, cattle records all duly checked and signed, will lean against the five-barred gate, roasting in his serge, determined to uphold the dignity of the law.

He fights the desire to sleep brought on, no doubt, by the tumbler of home-made wine he declared to be as harmless as the milk it stood by on the dairy slab.

He watches as we each in turn get wet with splashing spray and all the flock are dipped but one.

Bill the ram, whose head can split a stake and who once chased a would-be suitor, all Sunday dressed, to monkey climb a tree and kept him there all afternoon.

Whatever else the constable will enter in his books, he can be sure that no tick or warble fly will molest him on his journey home, for Bill decides that they will both take the waters and charges smartly from behind, sending the policeman jet propelled into the dip.

Soon after, hysterical with mirth, I pump clean water from the well over the head of the law, now minus tunic and dignity and wondering what to tell his sergeant.

Paradise is an old white house with barn-like door flung open wide all day, although everyone is busy round the farm.

No harm would come from folks who might come by. The gipsy family who turn up like magic every year in early June and stay until the harvest's in the barn would never steal from such as we.

This is a place of laughter, hard work and content, although poverty is only a ruined summer's crop away.

Paradise is another time, another place, before little men with measuring tapes and marking posts tore out the heart of Twelve Acre field and built the rows of three-up, three-down with bath and outside w.c.

Where the song thrush sang in the hawthorn bush, the ice-cream van ding-dongs its tin tune chimes.

The copper beech is gone and yet the council man plants saplings to be hacked to bits by children who don't care.

The barn that generations of my kind stacked high with corn now houses roadmen's brooms and the old house, defiled with plastic tiles and stainless steel, its dark beams hidden like a shameful past, will still stand strong when all the rest are slums.

The occupants can never really know what spring and summer really mean, except that cricket alternates with football on T.V.

The tenant planting up his hanky of a patch will never know that the root he curses as he breaks his fork was a tree that once bore fruit fit to send to London for a King.

And a minute's walk away the old farm lane, all overgrown with bramble, leads to nowhere any more.

It used to lead to the chestnut spinney, notorious since the time when Jack the shepherd was full of beer and song one Saturday night. He decided that a nap would help his head and went to sleep upon a pile of chestnut poles.

Made restless by the beer and deeply asleep at that, he was found, firmly wedged, by Miss Woods, the spinster organist Matins-bound.

Her efforts to release him and the fact that eucharist was said instead of sung that day made a tale that still makes people smile.

The lane stops dead where, on concrete stilts, the motorway, Common Market bound, strides across the country to the coast and paradise is gone from here.

Paradise is like the old white jug smashed a thousand ways and unless there is another time and another place, can never be regained.